Transferring Your
Skills into the W

D0371402

Are you seeking to use your subject knowledge and teaching skills beyond the classroom?

Many teachers don't recognise the vast range of skills, expertise and experience they possess. *Transferring Your Teaching Skills into the Wider World* will help you focus on how you can use your many transferable skills in a variety of contexts and settings across the educational sector and beyond.

Deborah Lewis and Hilary White identify the skills developed through a teaching career and match them with the wide range of jobs open to teachers looking for a new direction. This highly practical handbook:

- Illustrates the diverse ways in which you can utilise your teaching skills and experience;
- Surveys a wide variety of education related jobs and training options, using case studies to explore their advantages and disadvantages;
- Explores the opportunities open to teachers seeking a complete career change;
- Gives helpful advice for those wishing to develop their career within education.

The case studies are inspiring examples of individuals who have drawn on their teaching experiences to expand into other areas, describing the route they took and showing how they utilised their teaching expertise. Tips and hints show how you can follow a similar path.

Transferring Your Teaching Skills into the Wider World is essential reading for any teacher looking for guidance on how to change or develop their career whilst making the most of their existing skills and experience.

Deborah Lewis is an education consultant and additional inspector for schools. **Hilary White** is an early years specialist and writer.

Transferring Your Teaching Skills into the Wider World

Life Beyond the Classroom

Deborah Lewis and
Hilary White

Routledge
Taylor & Francis Group

LONDON AND NEW YORK

First published 2008
by Routledge
2 Park Square, Milton Park, Abingdon, Oxon OX14 4RN

Simultaneously published in the USA and Canada
by Routledge
270 Madison Ave, New York, NY 10016

Routledge is an imprint of the Taylor & Francis Group, an informa business

Typeset in Garamond by
Keystroke, 28 High Street, Tettenhall, Wolverhampton
Printed and bound in Great Britain by
TJ International Ltd, Padstow, Cornwall

British Library Cataloguing in Publication Data
A catalogue record for this book is available from the British Library

Library of Congress Cataloging in Publication Data
Lewis, Deborah, 1960–
Transferring your teaching skills into the wider world : life beyond the classroom /
Deborah Lewis and Hilary White.
p. cm.
1. Career changes. 2. Teaching—Vocational guidance. I. White, Hilary, 1960– II. Title.
HF5384.L49 2008
650.14—dc22
2007021227

ISBN 10: 0–415–42867–x (hbk)
ISBN 10: 0–415–42870–x (pbk)
ISBN 10: 0–203–93609–4 (ebk)

ISBN 13: 978–0–415–42867–5 (hbk)
ISBN 13: 978–0–415–42870–5 (pbk)
ISBN 13: 978–0–203–93609–2 (ebk)

Contents

Tables

Acknowledgements

With grateful thanks to Endaf Lewis, Michael White,
Tess Baker-Hytch, Kevan Bleach, Sarah Cole,
John Connor, Dr Malcolm Davison, Meg Fletcher,
Janet Gorton, Geoff Hancock, Sally Hyman, Helen Jefferis,
Carwyn Jones, Geraint Jones, Sian Martin, Kate Mears,
Chris Millican, Simon Moody, Catherine Murphy,
Richard Nixon, Tish Page, Zia Perriman, Roy Pumfrey,
Jean Rawlings, Catherine Raynor, John Reay, Brian Rogers,
Dawn Sharp, Karen Sherwood, Steve Tibbs, Dave Vizard,
Joe White, Hannah White, Peter Wild and Alf Wilkinson.

Abbreviations

A level	Advanced level
AfL	Assessment for Learning
Becta	British Educational Communications and Technology Agency
BPS	British Psychological Society
CCEA	Council for the Curriculum, Examinations and Assessment
CPD	Continuing Professional Development
CPE	Common Professional Examination
CRB	Criminal Records Bureau
CV	curriculum vitae
DCSF	Department for Children, Schools and Families
DELLS	Department for Education, Lifelong Learning and Skills
DT	design and technology
EAL	English as an Additional Language
EBD	emotional and behavioural difficulties
EBP	Education Business Partnership
ECDL	European Computer Driving Licence
EdD	Doctor of Education
FE	further education
GCSE	General Certificate of Secondary Education
HE	higher education
HLTA	higher-level teaching assistant
HMI	Her Majesty's Inspector
ICT	information and communication technology
INSET	in-service training
ISC	Independent Schools Council
ISI	Independent Schools Inspectorate
IT	information technology

ITT	initial teacher training
LaL	Literacy and Learning
LiL	Leading in Learning
LSC	Learning and Skills Council
MFL	modern foreign languages
NAA	National Assessment Agency
NCSL	National College for School Leadership
NPQH	National Professional Qualification for Headship
NQT	newly qualified teacher
NVQ	National Vocational Qualification
NWR	National Women's Register
Ofsted	Office for Standards in Education
OTT	overseas-trained teacher
PE	physical education
PGCE	Postgraduate Certificate in Education
PPA	planning, preparation and assessment
PSHE	personal, social and health education
PTA	parent–teacher association
QCA	Qualifications and Curriculum Authority
QIA	Quality Improvement Agency
QTS	Qualified Teacher Status
RISP	regional inspection service provider
SAD	seasonal affective disorder
SAT	Standard Attainment Test
SIP	school improvement partner
SNEC	Secrétariat National de l'Enseignement Catholique (Secretariat for Catholic Education, Rwanda)
SNS	Secondary National Strategy
SQA	Scottish Qualifications Authority
SSAT	Specialist Schools and Academies Trust
TA	teaching assistant
TDA	Training and Development Agency
TEFL	teaching English as a foreign language
UCAS	Universities and Colleges Admissions Service
U3A	University of the Third Age
VSO	Voluntary Service Overseas
WEA	Workers' Educational Association
WI	Women's Institute
WJEC	Welsh Joint Education Committee
WSI	whole-school initiative

Introduction

The world of education is constantly evolving, and many teachers no longer choose to spend their entire working lives based in a school or college. While your training and expertise will stand you in good stead for any workplace, a change of job does not have to mean the end of your career as an educationalist. As we set out to demonstrate in this book, there are numerous jobs that will take you away from a traditional school or college-based role but keep you within the field of education and enable you to make direct use of your skills and experience:

Chapter content

The book is divided into six chapters. Each chapter focuses on a different set of skills and competencies, and explores a range of associated jobs:

- **Chapter 1** covers jobs that make particular use of your generic teaching skills. Some of the jobs are voluntary or part time, others can be developed into a full-time career with the potential to provide a good income. The chapter begins with a survey of generic teaching skills and how they fit into the wider field of education. Although this survey will probably not tell you anything you do not already know, it can be useful to set down on paper just how many skills you possess – particularly when it comes to compiling a skills-based CV (see page 229) or writing letters of application.
- **Chapter 2** covers jobs that enable you to make particular use of your subject knowledge, interest and expertise. The introduction to this chapter divides subject knowledge into different categories and links each category with relevant jobs; for example,

if you have years of proven experience helping children towards exam success, you might consider working within the examination industry or undertaking individual tuition; if you enjoy developing activities and resources for your subject, you could write textbooks or articles for educational publications.

- **Chapter 3** covers jobs that require school- or college-based leadership and management experience. Whether you have worked at middle leadership level as a subject or year head, or reached senior leadership level as an assistant head, deputy head or headteacher, your experience and expertise are needed throughout the field of education. The jobs in this chapter include inspection, advisory and support roles, and positions that require strategic planning capabilities. As with Chapter 1, the chapter begins with a brief survey of leadership and management, which can be used to remind yourself of just how many skills and competencies you possess.

- **Chapter 4** is aimed at individuals who want a complete change from teaching. The chapter is divided into three broad sections, 'professional roles', 'running your own business' and 'retirement opportunities'. Inevitably, the jobs we survey make up only a tiny proportion of what is available, and they range from working voluntarily for a charity to retraining as a solicitor or becoming a management consultant.

- **Chapter 5** looks at the practical implications of making a career move. It begins with a section on auditing your financial circumstances, as a preparation for deciding which direction to follow. The second section focuses on 'making choices', with a set of questions designed to help you decide what kind of job to go for. A number of education-related jobs are freelance, part time and/ or short term. With this in mind, the third section looks at the ins and outs of developing a portfolio career and the practicalities of becoming self-employed.

- **Chapter 6** is for those who decide to stay where they are. Although teaching is stressful, demanding and hard work, it also has the potential to be immensely fulfilling and rewarding. The chapter begins with a list of reasons for remaining in teaching (and some may be surprised at just how long the list is!). The rest of the chapter is made up of tips from practising teachers on how to reduce your stress levels, manage your workload, improve your health and well-being, and cope with potentially difficult one-off events such as inspections, trips and parents' evenings.

Case studies

Every job surveyed in Chapters 1–4 includes either a case study or several examples of individuals who are doing or have done the job in question. Although each case study talks about their own particular job, as a group they flag up a number of interesting points for anyone who is considering a career move.

Without exception, every case study has found their teaching experience and expertise to be invaluable. A number of them point out that the competent teacher has highly transferable skills and a set of experiences that enable them to stand out in the workplace. When asked what advice they had for others, the general message was to have confidence in your capabilities and not to undersell yourself. As one of our case studies, Geoff, sums up: *'Have degree . . . have teaching skills . . . will travel!'*

It is also interesting to note how many of our case studies took on their new roles almost by accident. Perhaps an opportunity arose as a result of working in other education-related jobs, or they heard about a job through contacts. Although you may come across a number of opportunities that are less than appealing, the experiences of our case studies suggest that you should consider anything and everything as a potential stepping stone. The world of education is forever evolving, and new developments often generate new career opportunities. The jobs we have featured in this book tend to be generic in the sense that you should be able to find similar roles anywhere in the country. However, educational provision varies from area to area, and there are also a number of 'one-off' jobs throughout the field of education. If you are looking to develop your career, keep a constant eye on the local press, the education press and the internet. Be prepared to network and explore any option, however uncertain you might be. You never know what delights an obscure and tedious-sounding job title might be hiding!

Perhaps the most important theme to emerge from the case studies as a group is the general lack of regret. The vast majority enjoy their new roles and would not now choose to return to a traditional teaching and/or leadership and management role, although many work hard to maintain their links with schools and keep their skills up to date. Nevertheless, there are downsides for all of them. When we asked them to describe the disadvantages of their new working lives, the issues that came up most regularly were the loss of school holidays, no longer having regular contact with young people and, for the self-employed, the insecurity of their income in comparison with teaching. Overall, however, the stories the case studies have to tell confirm that there is an exciting, fulfilling and diverse set of opportunities out there for anyone who wants to develop their career beyond the school- or college-based setting. The generous contribution of our case studies has helped to bring alive the wider world of education-related work, and we are very grateful to them all!

Chapter 1

Effectively transferring . . . your teaching skills

Teachers often undervalue themselves as professionals and fail to realise just how wide a set of skills they possess. If you want to develop your career in education beyond the classroom, or even change to something completely different, it can be useful to reflect on just how many generic and transferable teaching skills you have:

Communicating to groups

Communicating effectively to a group of individuals is central to the teacher's role. It's a skill that teachers tend to take for granted and yet it is a highly sophisticated and complex form of communication. Whether you are new to the classroom and focusing solely on your own class, or a deputy head liaising with groups of colleagues, parents and governors, you will constantly be developing your ability to speak with clarity, use your voice to add meaning to what you are saying and project your personality to capture your audience. Even the apparently simple skill of scanning the group so that everyone falls within your gaze is not to be taken for granted. Try watching a hesitant or inexperienced speaker in action, and you will discover just how many communication tricks and techniques you use – without even being aware of them.

A major part of being able to communicate to groups lies in the ability to assess your audience and respond accordingly – something that most teachers become very skilled at. The average school day encompasses a dizzying number of changes; the typical secondary school teacher may well start off with a presentation to their departmental colleagues, spend the morning teaching Years 11, 7 and 9, the afternoon working with Year 13 and the evening introducing GCSE options to groups of parents. All of this demands a high degree of sensitivity to your audience's reactions, along with the need to assess and adapt to their prior knowledge and level of understanding. In order to succeed, you have to be able constantly to 'read' a group and adjust your delivery. Are they interested and listening? If not, what can be done to reclaim their attention? Is it time to pick up pace, slow down or repeat what you have just said in a different way? Most speakers do not run the risk of mayhem if they fail to pitch their content to suit the audience. You, on the other hand, are honing your presentation skills on your pupils – one of the most honest, critical and unforgiving groups in society.

Public speaking and communicating to groups of people is often cited as the most terrifying experience that ordinary people have to contend with. This is not to say that teachers do not feel the same when confronted with delivering a speech at a wedding, contributing to a public meeting or making a presentation. However, once a teacher, always a teacher. Even if your knees are knocking, you know you'll get by because you have done it all day long, day in, day out, term after term, year after year. Through sheer experience alone, your group communication skills will give you the edge over many others in the jobs market who have not had your educational training or experience.

Managing challenging behaviour

Managing challenging behaviour is perhaps the most difficult and demanding aspect of any teacher's role. It is certainly the aspect of today's schools that receives the most media attention.

As a teacher, you will have learned to be proactive in preventing problems before they arise. An experienced teacher knows how to pace a lesson so that the children are never bored or inactive; they can walk into any classroom and immediately spot organisational aspects that could lead to problems; they know when to be flexible and when to hold firm to their boundaries. Keeping an eye out for potential problems and having a toolbox of techniques to prevent them from occurring becomes second nature – an extremely useful skill to have in all aspects of life, quite apart from the jobs market.

But – however well you plan your lessons and your teaching space, problems will arise. This is when the teacher's legendary antennae come in useful – the 'eyes in the back of your head' that enable you to sense when something is up. This level of awareness is a special skill in itself, but it doesn't stop there. Having sensed that a situation has arisen, you must then decide how to deal with it – and quickly, before things get out of hand. Not for you the luxury of planning your response, or dealing with just one tricky individual at a time. A significant part of your role is the ability to assess quickly the input of each individual in a group situation, even when you haven't witnessed what happened.

This is the troubleshooting element of the teacher's role, but there are also those children who require an individual approach with specialist care and attention. This might involve you in liaising with parents and carers, support workers and, in some cases, social services. Your handling of such situations involves a high degree of compassion, sensitivity, and understanding of child development and human nature. Whether challenging behaviour demands an immediate and instinctive response or a carefully considered long-term approach, as a teacher you are required to deliver both – and often at a moment's notice!

Planning lessons and time management

Planning is the part of teaching that goes on behind the scenes – the bit that the general public don't take into account when they complain about teachers clocking off at 3.30 p.m. every afternoon! As with managing groups and challenging behaviour, it's a complex task involving many different skills and capabilities.

First of all, you have to know and understand the huge amount of documentation that accompanies any school-based curriculum. You then have to plan content and delivery, incorporate cross-curricular themes, establish short-term and long-term objectives, and prepare resources, all pitched at the ability level of your students and organised so that you can get through what you have to in the given time. And if a group needs longer on a particular topic, or you miss some crucial lessons, you will have to adjust and adapt your future lessons to make up the time; the date of the GCSE drama practical can't be shifted just because you have lost a chunk of lesson time to bank holidays and INSET . . . The teacher who is efficient and on top of their planning has organisational skills second to none.

Planning lessons and resources also brings out the creativity in a teacher. How can you display the latest incarnation of Unifix blocks in a way that encourages your Year 2 class to use them productively? What can you do with *A Midsummer Night's Dream* to spark interest in a group of switched-off 13-year-olds? If you weren't much of a researcher, graphic designer or ICT expert before you started teaching, you will be after a few weeks! Many teachers also develop a new way of looking at the world, with every object, scenario or event offering the potential to be translated into a learning experience. It may be a cliché, but as a teacher you will constantly have to 'think outside the box'. By its very nature, the job of teaching makes you resourceful, creative and free-thinking – highly transferable skills to have under your belt, whether you are planning to stay within the field of education or move to a completely new area.

Liaising with colleagues and parents

Although the bulk of your working day is spent with your students, the modern-day teacher is increasingly expected to work within many different teams. Even NQTs have to manage classroom assistants, technicians and students, while tasks such as planning the curriculum, sharing resources and disseminating information from courses necessitate working closely with colleagues.

The many different roles of the teacher also mean that you will liaise with colleagues in a variety of circumstances. Planning a series of lessons with your subject leader is quite different from acting in conjunction with your pastoral leader to manage a child's behavioural difficulties. Schools also tend to be highly structured. Although many institutions work hard at being democratic, the leadership and management structure is usually well established. The average secondary school teacher is accountable to a curriculum leader, a pastoral manager, a senior management team and a headteacher – and that's without including the governing body and the local authority. If you have worked within the management structure of a school, you have certainly had plenty of experience of being managed!

Most colleague liaison involves a familiar set of people, with whom you can develop a day-to-day, ongoing relationship. There is, however, another form of team co-operation that is becoming increasingly common and stands you in good stead if you want to transfer your skills to other jobs. Many schools now function in clusters or federations in order to share resources, planning and expertise and offer support and advice. This gives you the highly valuable experience of networking and sharing good practice with fellow professionals. Liaising with teachers at other schools requires a different approach from working day to day with your own colleagues – and it constitutes a very useful experience to have under your belt if you are considering roles such as consultancy, mentoring or conference work.

Dealing with parents provides yet another form of liaising with adults. Parents' evenings and *ad hoc* phone calls and meetings are the teacher's equivalent of customer services. The difference is that you are providing a service involving the customers' most precious commodity – their children. If you can handle the fears, anxieties, prejudices, misunderstandings and at times anger that many parents feel in relation to their offspring, you can handle just about any tricky customer. Liaising with parents will give you a set of skills and experiences that you should make the most of if you plan to move into any form of sales or marketing.

Self-motivation and self-assessment

Although teachers are far more monitored, assessed and 'supported' than ever before, you are still a lone professional for much of your working day. Being able to motivate and assess yourself is pivotal to your success as a teacher. There is now a culture in the teaching profession of frank and open self-assessment, and teachers constantly have to take on board feedback from students (which tends to be direct and often frighteningly accurate . . .). In the end, your survival is dependent to a large extent on your own self-assessment and willingness to adapt your practice accordingly. If your class are yawning and gazing out of the window, you have to face the fact that your lesson may be dull – and make the necessary changes to recapture your students' attention. Facing such immediate and stringent feedback day after day is not easy! This mode of operating makes for a tough, self-reliant worker who can motivate themselves, assess themselves independently and constantly improve on their performance – great qualities to have in any job.

These are just some of the generic skills that teaching gives you. Making a list can be a useful preparation for convincing the non-school-based employer just how much you have to offer. Use the summary below as a starting point and fill in the spaces with your own personal additions:

- presentation and public speaking skills;
- working with government directives, initiatives, regular curriculum changes . . .;
- planning and preparation of resources – research, ICT and graphic design skills;
- time management;

- working in teams with both familiar and unfamiliar colleagues;
- working within a management structure;
- providing parents with quality 'customer service';
- assessing your audience and adapting your delivery to suit their requirements;
- managing challenging individuals in both 'on the spot' and long-term situations;
- the ability to 'think on your feet';
- creativity, resourcefulness and the ability to 'think outside the box';
- self-motivation;
- self-assessment – accepting feedback and adapting your provision accordingly;
- a thick skin!

- . . . .
- . . . .

SO WHAT'S OUT THERE? . . . JOB OPPORTUNITIES

Mentoring

What?

Mentors give support to students in schools or colleges on an individual or small group basis. The majority of mentoring jobs are paid, but there are also opportunities to work in a voluntary capacity. Mentoring schemes are organised and run in a number of different ways:

- Some schools set up their own programmes, using staff members and external mentors with appropriate skills. A typical focus might be to target borderline C/D-grade GCSE pupils.
- A number of schemes are run by private companies and bought in by schools and colleges. The focus tends to be academic mentoring to raise achievement and improve learning, for example the development of study skills.
- The government-funded Learning Mentors initiative offers pastoral care with the aim of helping pupils to improve their levels of achievement and increase rates of attendance.

In some respects, the mentor's role overlaps with that of the teaching assistant. However, mentoring schemes are regarded as a complementary service, rather than a support role that is managed by a teacher within the classroom. Occasionally, the mentor's role might include giving support to adult staff working with young people, as well as the young people themselves.

Where?

As a mentor, you will be located in schools or colleges. Although any school may decide to use mentors, the majority of job opportunities tend to occur in inner-city, urban and deprived areas. Unlike teaching assistants, mentors usually work with pupils outside the classroom.

When?

Your timetable will be flexible to fit in with the pupil and the school. You will, however, mostly work within school hours and term-times. Occasionally you may be required to attend after-school meetings to discuss the children you are working with, and some schemes also offer support during holidays.

Who?

To be a successful mentor, you have to be able to form a good rapport with pupils – and quickly! All the usual skills involved in working with demanding pupils come into play, for example patience, consistency, flexibility and the ability to communicate and set boundaries. Mentors come from all walks of life, but in practice many have had experience working with young people. Teaching provides an excellent background, particularly if you have had previous pastoral responsibility. Some schools and colleges require mentors from a particular ethnic or linguistic background. Specific life experiences can also give a mentor an advantage in making links with particular pupils. As the mentoring system develops, there are increasing opportunities to specialise in areas such as family liaison or specific needs.

How?

Schools and colleges often advertise locally for mentors. It is also worth investigating whether private education companies are carrying out any schemes in your area. If you are currently in a teaching job, discuss your interest in mentoring with your line manager, as there may be opportunities within your own school or other schools and colleges in the locality. If you are appointed by an education company or organised scheme, you may be offered a short training course; for example, the Learning Mentors initiative runs a five-day introductory programme. Government-funded training opportunities should also be available at a local level, and there are NVQs aimed at individuals working in learning development and support services. Any educational coaching or generic mentoring courses are relevant, and although mentoring is a different process from counselling, the skills developed through a counselling course can prove to be very useful. For more information about recruitment and training opportunities via the Learning Mentors scheme, visit www.standards.dcsf.gov.uk/learningmentors.

Why?

Mentoring enables you to establish closer contact with pupils than is usually the case for the classroom teacher. This is a role to consider if you enjoy one-to-one involvement and have an interest in the pastoral care of challenging and underachieving pupils. If you work for an education company or the government's Learning Mentors scheme, you should also get the opportunity to visit and work with pupils in a variety of different settings.

Case study

From head of year to . . . Academic mentor

When Jane left her job as head of year in a large comprehensive to move with her husband to a new area, she decided to look for education-related roles outside the classroom. She had been working in the conference department of an education consultancy group for a couple of years when she was invited to become involved in a new mentoring scheme they were establishing.

Q What attracted you to the mentoring role?

A *I had always missed having contact with pupils, and as my role as year head had given me a considerable amount of pastoral experience, I felt well qualified to take part in the scheme. I wasn't particularly looking to expand my working life, but when I was offered the opportunity to become a mentor, it seemed too good to pass up!*

Q What does the work involve?

A *I am currently working with disaffected Year 11 pupils who are underachieving. My role involves motivating them, forging positive relationships and offering study skills and strategies. Each week, we get together to agree on targets and then meet the following week to review progress.*

Q What is it about mentoring that you most enjoy?

A *Without question, what I most enjoy is the opportunity to give pupils my undivided attention. This special and supportive one-to-one relationship is invaluable and, for some children, the only positive attention they get. I also enjoy the challenge of stepping outside a traditional teaching role. Although I'm not an English specialist, on one occasion I ended up teaching Seamus Heaney's poetry in order to meet the needs of a particular group of pupils!*

Q What are the other advantages of the role, apart from the satisfaction it gives you?

A *The flexibility of the work fits in well with my domestic and other work-based responsibilities. I also enjoy being able to draw fully on all those years of teaching experience. Apart from forming relationships with and supporting the pupils, I have to plan sessions, prepare resources, keep records and liaise with senior leaders and other staff over the pupils' needs and progress.*

continued

Q And the disadvantages?

A *My working day can sometimes be a bit disjointed; not all the schools are local, and I often end up travelling long distances. I am not paid for preparation or record keeping and I have to be careful to keep that side of the work under control – although this is something that teachers are used to! Overall, however, I love the work and would recommend it to any teacher who wants to make a difference.*

Other opportunities

Working for Connexions

Connexions is a government-funded agency with responsibility for providing support, advice and guidance to young people in England aged 13 to 19. Its aim is to help young people progress smoothly into adult life and give information about learning, personal development and job opportunities. Qualified Teacher Status is one of the recognised professional qualifications needed to become a Connexions personal adviser, and teaching experience provides an excellent background for this kind of work. For more information, visit www.connexions.gov.uk.

For information about working in a government-funded careers service throughout the rest of the United Kingdom, visit:

Wales: Careers Wales   www.careerswales.com
Scotland: Careers Scotland   www.careers-scotland.org.uk
Northern Ireland: Careers Service NI   www.careers serviceni.com

Other opportunities

Becoming an educational psychologist

Educational psychologists work with children who are having difficulties within an educational setting. The role includes assessing a child's emotional, social and learning needs through consultations, observations and liaising with parents, teachers and other professionals. Educational psychologists can also be involved in policy setting, research, the provision of INSET training and running parent information sessions.

If you wish to train as an educational psychologist and do not have a psychology degree, you will need to take a conversion course accredited by the British Psychological Society (BPS). You will then undertake a three-year doctorate training programme, which includes supervised professional placements. Once you are fully qualified, you will need to keep up to date with the latest research and developments in your field. For more information, visit the BPS website: www. bps.org.uk.

Working as a teaching assistant

What?

Teaching assistants (TAs) have become an increasingly important part of school life over the past few years. Also known as learning support assistants, classroom assistants or curriculum assistants, they take on a variety of different tasks, for example working on a one-to-one basis supporting a child with special needs, working within a secondary school department helping individuals and small groups, or assisting teaching staff with displays, resources and other aspects of preparation and planning. Many teachers now wonder how they ever coped without TAs.

Where?

Depending on your role, as a TA you will either work within the classroom or take individuals or small groups out of the classroom. A curriculum assistant, whose main role is to help with the preparation of resources, will be based in a departmental office or the work area of a staffroom.

When?

Although some TAs work a full week, the majority of jobs are part time. A TA's working day will usually end when the children go home, and as a TA you also get school holidays, although preparation work can spill over into evenings and weekends.

Who?

In most cases, no specific qualifications are needed, although once in the job, some schools encourage TAs to work towards appropriate NVQs. An increasing number of ex-teachers are becoming TAs, either as a stepping stone for getting back into teaching after a break or because they want to continue working with children but no longer want the stress, responsibility and workload that is the lot of most teachers. Being an ex-teacher will often put you in a strong position, particularly when it comes to being selected for interview. However, once you get to the interview you are likely to find yourself on a level playing field. One secondary school subject leader told us that she recently chose an unqualified applicant over an ex-teacher, based on her judgement that the former would relate better to the pupils on a small-group and one-to-one basis.

How?

TA posts are usually advertised in the local press, along with other county or school vacancies. Jobs are like gold dust in some areas because they fit in with school hours; volunteering as a parent helper in a primary school can put you in a good position to move into paid work. Applications are similar to teaching posts; contact the school for an application form or send in a letter of application and CV. Although schools vary in what they are looking for, an interview for a TA post will tend to be less in-depth than an interview for a teaching job.

Why?

Becoming a teaching assistant may seem an unusual career move for a teacher, but it is a job that holds many advantages. If you can afford to take a cut in salary, you can potentially have all the pleasures of teaching, without many of the disadvantages. Not for you the pressures of marking, report writing, parents' evenings and taking overall responsibility for the learning, welfare and development of scores of children. The TA's job tends to be quite organic and it is often possible for the role to develop in ways that will make the most of your particular skills and strengths. There are also opportunities for an experienced TA to undertake additional training and become a higher-level teaching assistant (HLTA). For more information, visit www.tda.gov.uk/support/hlta/.

Although you should find the job less demanding than teaching, you need to make sure that you are not inadvertently used as a low-paid teacher. Schools are hard pressed, and with the best will in the world it can be difficult not to exploit a capable pair of hands. Be clear from the start about what your role involves and how much you are willing to give, over and above your job description. Of course, no school employee gets a totally easy ride, and TAs work extremely hard. However, if you are looking for a less stressful school-based job that really does fit into school hours, this is one option well worth considering.

Case study

From primary school teacher to . . . learning support assistant

Christine left her job as a primary school teacher to start a family. When she decided it was time to go back to work, she discovered that things had moved on and that she had missed out on some major changes and initiatives. Here she describes why she decided to become a learning support assistant rather than return to teaching, what her job involves and how it has developed over the years:

continued

When I spotted an advertisement for a learning support assistant at my local comprehensive, I realised that the job would fit in with my own children's schooling and use my teaching skills. With so much having changed during the years I was out of teaching, it seemed a better option than looking for a teaching job. That was eleven years ago, and I am still here! My current role involves supporting pupils within the classroom, particularly those with literacy difficulties. I also work on a one-to-one basis helping pupils with organisation, study skills and coursework. My teaching experience and qualifications have led to further opportunities and I have developed my role through doing a course in special needs and taking on some SEN teaching responsibilities – for which I am remunerated.

I have found my teaching experience invaluable and I constantly draw on my ability to communicate with pupils, address their varying needs, and organise, plan and prepare resources. I have also used my knowledge of the primary curriculum, adapting it to help me support secondary-aged pupils with literacy difficulties. Thanks largely to my teaching background, I am also able to play a much more informed role in implementing departmental initiatives than is typical for a teaching assistant.

Overall, there have been few disadvantages, although I would advise ex-teachers to prepare themselves for taking a back seat. Because I moved from the primary to the secondary sector, this was easier for me, as I was not familiar with the system, but I realise that it might have been harder to relinquish control had I become a primary school teaching assistant.

Other opportunities

Working for a teaching union or professional association

The teaching unions and professional associations offer both paid and voluntary job opportunities. Your responsibilities as a paid union officer will include tasks such as assisting with individual casework, supporting local associations, negotiating with local authorities and assisting with training programmes. If you are a voluntary school-based union or association 'rep', you will be responsible for recruiting new members, representing the members in your school and acting as a communication link between members and the union offices. To find out what opportunities are available, visit your union's or association's website.

Assessing NVQs

What?

National Vocational Qualifications (NVQs) are organised and accredited through awarding bodies such as City & Guilds. Unlike the traditional 'coursework-and-exam' route, NVQs enable individuals to work towards a qualification within the workplace by demonstrating competency in their current role. This is actioned through compiling a portfolio that presents evidence of the candidate's experience, knowledge and practice. In this respect, the NVQ differs from taught courses, where students are required to study, learn new information and skills and revise for examinations, although in some instances NVQ candidates may be required to attend courses to provide underpinning knowledge.

The NVQ assessor's role is to manage the qualification and assess the candidate's competence and portfolio. The assessor also acts as mentor, visiting the candidate in the workplace and offering support and advice wherever necessary. Assessment visits include checking newly gathered portfolio evidence against the established standards for the qualification, signing off any units that have been completed, planning for the next stage of activities to gather evidence, observing the candidate at work and meeting with the employee's manager, where appropriate.

Where?

Most meetings with the candidate you are assessing will take place in the workplace. For many assessors, one of the advantages of the job is the chance to access a wide variety of different locations and work-places; for example, a childcare assessor will visit playgroups, daycare establishments and even home-based childminders; an assessor for teaching assistants might visit early years, primary and secondary settings. If you are employed by a training company, you will mostly complete administrative and paperwork tasks at home, although you will nominally be linked to the training company's offices. If you are employed by an FE college, you will usually be college based, with easier access to administrative support.

When?

Assessment visits are timetabled to fit in with your candidate and their workplace. Visits can last for anything from an hour to three hours, depending on your agenda and what you and the candidate need to cover. The number of visits you make will depend on the needs of the candidate. On average, you can expect to visit each candidate every three to four weeks. Full-time employed positions occasionally come up, but the majority of NVQ assessors work on a part-time or freelance basis.

Who?

Apart from undergoing specialist training (see 'How?', below), you also need experience in one of the occupational NVQ areas. For example, early years teachers are well placed to assess childcare quali-fications, and any teacher with management experience can go on to assess management and administration qualifications. Although you do not need to be a qualified teacher to become an NVQ assessor, you will draw on many of your teaching skills: for example, the ability to encourage and motivate individuals; to plan and manage your time and that of your candidate; to work towards a goal; to assess the candidate's written evidence and performance; and to discuss with a candidate, in a constructive and supportive manner, where improvement is necessary.

How?

To find out more about becoming an NVQ assessor, contact local training companies or FE colleges, many of which run NVQs with taught elements. Some training companies will train you for free as part of the recruitment process, whereas others advertise for qualified assessors. If you want to organise your own training as an NVQ assessor, contact a training company or FE college. You can work at your own pace, but most candidates complete the qualification well within a year of starting.

Why?

Becoming an NVQ assessor keeps you within the field of education, but at the same time introduces you to a very different way of working with your students. If you are starting to feel confined within the four walls of the classroom, working as an NVQ assessor gets you 'out and about' on a regular basis. The role also enables you to work with adults, and, for some teachers, supporting individuals with their vocational and work-based training can prove to be more rewarding than school or college-based teaching.

Case study

From English teacher to . . . NVQ assessor

Liz began her career as an English teacher in a large inner-city comprehensive. Over the years, she moved schools several times in order to gain promotion, and she was a senior teacher with responsibility for pupil welfare when she developed health problems. She describes how she became an NVQ assessor, what the job involves and how she has developed a new career:

continued

Q Explain how you became an NVQ assessor.

A *I had to give up teaching due to health problems. My health eventually improved enough for me to return to work, but I decided I no longer wanted the stress of a senior teacher's position. I was quite happy to go back into teaching at a lower scale, but I also fancied a change and I started looking out for other options. Although I knew little about NVQs, an advertisement in the local paper caught my eye. A training company was asking for NVQ assessors with experience of teaching or training and offering to train successful candidates for free.*

Q So you decided to go for it?

A *Yes, I applied and went through a selection procedure. This involved attending an observed group interview with role-plays. Although, like any interview, it was a bit gruelling, it did not compare to the stress of the three-day interview procedures I went through to win my management posts. Anyway, I got through it all in one piece and, based on my leadership and management background, the company appointed me to assess the Customer Service and Management NVQ.*

Q Do you enjoy the work?

A *Very much so. After years of being based in schools, I enjoy travelling to different workplaces and I'm always fascinated to get an inside look at, among other places, leisure clubs, garden centres, estate agencies and recruitment consultancies. I also love the flexibility of being able to plan a timetable that gives me some free time during the day. The work brings me into contact with a wide range of people from different age groups and backgrounds, and with a variety of needs and requirements.*

Q How do you use your teaching skills?

A *In many different ways. I see several similarities between the NVQ candidates and some of my ex-pupils. Motivating a disenchanted, time-stretched worker who doesn't really want to do an NVQ is not that dissimilar to motivating a switched-off* teenager who cannot see the point of studying Shakespeare! I also have to communicate with managers and other training company personnel, and I am constantly drawing on my past experience of interacting with parents and colleagues in school. Apart from the human interaction, the organisational side of the work is hugely important. Record keeping is central to the NVQ system and although, like many teachers, I found it a burden in the classroom, my experience is now standing me in good stead. Timetabling and time management are also essential skills. If you don't plan your visits carefully, you can spend most of your day driving back and forth across the countryside!

Q Explain how your career as an NVQ assessor has developed.

A In spite of my intention to have a less stressful working life, I found myself looking for promotion and I am now an internal verifier. This qualification enables me to monitor the work of other assessors and run my own assessor training sessions.

Q Do you have any tips or advice for teachers who would like to follow a similar path?

A The NVQ system demands a different mindset from the traditional taught-and-examined course. If it is new to you, I would recommend getting to know the system thoroughly before making a decision to go ahead. I would also recommend approaching your continuing professional development co-ordinator, as there may be opportunities to assess candidates following an NVQ for teaching assistants in your school.

Q Are there any disadvantages to the role?

A Only the pay! If you work solely as an NVQ assessor, you will probably end up taking a salary cut, and as it is not that easy to find full-time posts, you may need to regard your new role either as a second income, a top-up for early retirement or as part of a work portfolio.

Working as a supply teacher

What?

To work as a supply teacher, you need to be a qualified professional with the necessary skills to cover for an absent colleague, sometimes at very short notice and occasionally on a long-term basis. Your role will, however, vary enormously from class to class and school to school. Although the absent teacher should have left work for his or her class, this is not always the case, and you need to have several activities at your fingertips in case of emergencies and/or be ready to liaise with a curriculum or key stage leader. As a supply teacher, you will be expected to cover all aspects of the absent teacher's role. This can include anything from break duty to helping out on a school trip. If you happen to be working in a school during an Ofsted inspection, you could also be inspected as part of the evaluation of teaching and learning for that school.

Where?

In the early stages of your career as a supply teacher, you will have to be willing to go wherever you are needed if you want to form links with the schools in your area. Once you are more established, you can exercise greater control over where you choose to work. If you are prepared to travel, you will have access to a wider range of schools, although if you live too far away, a school will not have the option of calling on you at the last minute.

When?

As a supply teacher, your working hours will vary from week to week, and you will also have to be available when schools need you. Mary worked as a primary supply teacher for a number of years and in some cases was telephoned at 8.30 a.m. and asked to arrive at a school within twenty minutes. On other occasions, she would be booked weeks in advance. Jobs vary in length, and can range from just half a day to a couple of weeks, or even a short-term contract.

Who?

To work as a supply teacher, you need to have Qualified Teacher Status. Opportunities are available in all sectors, from early years to secondary, and you do not necessarily have to restrict yourself to the age group you trained for. Although Mary was a qualified primary school teacher, she agreed to take on some supply teaching at a nearby middle school. She found the experience a refreshing change and, as a result, is planning to offer her services to some of the secondary schools in the area.

Supply teaching works well as a flexible part-time job that can be combined with a young family or used as a means of getting back into teaching after a break. Many retired teachers also return to their schools in a supply capacity to supplement their pensions. Such teachers have the advantage of being established at the school and so avoid the disciplinary challenges that can be the lot of the ordinary supply teacher – although some find that they lose their 'status' with the pupils within a couple of years.

Currently, it is possible for an NQT to work as a supply teacher for up to four terms after finishing training, but it will only count towards your induction period if the placement lasts for more than one term. After the four terms are up, you are only allowed to teach in a supply capacity if a placement lasts for more than one term and so counts towards your induction period. For more information, visit www.teachernet.gov.uk/professionaldevelopment/induction.

Occasionally, a teacher will choose to make a career out of supply teaching. Having completed a primary training course as a mature student, Bella found it difficult to get a permanent job. She started taking on supply placements and managed to achieve Qualified Teacher Status through a series of short-term contracts. As a single mother, she found the flexibility of supply easier to cope with than the commitment of a long-term post, and she made a career decision to become a professional supply teacher. She ensures that she always has a minimum number of schools using her regularly at any one time and regards setting up and maintaining links with schools as an essential part of her job. If she feels that she is losing touch with a school, she sends a card at the start of each term, reminding the school that she is available, and at the same time she works hard to keep adding new contacts to her list. This system gives her more than enough work to support herself and her family, and she would not now choose to take on a permanent position.

As a supply teacher, you need to be able to hit the ground running. Pupils have always tested supply teachers to the limits, and even younger children are experts at taking advantage of a teacher who doesn't know the system. To survive as a supply teacher, you need confidence, sharpness, the ability to convince the class that you have authority and the ability to make a positive impact in a short space of time.

How?

There are several routes to becoming a supply teacher. One option is to ask your local authority to add you to the list which is regularly circulated to all schools in the area. Joining a supply agency is another possibility; find out what is available by doing an internet search, looking in the business section of the telephone directory or checking the advertisements in the education press. One of the best options is to make personal contact with schools. Mary took her CV to a number of local primary schools and introduced herself to the headteacher. She was surprised and pleased at how much work this generated, and once she was established, certain schools went on to use her regularly. She does, however, warn that relationships can be precarious; she recalls having to cancel a school that had booked her well in advance, and to her great regret she was never again invited back.

Why?

Supply teaching offers many advantages. The flexibility of the role is a great plus – you can always say no if you are not free on a particular day, although you do need to bear in mind that the more available you are, the easier it is to build up a strong relationship with a school. If you enjoy being in the classroom, but dislike the paperwork that accompanies the modern-day teaching role, you may find that supply teaching offers you a better work–life balance. This is not to say that there is no marking and preparation, but your paperwork burden will be considerably less than that of the regular teacher and you will avoid the many meetings and parents' evenings that permanent teachers are required to attend.

Supply teaching also gives you an insight into lots of different schools – fascinating for anyone who is interested in education as a whole. You will quickly learn which schools and/or departments have a robust disciplinary structure and offer good support systems to supply teachers (and as you become established, you will increasingly be able to pick and choose the schools where you work). If you are in the early stages of your career or looking to go back into school after a career break, you can learn a huge amount from your different placements. Unlike many education-related jobs, the pay is commensurate with that of the permanent main-scale teacher, although most supply teachers end up working part time, and you do not get paid in the holidays.

And the downside? If you want a regular working timetable, like to be able to plan in advance, see a topic through and watch your pupils' development across the year, then supply teaching is probably not for you. You will also have to cope with some hair-raising situations, and although you are working as a qualified teacher, you may not be accorded the same status and respect as a permanent teacher. At the same time, if you can establish yourself as reliable, there is the potential to become a highly valued part of the schools where you work. As a regular supply teacher, you are also in a strong position to take on a permanent contract if this is your ultimate goal.

Other opportunities

Working as a cover assistant

A number of larger schools are now appointing cover assistants. Like teaching assistants, cover assistants do not have to be trained teachers, and they are part of the permanent staff with the specific job of standing in for absent teachers. Any school that employs cover assistants will tend to use them before calling in a supply teacher. Although this can reduce work opportunities for external supply teachers, becoming a cover assistant offers a different kind of opportunity for a trained teacher who is happy with a supply role but wants the stability of working within just the one school.

Invigilating examinations

What?

Many schools and colleges employ outside staff to invigilate both public and internal examinations. Invigilators are central to the smooth running of the exam system, and the role includes a number of responsibilities such as putting out and collecting question papers and resources, supervising the candidates as they enter and exit the examination room, and ensuring the appropriate conduct and behaviour of candidates during the exam itself.

Where?

The work is located wherever the school or college holds its examinations: halls, gyms, dining rooms and classrooms for small groups of candidates. If you are missing that unique school odour of yesterday's dinner combined with old trainers, then this is the job for you!

When?

Apart from short periods of training, invigilation work is restricted to examination periods. The busiest times tend to be May/June and January, although modules can take place at other times throughout the year. As the exam timetable is dictated by the awarding bodies, there is little flexibility over the dates and times you will be required to work. Many schools do, however, give you the opportunity to let them know in advance the times and days when you are available. The length of your working day will vary, depending on the exam timetable and the needs of the school or college. On some occasions, you may only be required to work for a morning or afternoon; on other occasions, you may be needed for the whole day, particularly if you take on the role of senior invigilator (see case study below).

Who?

Although you do not need any special qualifications to work as an invigilator, it is a job that is often taken on by ex-teachers – and with good reason. Invigilators play a crucial role in establishing the kind of environment where candidates can give of their best, and your ability to assert your authority and handle large numbers of pupils will prove invaluable. Many schools and colleges are delighted to have competent ex-teachers in the role, so make the most of your CV and experience when you apply.

How?

You will often find adverts for invigilators in the local press. It is also worth ringing around the schools and colleges in your area to ask if they have any vacancies. Following the application and interview process, most schools and colleges will offer a short training session to successful candidates.

Why?

If you have retired or taken a career break, invigilating examinations will take you back into school, but without the pressures of having to plan, mark or teach on a day-to-day basis. Although the work is not particularly well paid, it provides a useful income boost in the run-up to the summer holiday and during the post-Christmas period.

Case study

From retired deputy head to . . . exam invigilator

After nearly forty years as a teacher, and latterly a deputy head, Rhys missed having contact with both children and colleagues, and he decided to look for a part-time job. Here he describes how he became an invigilator, what the work involves and why he enjoys it so much:

When I saw a newspaper advertisement for invigilators at my local comprehensive school, I decided to send off for an application pack. The school seemed pleased to have an experienced teacher in the role and appointed me to work as part of a team covering Year 9 SATS, Year 10 internal exams and Year 11 GCSEs.

The job has turned out to be just what I was looking for. It takes me back into school but does not get in the way of my other hobbies and interests. I particularly enjoy being able to use my many years of experience, without the day-in, day-out responsibilities of classroom teaching. Although you don't need to be a teacher to work as an invigilator, my teaching skills have proved

continued

invaluable. I am used to managing large groups, dealing with nerves and creating the calm atmosphere required for an examination. I also have to record any incidents that occur, and my years of experience within the education system have helped me considerably in making on-the-spot judgements over what is and isn't of importance.

After a year in the job, I was promoted to senior invigilator. This new role involves managing a team of invigilators, ensuring that the correct question papers are in the right rooms, collected in the right order, checked against the official register and sealed in the correct envelopes. As an experienced teacher, my organisational skills, attention to detail and commitment to the examination system have stood me in good stead. I know all too well the potential for disaster if the system breaks down and things are not done correctly!

I would certainly recommend the job to anyone who is happy to deal with large groups of students and play what is actually a very important role within the current education system. The only downside is the pay, which probably doesn't reflect the degree of responsibility you are taking on. It's not a problem for me as I have a pension, and I do the job for the enjoyment rather than the money. However, if you need a part-time job for financial reasons, you may have to take on other work throughout the rest of the year, or look elsewhere.

Running extra-curricular clubs and activities for children

What?

There is a wide range of options if you want to become involved with activities for young people outside school. The following list covers just some of the possibilities:

- **Brownies, Guides, Cubs and Scouts**: the Guide and Scout movements offer work opportunities at many different levels. For example, roles within the Guides range from simply sharing your hobbies and skills as an adviser, to becoming a commissioner with responsibility for organising and supporting groups throughout your region. You can also choose the age range you prefer: the guiding movement includes Rainbows for the five to seven age group, Brownies for sevens to tens, Guides for tens to fourteens and a Senior Section for older teenagers and young adults. The Scouting movement is open to both boys and girls, and offers Beavers for the six to eight age group, Cubs for eights to tens and Scouts for older children and young teenagers.

- **Youth clubs**: the youth club movement was set up to help young people develop physically, mentally and emotionally through leisure-time activities. Youth clubs tend to be small, community-based groups, often located in a community centre. Some youth clubs are affiliated to the local authority and receive grants, others are run by independent bodies such as local church groups.

- **Religious and cultural clubs and groups**: if you represent an ethnic or cultural minority or are a practising member of a religious group, there may be opportunities to help children learn about their religious or cultural background in an out-of-school setting. Examples might include working with an Islamic study group, setting up a Saturday school to help children explore their native family culture, or leading a Church of England Sunday school session.

Where?

Your working environment will vary, depending on your role. Brownies, Guides, Scouts and youth clubs often use local schools, community centres, village halls or even their own scout huts. Religious groups tend to meet in a place of worship; for example, our case study Helen ran her Sunday school in the church vestry while the service was taking place in the main body of the church. Cultural Saturday schools are often held at a community centre or even in the home of the individual running the group.

When?

Depending on your role, your working hours tend to be evenings, weekends and holiday periods. If you work within the Scout or Guide movement, you will probably be involved in taking your group on summer camp. Activities for younger children are usually held soon after the end of the school day, whereas groups such as youth clubs will meet later in the evening – something to consider if you are fitting the role around your own family.

Who?

Whatever the activity or age group, teaching experience is invaluable. You will also need the necessary skills, interests and background to meet the requirements of the role you take on; for example, some expertise in sport, drama or art is a distinct advantage if you plan to work in a youth club. Bear in mind that most extra-curricular clubs provide leisure activities for children and are therefore less structured than schools. If you suspect you might find it difficult to adapt to the more liberal environment of a non-school-based group, this may not be the role for you. As most of the roles are voluntary, you also need to consider whether you require an income.

How?

- If you want to work for the Guide or Scout movements, contact local groups to find out what opportunities are available. To get an idea of some typical roles, visit www.scoutbase.org.uk or www.girlguiding.org.uk.
- To find out more about youth clubs in your area, contact your local authority. Searching for 'UK youth clubs' on the internet will also provide you with both local and national information and job opportunities.
- If you want to work within a particular cultural or religious setting, asking parents what is available is often the best way to make first contact with a group. If you perceive that there is a need or interest that is not currently being met, you could also consider starting your own group. Contact Ofsted to establish whether you need to register your group and meet any requirements and regulations such as CRB checks and taking out insurance. Contact details for Ofsted can be found on their website: www.ofsted.gov.uk.

Why?

Working in a youth club or a Guide or Scout group is a good way of contributing to your community, and your teaching skills and experience will be much appreciated. You should also be able to add to your own skills set, with a number of organisations offering a range of training opportunities; for example, if you volunteer to work in a youth club, you may be able to take courses in subjects such as first aid or drug awareness. A major advantage of this kind of work for many teachers is the chance to spend time with young people, without the pressures of syllabuses, examinations and bells. As with our case study, Helen, working in a voluntary capacity can also enable you to 'keep your hand in' during a career break. It can help you decide whether or not you wish to go back into teaching, and makes a useful addition to your CV if you are planning a return to the classroom, or are at the early stages of your career.

Case study

From primary school teacher to . . . Sunday school leader

Helen had always been a regular churchgoer, and when she started to introduce her own children to the Sunday school group, the education co-ordinator invited her to help with organising the group:

Q What age group did you work with?

A *As the congregation was quite large, the church ran two sessions, one for younger children and one for the over-eights. The education co-ordinator knew I was a Key Stage 2 teacher before having my family, and he was delighted when I agreed to teach the older children. He usually found it hard to staff the eight-plus group as they were perceived as more of a challenge to handle.*

Q How important were your teaching skills?

A *As an ex-teacher, I found the planning of resources and lessons came naturally. I was, however, surprised at how much the role differed from that of the classroom teacher. Without teacher status or established school systems to fall back on, I was totally reliant on my own skills in handling children,*

continued

managing the group as a whole and planning sessions that would hold the pupils' interest. My new role certainly helped me to brush up on my teaching skills!

Q You are now back in teaching. Did your Sunday school role play a part in your return?

A *Yes, very much so. It gave me the confidence I needed to get back into the classroom – first as a supply teacher and then as a permanent part-time member of staff. I was able to add the experience to my CV, and during my interview I talked about what the work involved and how it had kept my teaching skills alive.*

Q What were the advantages of the role?

A *Apart from providing a stepping stone back into teaching, running the Sunday school helped me to feel a much more integrated member of both the church and the wider community. I also enjoyed helping the children to explore issues that are important to me, and I was free to use activities I love, such as art and drama.*

Q And the disadvantages?

A *Other than lesson preparation on a Saturday night, the only real downside occurred when I had to be firm with the children of friends from the congregation. That was tricky at times! Overall, though, I would recommend a similar role to anyone who wants to maintain or develop their teaching skills and make a voluntary contribution to their community.*

Other opportunities

Purchasing a subject franchise

Purchasing a subject franchise is another option for those who would like to run an out-of-school activity for children. See page 84 for more details.

Working in out-of-school clubs and summer schools

What?

- Out-of-school clubs provide a 'wraparound' service for parents who work or are in training and need childcare outside school hours. They usually function before and after school, and offer activities such as art and craft, games, sports, drama and dance, along with the opportunity for children to read or relax in a quiet area. There are many different providers for this kind of care, ranging from local authority-run facilities to voluntary organisations and employer-sponsored schemes. Currently, any out-of-school club that offers care for the under-eights must be registered with Ofsted and meet national standards. Working in an out-of-school club is a salaried role, although the pay is not commensurate with that of a teacher.
- Summer schools cater for all age groups and offer a wide range of courses, including music, art, dance, drama, provision for the gifted and talented, help with GCSEs and language courses. For several years, our case study, Simon, has combined his full-time job as a drama teacher with running a holiday sports play scheme. Organised by the local community education office, the scheme operates during the summer and Easter holidays and caters for children between the ages of 7 and 13. It aims to provide holiday childcare for working parents and give children the opportunity to experience and develop their skills in a range of different sports.

Where?

Most out-of-school clubs are located on school premises, enabling children to move seamlessly from classroom to after-school care. Many clubs aim to use outdoor facilities as much as possible, and clubs that offer daytime holiday care may also arrange trips and outings. Although summer schools can take place in a variety of locations, they are usually based in schools.

When?

Working in an out-of-school club involves early starts and late afternoon hours, and you may be required to offer daytime provision in the holidays. Summer schools take place during the long school holiday, with some schemes also running at Easter. Although summer schools vary in duration, each course typically lasts for a fortnight. You may work for just a two-week stretch, or you may be given the opportunity to teach more than one course throughout the holiday. Some schools are residential, which could require you stay away from home for the duration of the course.

Who?

Although you do not have to be a trained teacher to work in an out-of-school club, your teaching skills will come in very useful. Most out-of-school clubs are aimed at the primary age group, so you need to be willing to work with younger children. The ethos and atmosphere of the out-of-school club are quite different from those of the classroom. Although the children are still within a structured care setting, they have finished their school day and need to relax and let off steam. When considering this kind of work, ask yourself how easy you will find it to adjust from the teacher's role to the somewhat different emphasis of the childcare provider.

To work in a summer school, you need to have the necessary teaching skills, experience and qualifications. Although he is a drama teacher, Simon had taught sport in previous jobs and draws extensively on his experience of organising games, managing space, time and resources, and handling large groups of children.

How?

Contact local schools to find out whether they are running an out-of-school club that you could become involved with. You can also visit www.childcarelink.gov.uk and search for out-of-school and holiday clubs in your area.

To find out what summer schools are available, try contacting schools in your area. If you are currently in teaching, your own school may offer opportunities. Simon heard about his job through the local community education department, who were based at his school and knew that he was looking for holiday work. If you are happy to teach on a residential course, it is also worth contacting the larger independent schools across the country, as they often host a variety of holiday courses and activities. For a comprehensive list of summer schools, visit www.summer-schools.info.

Why?

Working in an out-of-school club is a good choice for someone who has taken early retirement, or who wants to 'downsize' or make a preliminary move back into teaching after a career break. The role also offers teachers the opportunity to spend time with children in a less structured setting than school – although when it comes to planning activities and creating a positive environment, your teaching experience will prove very useful. On the downside, your day can be rather fragmented – something to consider if you need to fit your working hours around your own children.

In contrast to an out-of-school club, working in a summer school can be combined with a full-time teaching career. Simon took on his role as a holiday play scheme leader because he had a young family and needed the extra income. Working in the holidays was the obvious way to earn more money, and it has proved to be a financial lifesaver. The job does, however, prevent him from spending time with his family, and he also advises any teacher to consider carefully whether they can afford to miss out on the 'recharging' opportunities of the holidays. On the plus side, he enjoys the chance to spend time with children in a more relaxed and informal setting. As a secondary school teacher, he also finds it both interesting and fulfilling to work with a younger age group.

Other opportunities

Working in an American summer camp

If the prospect of working with children in the United States appeals, consider applying for a job in an American summer camp. For the past seven years, Philip has spent July and August working for a summer camp located in New York State. He started out at the age of 19 as a lifeguard, counsellor and group leader, before attending university and training as a teacher. He is now Assistant Head Counsellor, a role that includes responsibility for welfare, safety, the organisation of activities and the deployment of staff.

---

continued

For Philip, there are numerous advantages to the role. He values the break it gives him from the United Kingdom and the chance to get right away from school. He also enjoys the very different experience of working with American children. The one difficulty is getting leave from school; unfortunately, the camp dates don't coincide with the British summer holidays, and each year he has to beg for time off. It is, however, a role he would recommend to anyone who wants the challenge of working with young people in another country.

Working for charities and places of interest

What?

Charities, monuments and places of interest offer various education-related roles, both paid and unpaid. The following are just a few examples:

- **Education officers**: most charities and places of interest employ education officers, and they welcome volunteers or job applicants with teaching experience. If you have ever organised a school trip, you will have some idea of what the education officer's role involves: planning activities and developing resources, liaising with schools, conducting school parties around the site and ensuring that pupils have a productive visit.
- **Visiting speakers**: many larger charities send speakers into schools. When Pamela retired from her job as a primary school teacher, she wanted to continue working with children, and she took on the role of schools liaison officer for a children's charity. Not only did she enjoy contributing to assemblies and theme days, but also the schools she visited welcomed her input; as she was an experienced teacher, they were able to leave her to it and snatch a few moments of non-contact time!
- **Specialised posts**: some larger charities and museums also have education-related posts with a more specific brief. For example, at the time of writing, Save the Children was advertising for volunteers to run a new initiative helping UK schools gain an insight into the lives of children from developing countries.

Where?

With such a wide variety of roles to choose from, you should be able to find a working environment to suit your needs and personality. If you love ancient buildings and artefacts, you will probably enjoy the characterful surroundings of a museum or historical monument (although you may end up with less than state-of-the-art facilities); if you want to be surrounded by architectural beauty and a spiritual atmosphere, look for work in a place of worship; and if you like being outdoors, try the National Trust or English Heritage. Some roles may also be office or even home based, with visits to schools and colleges as part of the package.

When?

Your working timetable will vary, depending on where you work and your particular role. If you are a volunteer, there may be scope for you to dictate your own working hours. Retired university lecturer Brenda volunteered to organise an exhibition for her local museum, based on the life and times of a local Victorian geologist. Given her experience, the museum were more than happy to let her manage and organise the project, and, along with it, her own timetable. Similarly, Pamela was usually able to organise her school visits to suit herself. Other roles will, however, involve a more regular commitment and the possibility of weekend work – shifts as an education officer or guide, for example. Take into consideration whether you want flexible working hours or a set timetable when choosing which roles to go for.

Who?

Whatever your skills, requirements and level of previous experience, you should be able to find a role to suit you. Retired teachers have always made a significant voluntary contribution to local charities, churches and museums. Alternatively, you can carry out voluntary work alongside a teaching job or use it as a stepping stone to salaried work (see the following case study). If you need an income, try approaching the larger charities, cathedrals and museums, as they are usually in a better position to offer paid employment.

How?

There are various ways of finding out what is available. Look out for adverts in the local press and try ringing museums, churches, cathedrals and historical monuments in your area to offer your services. Many charities also use their shop windows as a means of advertising for volunteers, while the larger organisations have websites with a 'jobs and volunteers' section.

Why?

Working for a charity, museum or place of interest enables you to give something back to the community, and you should find that your teaching skills and experience are very much valued by the organisation you work for. You can also follow your heart when deciding where to offer your services: working for charities devoted to animals, children, the developing world or specific medical conditions; supporting places of worship if you have religious faith; or helping out in museums and places of historical interest if you value Britain's heritage. Many retired people also find voluntary work a useful way to make new contacts and keep active, while those still in teaching can gain access to a whole new range of experiences.

Case study

From religious education teacher to . . . Cathedral Education Officer

Tess combines a part-time job teaching RE with her voluntary role as an education officer at Salisbury Cathedral. Here she explains what the work involves and why it is such an important part of her life.

I began working at Canterbury Cathedral as a student and spent an idyllic summer living in the cathedral precinct and training to be a guide. When I moved to East Anglia, I approached Lincoln Cathedral and was given my first taste of working with school parties. Ten years ago, yet another move brought me to the education office at Salisbury Cathedral, where I am still working today.

My role as an education officer involves developing and running workshops for secondary-aged pupils. These can range from inter-faith days working with representatives from other religions to interactive activities inspired by the cathedral and its treasures. I constantly draw on my subject knowledge and teaching experience to plan my workshops, and as a secondary school teacher I am happy to work with teenagers – an age group that many volunteers prefer to avoid. I did, at one point, consider taking on a salaried post as Cathedral Education Officer. In the end, I decided against it only because the holidays did not compare well with those of the school teacher. I now combine my voluntary role with a four-day teaching week at a secondary school, and I find that the two different settings give full scope to both my enthusiasm for education and my Christian commitment.

I would advise any interested teacher to approach their nearest cathedral and explore all the options. I love the work, and although I draw extensively on my teaching skills, my experiences at the cathedral have made an equally positive impact on my role as a classroom teacher. In my case, I do have a theology background, but this is not an essential, and I'm sure that any cathedral would welcome a willing volunteer teacher with open arms!

Teaching adults in the community

What?

There are a huge number of options if you want to teach daytime or evening courses, run workshops or organise activities for adults within the community. The following list covers just some of the major UK-based adult education providers:

- **Local authorities**: local authority adult and community education departments offer a wide variety of learning programmes, courses and activities. A student may come out at the end of a course with an ECDL (European Computer Driving Licence) qualification in computing, a GCSE in maths, or simply a new set of skills, interests and friends. Typical courses might include

'Understanding What Your Children Learn at School', 'Cooking on a Budget', A level sociology or 'Computing for the Terrified'.

- **Further and higher education (FE and HE) colleges**: colleges of FE and HE run a range of part-time qualifications, including GCSEs aimed at adult learners or students who want to retake a qualification at a later stage in their education. Some HE colleges also offer opportunities for experienced teachers to act as visiting lecturers on a PGCE (Postgraduate Certificate in Education) or MEd programme.

- **The Workers Educational Association (WEA)**: the WEA is a charity operating at local, regional and national level to promote learning for life. It offers a wide variety of accredited and non-accredited courses covering areas of interest such as the visual and performing arts, humanities and literature, ICT and staff development. It has a particular commitment to those who missed out on education in the past.

- **The University of the Third Age**: known affectionately as the U3A, the University of the Third Age is yet another national organisation that offers teaching opportunities. With its unique and well-respected approach to learning, it caters for the older person who is no longer in full-time employment, although there are no minimum age requirements. Rather than providing pre-ordained courses and activities, it enables local people to set up their own 'interest groups'. The groups remain small and are generally held in people's homes to create an informal, friendly atmosphere and keep costs low. A member may offer to lead a group if they have a particular body of knowledge, although it is central to the philosophy of the U3A that no one needs qualifications to join and no qualifications are awarded. As an alternative, the group may choose to ask an outside tutor to contribute. The U3A also runs summer schools and online courses.

- **Privately run courses**: it is always worth looking out for privately run courses within your field of expertise. For example, some craft shops organise their own needlework and papercraft classes; gyms run sessions in fitness, Pilates and yoga; swimming pools run life-saving courses, water aerobics and swimming lessons; museums and art galleries offer courses and talks on subjects such as local history and art appreciation; and there are a number of private cookery schools. All these organisations need tutors with teaching experience and knowledge of their subject.

Where?

Most local authority adult and community education departments are linked to a community or extended school, and you will often teach your course on school premises. This is useful if you need resources such as computers, a stage for performances or a gym area for fitness-related activities. Courses may also be spread around the locality to make them accessible to more people (particularly the case in rural areas, where you could find yourself located in a village hall or community centre). The teaching locations for other organisations will also vary. The WEA often provides courses in conjunction with local organisations and community groups, and it uses a similar range of locations, whereas many U3A groups take place in people's homes. One of the challenges of teaching community-based courses for adults is the need to adapt to and make the most of a variety of different teaching locations.

When?

Adult education courses and activities take place throughout the day: mornings, afternoons, evenings and, in some cases, weekends and during holidays. This enables you to fit the job around commitments such as childcare, other part-time work or hobbies.

Who?

With such a huge remit, teaching adults in the community offers opportunities in just about any subject area. If you want something that taps into your years of experience and expertise, look out for roles such as visiting lecturer on a teacher training course; for something more relaxed and informal, investigate the U3A or a privately run interest-based course such as cookery or craft; to make double use of your years of lesson planning and syllabus knowledge, consider teaching a part-time GCSE. Many teachers supplement their income by running evening classes in addition to a full-time job.

In some cases, you also need to look into whether you are suitably qualified. In order to work for a local authority adult and community education department, even experienced teachers may have to obtain a further qualification for teaching adults (contact your local FE college for information on possible courses). Specialist training might be required to teach classes such as Pilates or yoga, and it is also worth checking whether you will need to organise your own insurance (for more information, see pages 207–8).

How?

If you want to work for an adult and community education department or FE or HE college, contact your nearest community education office, local authority or college to find out what skills they are currently looking for. It is also worth checking local newspapers, as both adult and community education departments and FE or HE colleges often advertise for specific tutors. If you contact your local community education office and get the chance to discuss your options, consider suggesting some of your own ideas for courses that you could teach. Some adult and community education departments are happy to advertise a course designed by a tutor and then run it if they get enough takers to make it financially viable.

The WEA has an extensive website with a jobs section, informing you of how to apply online or by post (visit www.wea.org.uk for more information). The U3A also has a detailed website explaining its unique philosophy of learning, and giving information about how to find groups in your area or set up your own group (visit www. U3A.org.uk).

Why?

Working with adults who have chosen a course of their own free will can be a more straightforward experience than teaching certain schoolchildren – although, as our case study, Sarah, points out, handling a difficult adult can be every bit as challenging as handling a difficult child! With so many possibilities, you can get right away from the pressures of syllabuses and examinations by choosing to focus on a hobby. Alternatively, you can make good use of your experience as a subject teacher by running a part-time GCSE or A level course. If you have a family to look after, the flexibility of the working hours can also be a great advantage, as Sarah describes.

Case study

From physics teacher to . . . adult education tutor

Sarah taught physics at her local comprehensive school before leaving teaching to start a family. When her younger daughter was 3, she felt it was time to return to part-time work, and she started exploring her options:

Q Why did you decide to teach adults, rather than go back into the classroom?

A *I wanted to utilise my teaching experience and qualifications but did not want to face the challenges of school teaching at the same time as caring for a young family. A friend suggested adult education and I contacted the local community education centre to find out whether there were any roles that might fit my skills and experience.*

Q And were there?

A *Yes – I was very much in the right place at the right time. My decision to return to work coincided with a surge of interest in computing, and as I had good computer skills, I started teaching classes in computing to adults. Over the years, this has included courses such as 'E-mail and the Internet', 'Computers: From Terrified to Terrific' and ECDL courses.*

Q Were you able to fit the work around your young family?

A *The job offered all the flexibility I wanted, and in the early days I neatly solved the childcare problem by only teaching evening classes. Once my daughters had started school, I was able to take on additional morning and afternoon classes to fit in with school hours. Now that they are teenagers, I can work more or less whenever I want to. The hours have grown along with my family!*

Q Apart from the flexibility, what are the other advantages of the work?

continued

A *In the early days, I loved the opportunity to spend time with adults, and found myself looking forward to my evening classes after a day at home with toddlers. Although I am no longer quite so desperate for adult company, I still enjoy my students, most of whom are a delight. I also enjoy the variety; courses such as 'E-mail and the Internet' are based around my students' needs, and no two courses are ever quite the same, although accredited courses such as the ECDL do involve following a syllabus.*

Q And the disadvantages?

A *They are few and far between, but no job is perfect! Although the majority of my students are a pleasure to teach, some can be quite insecure, and I have found that challenging adults need to be handled every bit as sensitively as challenging children. As I am based at my local community school, I have to plan the timings of my sessions around the school day; many of the students are unnerved by large groups of schoolchildren and I try to ensure that they arrive, depart and take coffee breaks when the pupils are in lessons – not always as easy to manage as it might sound! Over the years, I have also gained the impression that adult education tutors do not have the same standing as schoolteachers – something to consider if job status is important to you.*

Q But you would still recommend the job to others who want a change from school teaching?

A *Oh yes, definitely. Not only is the job fulfilling in itself, it can also lead on to other things. Now that the girls are older, I have been able to expand my career into other areas of computer teaching and IT support. Much of this work developed from networking through my adult education work and meeting a wide range of adults in the community. Twelve years on, I regard my transition into adult education as the best career move I have made so far.*

Other opportunities

Becoming a visiting speaker

Groups such as the Women's Institute (WI) or the National Women's Register (NWR) regularly engage visiting speakers to contribute to their meetings. Speakers' topics vary considerably and can range from the story of an expedition with accompanying video to your (preferably humorous) experiences as a teacher, parent, cook or any other role. One popular and successful speaker in Gloucestershire simply told everyday tales of her life as a farmer's wife in the 1960s and 1970s, relying on her skills as a comic and storyteller. If you think you can speak on a topic that would be of interest, are happy to work in the evenings and don't expect to be paid much, try contacting groups in your area and offering your services as a visiting speaker.

Other opportunities

Teaching English as a foreign language (TEFL)

Traditionally, a TEFL qualification was used as a means of working abroad. However, with organisations such as the National Health Service employing an increasing number of overseas staff, UK-based opportunities for teaching English as a foreign language are growing. To find out about training options, carry out an internet search for 'TEFL' or 'teaching English as a foreign language'.

Working as a voluntary teacher overseas

What?

There are many charities and organisations that arrange for teachers to work overseas in a voluntary capacity. One the best known is Voluntary Service Overseas (VSO), a leading international development charity with a focus on promoting innovative approaches to global volunteering. Its central ethos is to pass on skilled professional expertise to local people so that when a worker returns home, their skills remain in operation within the community. Recently, the VSO's recruitment policy has changed, and it now seeks experienced professionals, rather than school leavers. There is always a need for teachers, and at the time of writing, VSO was particularly asking for applications from headteachers and those with education management skills. As well as teaching abroad, volunteers also work with overseas ministries of education, local education authorities, teacher training colleges and teaching inspectorates. There are also opportunities to become involved with curriculum development, monitoring and evaluation, training, and school management.

Where?

VSO works in over forty countries across Africa and Asia. Working environments vary depending on where you are posted, although all volunteers are provided with accommodation.

When?

Most VSO postings are for a two-year period.

Who?

Age limits for volunteers are between 20 and 75. In practice, however, teaching volunteers will be older than the lower age limit, as they are required to have a teaching qualification and some experience. Working for VSO is a major, long-term commitment rather than something that can be fitted around other aspects of your home and working life. In order to commit to the role, you need to be free of dependants and able to leave behind any home-based responsibilities for at least a two-year period. If you are looking for a major life change or have recently retired but still want to use your skills and experience in a completely different setting, then teaching in a voluntary capacity overseas is well worth considering.

How?

To discover more about volunteering for VSO, visit its website at www.vso.org.uk. Apart from general information, you can find out about specific volunteering jobs, as well as apply online, download an application form or order an application pack. If you prefer to speak to someone directly, the VSO switchboard number is 020 8780 7200.

Apart from VSO, there are many other organisations that arrange for teachers to work overseas in a voluntary capacity. An internet search for 'voluntary work abroad' should bring up lots of options.

Why?

If you are experienced and intrepid, working as a voluntary teacher overseas offers a huge adventure, at the same time as enabling you to make a difference. If you are feeling a bit jaded about teaching, the work may also rekindle your enthusiasm – it's not unusual for a stint with VSO to remind teachers of why they joined the profession in the first place. Many teachers also find that voluntary work overseas is good for their professional development, offering a much wider range of experiences than would have been possible in the United Kingdom. Taking a sabbatical to teach abroad is increasingly seen as a positive career move, and over the past decade the vast majority of working-age VSO teachers have returned to teaching posts in the United Kingdom. The one thing that VSO does not offer is remuneration. It is, as its name suggests, a voluntary service, although volunteers are provided with a local-level allowance, air fares and insurance.

Case study

From primary headteacher to . . . VSO volunteer

As a retired primary headteacher with twenty-five years' experience, Meg Fletcher is typical of the type of volunteer VSO is currently recruiting.

continued

Meg works for VSO as an Organisational Development Adviser for the National Secretariat for Catholic Education (SNEC) in Kigali, Rwanda. The SNEC oversees 1,200 schools, which in total employ 13,000 teachers teaching a million pupils. As a result, any strategies implemented by the SNEC have a huge impact, and in spite of its influence across Rwanda, it still needs help with establishing best practice, gathering information, identifying student needs and developing strategies for growth.

This is where Meg comes in. At the SNEC, she is working specifically on its strategic overview and long-term development plans. 'My role is to assist people in developing their ideas in relation to education,' Meg says. 'People here are very clear about what they want; it's just that they don't have any experience of how to get it. I've got twenty-five years' experience as a headteacher so I know what questions to ask and how to set achievable goals.' As an example of using her educational and management skills, she cites her involvement with a Canadian-funded project to introduce ICT to Rwandan schools: 'In the years I worked as a teacher in England, I saw how computers became more prevalent in schools and so I understood how an effective ICT programme can work. I also saw how it could be done better – in the implementation and the training. So when drawing up this business plan, I knew who to ask about certain things, and what to ask. It's from the business culture in Britain that I've managed to do this.'

Although Meg is putting a lot into the programme, she is getting a lot out of it. She is inspired by her local colleagues' faith that they can build a more positive future for Rwandan schoolchildren, in spite of the appalling events that took place during twelve years of genocide. She also values the respect with which she is treated by young and old alike, and the belief that her years of experience have made a positive difference. 'I can see now, after being here for a while, that life doesn't stop when you retire. People say that in Rwanda, you get younger every year . . .'

Other opportunities

Teaching exchanges

Teaching exchanges are another option for teachers who want to work overseas for a limited period. VIF is just one company that arranges exchanges for teachers. For more information, visit www.vifprogram.com.

Contributing to education courses and conferences

What?

Contributing to education courses and conferences is an option for any experienced teacher who would like to share their expertise with their peers. Courses and conferences are mostly run by private companies or bodies such as the National College for School Leadership (NCSL), with the majority of delegates funded to attend by their schools.

There is a clearly defined difference between a conference and a course. Conferences tend to feature a high-profile keynote speaker, followed by presentations, seminars or workshops. Courses are less formal events, usually led by just one or two trainers. They tend to be more interactive than conferences, with a greater focus on offering practical strategies. Topics for both conferences and courses vary hugely, covering everything from the role of a year leader to managing a curriculum area or introducing new ICT technology. Whatever your area of expertise, you should be able to find work as a speaker or trainer, particularly if what you have to offer meets the demands of current educational practices and initiatives.

Most education and training companies also offer an 'in-house' service for schools and colleges that require INSET training. The company draws on a bank of trainers who are sent into a school or college in response to a request for a particular course or topic area. You can also liaise directly with schools and colleges to offer training tailored to individual requirements. In order to do this, you will need to operate as a freelance consultant (see 'How?', below, for more information).

Where?

Courses and conferences take place nationwide. They are mostly city based, with delegates attending from across the region. The venues are usually hotels, business centres or universities (a good lunch is one of the perks of both attending and speaking at a conference!). Most INSET training takes place on school or college premises, although schools and colleges will occasionally choose to run a training day off-site.

When?

Courses and conferences usually take place during weekdays, as they are regarded as part of the delegates' working week. Some courses are two-day, with an overnight stay as part of the package. Unless you live near the venue, you may need to travel the day before to make sure that you are ready for an early start – something that is worth considering when costing your time as a speaker or trainer.

Who?

To contribute to an educational conference or become a trainer, you need to be an experienced teacher with lots of examples of good practice to draw upon. You also need to be comfortable in the role of leading and training your peers. Many teachers, while excellent in the classroom, find it nerve-racking to give a presentation to a group of colleagues. If this is the case, the role may not be right for you, however much skill and expertise you possess. You also need to be a confident performer, as you will be speaking on a national stage with a demanding audience who want to come away feeling that your course or conference was worth attending.

Although you need an underpinning of sound teaching experience to become a speaker or trainer, you do not have to combine it with a current teaching role. However, if you have left the classroom altogether, it is essential to find other ways of keeping up to date with educational developments. These can include pursuits such as joining subject associations, taking on other educational roles (examining, inspection and consultancy work), maintaining links with schools where you have taught, and broad-based research. Given the constantly changing face of education, keeping abreast of developments is something to take into account when considering issues of workload and time management. Increasingly, you will also need good ICT skills. The PowerPoint presentation is now an integral part of many talks and courses, and you will be expected to be on top of whatever technology is required.

How?

Contact private education and training companies to discuss what they are looking for and whether it matches what you have to offer. Start by sending in a letter and CV, followed by a phone call. Companies are always on the lookout for good-quality speakers as well as up-to-the-minute ideas for conferences, so you should be well received. If you are currently in teaching, check the advertising flyers left in your pigeon-hole for names and contact details.

To set yourself up as an independent trainer, you will need to plan your own marketing strategy, organise your own contracts, provide your own resources and run the business side of your work. For more information on exploring the market and the practicalities of working freelance, see the next 'case study', and Chapter 5.

Why?

Speaking at education courses and conferences is a high-profile way to use your skills and experience. It makes an impressive addition to your CV if you are working towards promotion and can also be an effective way both to network and to market yourself. Compared with many extra-curricular education-related roles, the pay is quite good; for example, if you run a one-day training course on your own, you can expect to earn anything from £350 to £800, plus expenses. If you are still in teaching, some education and training companies will also fund supply cover so that your absence from the classroom does not impact on your school's finances.

The flexible nature of the work is another advantage. As you build up links with different training providers and individual schools and colleges, you can pick and choose your dates to fit in with your other commitments. However, if you are teaching full time, you will need to negotiate with your school over how often they are willing to release you. You also need to think very carefully about the effect too many absences will have on your classes. As an alternative, combining the role with part-time teaching or other education-related jobs gives you the best of both worlds.

Case study

From geography teacher to . . . behaviour consultant and trainer

Dave taught geography in a secondary school for several years, latterly taking on pastoral management roles and working as a local authority behaviour management adviser before starting his own training and consultancy business:

Q Why did you decide to make a move out of teaching and into a training and consultancy role?

A *After teaching for thirty years, I wanted a change of direction. As a local authority adviser, I had enjoyed my two-year stint working in schools and providing staff development activities, and I decided I was ready to meet the challenge of setting up my own company.*

Q Describe your business and what it involves.

A *I work throughout the UK with teachers, lecturers and support staff, providing guidance, advice and training on behavioural issues. I also work for a number of companies who run national training events and in-house courses tailor-made to meet the specific needs of schools and further education colleges.*

Q So contributing to courses and conferences is an important part of your business?

A *Yes, it is central to my working life. Apart from contributing to courses and conferences organised by education companies and training providers, I also run my own training courses.*

Q Describe a 'day in the life' of an education trainer.

A *Prior to the course, I plan and prepare the course content and organise the resources I intend to use. I avoid overnight stays wherever possible, so that often means an early start on the day of the course. When I arrive at the venue, I meet the CPD [continual professional development] co-ordinator if it's a school, or the course manager if it's a hotel or conference centre. I am* shown the room, set up my resources, equipment and the books I sell, and check that everything is ready. A school-based course usually begins at 9 o'clock sharp, whereas in a hotel the start is usually scheduled for 10.00 a.m. The length of the training day is about five to six hours' contact time, with a morning coffee break and an hour for lunch. I am usually the sole trainer, so it is full-on and intensive work. I include a variety of activities: group work, pair work, videos and audio information, as well as my presentations and input. There's a lot to keep tabs on! At the end of the course, I always reward the delegates with a glass star to illustrate motivational techniques and add a feel-good factor. They then fill out an evaluation form, and some stay behind to discuss issues arising from the course. When all the delegates have finally left, I pack up and either begin the (often long) drive home, or go straight to the next venue.

Q Your teaching skills must prove invaluable.

A As with all teachers, over the years I have developed an invaluable set of skills which I use constantly in my role as a trainer; for example, the ability to communicate effectively with both small and large groups, planning and preparing stimulating resource material, time management, and an extensive knowledge of the curriculum and pastoral care issues.

Q Do you have any tips or advice for people who would like to follow a similar path?

A To establish yourself as an independent consultant and trainer, you have to come up with a service that has a unique selling point. What can you offer that is new and different – and, most important of all, is it what people require? Do your research and bear in mind that some areas of the market are flooded. If you still feel you have a workable idea, develop a sound business plan, get a good accountant and consider making a gradual entry – by combining part-time freelance training and consultancy work with a part-time teaching job, for example.

continued

Q You clearly enjoy your work. Are there any disadvantages?

A *It can be a solitary existence. I miss the support of colleagues, and the social side of working in a school. Managing time is also a real challenge; the level of multi-tasking becomes quite extreme on occasion. Even if you have contracts with companies, the work can be uncertain; you tend to be fully booked a couple of terms in advance and then have nothing for the next term. However, I love the variety of working with people from lots of different institutions and visiting settings across the country. I also enjoy keeping abreast of new initiatives and building up a clear national picture on a range of issues affecting all schools and colleges. The advantages far outweigh the disadvantages!*

Visit Dave's website at www.behavioursolutions.com. He has also developed a website to support new trainers: www.yourpresentationsolutions.com.

Other opportunities

Designing and managing education events

Apart from requiring speakers and trainers, education courses and conferences also have to be marketed, designed and managed. For more information on these roles, see:

- 'Planning and directing education courses and conferences' (pages 148–52)
- 'From deputy head teacher to . . . events manager' (pages 180–2)

Other opportunities

Changing sector

If you need a change of direction but do not want to give up teaching, it may be worth considering a switch from one sector to another. Moving from secondary to primary is probably the most common, and as long as you have a teaching qualification, you do not currently have to retrain. One primary head we spoke to said that she would certainly consider any application from a secondary school teacher on its merits, although she would look for evidence of genuine interest and commitment. If a move into the primary sector appeals, it is probably wise to aim for Year 5 and 6 jobs until you become more established. You also need to gain some experience of working with the primary age group through supply teaching or liaison activities with your feeder schools.

In order to change from primary to secondary, you will need proven knowledge and expertise in your chosen subject. If the field is not particularly strong, it is more likely that the less traditional application will be given serious consideration. In the end, headteachers and curriculum leaders want the best person for the job; if you can demonstrate at interview that you have sound teaching skills and a good knowledge of your subject, your application should be as viable as any other. In the current climate, there are more likely to be opportunities for those who can offer a shortage subject such as science or maths. As there tend to be fewer candidates for mid-year vacancies, it may also be worth making initial applications for an Easter or summer start, and accepting that you might, initially, be offered a short-term contract.

Something else to consider is the differing requirements and challenges faced by the secondary and primary school teacher. You may have tougher disciplinary scenarios to deal with in the secondary sector, but you will only be spending a short period of time with your most challenging pupils. The primary school teacher has to cover the entire curriculum,

continued

but, unlike the secondary school teacher, does not have to deal with such a dizzying number of pupils across the school day. Some find it easier to work with primary-aged children than the adolescents of the secondary sector, but the closer pupil–teacher relationship in the primary school can be emotionally draining. Teachers are often surprised at the differences between the two sectors, and it is always a good idea to get some practical experience before making a final decision to move from one to the other.

If you are looking to change sector, be open-minded about the possibilities. A move does not just have to mean switching between primary and secondary teaching; nor do you have to remain in mainstream education:

- **From secondary to . . . specialist FE college**: *Mark was a deputy head in a comprehensive school before taking early retirement at the age of 52. He wanted to continue working and saw an advertisement for the post of Head of Key Curriculum in a college for students with severe learning difficulties. Initially, the job was a short-term maternity cover, but when the contract came to an end, he was taken on permanently as Extended Curriculum Co-ordinator. The role included managing staff and devising the curriculum – similar to his responsibilities as a deputy head in the mainstream secondary sector. Although Mark had enjoyed teaching pupils with learning difficulties in his previous job, he discovered that he had a lot to learn from working with these students, most of whom fell into the 18 to 25 age group. Although it proved to be a huge challenge, he ended up having the most fulfilling eight years of his working life. Inevitably, the college's approach to teaching and learning differed from that of mainstream education. With its focus on valuing whatever the individual managed to achieve, however little, Mark was at last able to escape the pressures of 'results' and 'league tables'. As he describes his work with these students, it is clear that they taught him every bit as much as he taught them.*

- **From mainstream primary to . . . Montessori nursery**: *at the other end of the age range, Jess decided to make a switch from teaching Key Stage 2 children to nursery education. During her years as a primary school teacher, she became increasingly frustrated by the restrictions of the curriculum and the necessity to be a 'sergeant major' in order to keep her class under control. She also started to realise that the younger the child, the more chance you have to instil an enthusiasm for learning. Looking around for an alternative, she became interested in the Montessori approach to education and decided to retrain as a Montessori nursery teacher. With the Montessori approach's focus on developing independence and treating each child as an individual, it turned out to be just what she was looking for. Now that the number of UK Montessori primary schools is growing, Jess is considering further training so that she can return to teaching her original age group. Whatever she decides, her future looks promising, and she has never for one moment regretted her decision to move sectors.*

Other opportunities

Becoming a school governor

School governors play an important part in school life, with responsibilities ranging from managing the school budget and appointing headteachers to ensuring that the school is meeting the National Curriculum. As a teacher or ex-teacher, you can stand for election at any local school as a community governor, stand as a parent governor at your child's school or represent your colleagues as a staff governor at your own school. Although being a governor is hard work and offers no financial reward, it is a fulfilling role and gives you a useful insight into this particular aspect of school leadership.

Chapter 2

Effectively transferring . . . your subject skills

Whether you are introducing 4-year-olds to the life cycle of a butterfly or teaching A level economics, as a teacher you need to have an in-depth and extensive knowledge of your subject. But what does this actually mean, and how can your subject knowledge be transferred into the wider jobs market?

A passion for your subject

First and foremost, a teacher needs to have sound generic teaching skills. However much you love your subject, it is your ability to deliver an effective lesson and manage your classroom that provides the underpinning for your teaching. Once you have these essential skills under your belt, you can then get on with the fundamental purpose of teaching: imparting knowledge, inspiring your pupils, preparing them for the world beyond the school gates and helping them to develop an independent and possibly lifelong interest in your subject.

Having an enthusiasm for your subject is an essential ingredient in the recipe for good teaching. For example, the most effective history teachers turn their lessons into gripping storytelling sessions; an art teacher who is genuinely excited by the possibilities of batik or junk modelling will transfer their enthusiasm to their pupils; the English teacher who enables young teenagers to recognise the relevance of Romeo and Juliet is providing a gateway into Shakespeare. When asked about the teachers they remember from their own school days, most adults will focus on a teacher's ability to transfer their enthusiasm for their subject. Since the beginning of time, countless destinies have been shaped by a talented teacher inspiring in their young pupils a love of maths . . . or geography . . . or PE . . . or Ancient Greek.

Tailoring your subject knowledge

Enthusiasm alone is not enough, however. In order to be a successful subject teacher, you also need to adapt your subject knowledge to suit the context within which you are teaching. What is relevant to a particular age group? How can the content of your lessons be developed to tally with the content of the curriculum? How should subject-related skills, facts and information be organised and presented, and what different teaching techniques and resources should you use for each element of your lesson? For example, an effective maths teacher will have an analytical knowledge of a mathematical operation and be able to break it down into clear steps, taking into account the aspects of the problem that typically cause students difficulties. The early years teacher exploring butterflies with his or her 4-year-olds must decide on the key points and how to present the information in a way that is clear and accessible for very young children. Not only are teachers required to have comprehensive subject knowledge (and in the case of early years, primary and an increasing number of secondary specialists, a wide range of subjects), they also have to understand their subject in relation to teaching. Being an expert on the First World War is a very different thing from being an expert on *teaching* the First World War.

Transferring your subject skills

Some teachers particularly love the activity of teaching – the element of performance, interacting with their pupils, planning, organising and managing the microcosmic world of their classroom. Others have a deep and abiding fascination for their subject and discover a particular skill in planning and developing lessons and resources, helping their pupils to do well in examinations, using ICT as a means of lesson delivery or enabling pupils with learning difficulties to get the most out of their subject. If you are looking to move beyond the classroom but want to use your knowledge, experience and love of your subject within an educational context, there are many different options. The following list breaks down 'subject skills' into different areas of expertise, and looks at which of the various jobs surveyed in this and other chapters might fit each area.

Subject knowledge

Do you have both a broad knowledge and an enduring interest in your subject? If so, consider the following:

- working for a subject association (page 84);
- writing education books and articles (page 101) – approach subject-specific publications with your idea;
- delivering talks and workshops in schools (page 89);
- contributing to an education website (page 97);
- teaching adults in the community (page 41);

Teaching for examination success

Do you have a sound understanding of the examination system and proven experience of helping your pupils to achieve exam success? If so, consider the following:

- tutoring (page 81);
- examining and moderating (page 76);
- working as a subject officer for an awarding body (page 73);
- writing education books and articles (page 97) – particularly revision guides;
- contributing to an education website (page 97) – create or contribute to a site devoted to revision.

Subject-specific pedagogy

Do you have a particular interest in the teaching of your subject, and subject specific approaches and methods? If so, consider the following:

- working in teacher training (page 64);
- working as an education consultant (page 132) – specialise in the teaching of your subject;
- writing education books and articles (page 101);
- delivering talks and workshops in schools (page 89);
- working as a subject adviser (page 68);
- contributing to education courses and conferences (page 51);
- planning and directing courses and conferences (page 148) – if you work freelance, you can focus on planning events based on your subject.

Developing ideas, activities, lesson plans and resources

Do you enjoy the creative side of your subject teaching – researching and planning activities related to your subject, coming up with fresh ideas and developing resources? If so, consider the following:

- writing education books and articles (page 101) – particularly subject specific, 'ideas-based' magazines;
- working in teacher training (page 64) – including running CPD courses;
- contributing to courses and conferences (page 51);
- contributing to an education website (page 97);
- working as an education consultant (page 132);
- working as a subject adviser (page 68).

A vision for the future

Do you have an interest in how the teaching of your subject might develop in the future, and want to play a part? If so, consider:

- working for government or a government-funded organisation (page 112);
- working as a subject officer for an awarding body (page 73);
- working in teacher training (page 64) – particularly a university post with a strong research element;
- writing education books and articles (page 101);
- working as an education consultant (page 132);
- researching your subject – if you have a special interest in an aspect of your subject and its future within education, look into doing a research Master's degree or PhD.

An interest in ICT

Do you have expertise in the use of ICT in relation to teaching your subject? If so, consider the following:

- contributing to an education website (page 97) – utilise your knowledge of how school IT networks operate and your ability to develop activities and resources for online use;
- working as a subject adviser (page 68) – specialise in the use of ICT within your subject;

- working as an education consultant (page 132) – specialise in the use of ICT within your subject;
- writing education books and articles (page 101) – specialise in the use of ICT within your subject;
- contributing to education courses and conferences (page 51) – specialise in the use of ICT within your subject.

Expanding your subject knowledge

If you want to expand your subject knowledge, investigate the following:

- join a subject association;
- take out a subscription for a subject-related magazine;
- attend relevant talks, lectures, workshops, conferences and summer schools;
- contact teachers in other schools with similar interests;
- make a book list and work your way through it;
- sign up for an Open University degree, a Master's or a PhD in your particular subject;
- explore relevant work experience, such as spending a week in a local radio station (media studies) or visiting a paint factory (chemistry);
- travel to appropriate places, particularly if you are a geographer, biologist, linguist, classicist or historian.

SO WHAT'S OUT THERE? . . . JOB OPPORTUNITIES

Working in teacher training

What?

All UK teacher training courses are degree-level qualifications, either a three- or four-year BEd for post-A level students or a one-year PGCE for postgraduate students. Some universities also offer BAs in early childhood studies and education studies, foundation degrees in education and taught doctoral programmes. Teaching degrees and postgraduate qualifications are available from early years to further and higher education – and they all offer job opportunities for the experienced teacher. Some typical job titles include 'Lectureship in Education (Modern Languages)' and 'Lecturer in Primary Education (Science)'. Although the roles and responsibilities vary, most jobs include lecturing on the theory and practice of education, observing and assessing students on teaching practice, carrying out research, and contributing to administrative and management processes within the department. There may also be opportunities to write for academic journals and publish education books, contribute to MEd degrees, become involved in delivering INSET and professional development courses, and design new courses.

Where?

Your work will mostly be university based, although you will spend time in schools observing students on teaching practice and liaising with staff. Research projects may also take you into schools. If you do not live near a university, you may have to consider part-time work, or even long-distance commuting. Early years specialist Helle lectured in a teacher training college in London. When she moved to mid-Somerset, she discovered that there were no similar job opportunities in her new and very rural location. Unwilling to abandon her career, she looked into commuting to London and, with the support of her head of department, was able to organise a two-day timetable of lectures and tutorials. Although this involved an overnight stay in London and a three-hour journey each way, the opportunity to continue her career and maintain her contacts more than made up for the inconvenience.

When?

As a full- or part-time university lecturer, you will work with students during university terms, although research, writing and planning may carry on throughout the holidays. Some part-time modular and MEd courses may also involve evening lectures. Many university education departments employ associate or visiting lecturers, who are seconded from school to work on a teacher training programme. The structure of the courses will vary from university to university, with some (including the Open University) offering flexible modular programmes.

Who?

To lecture on a teacher training course, you need to be a qualified teacher with proven successful teaching experience and evidence of 'continuing professional development'. It is also desirable (and for some jobs, essential) to have a higher-degree qualification such as a Master's, and experience of research, of working in a training or advisory role with colleagues and of a management role. Kevan is a secondary deputy head who has combined a part-time lectureship at a university in the English Midlands with a four-day teaching week. Over the years, his teaching career has progressed from teacher-in-charge of history to head of humanities and, ultimately, a senior leadership post. At the same time, he has delivered continuing professional development courses in schools across the country, been seconded to his local authority as an associate inspector for NQTs and pursued both an MA and an EdD. His extensive CV demonstrates the kind of background needed for a university-based role in teacher training.

How?

Check the education press for vacancies and do an internet search for 'teacher training jobs'. It is also worth contacting the school of education at your local university or the Open University to enquire about opportunities.

If your CV is a little sparse, you may need to plan for a career move in advance. Check the job specifications for various teacher training posts and start building up relevant experience. Look out also for useful contacts. As the tutor responsible for PGCE students in his school, Kevan was able to build up a good relationship with the staff at his local university. This led to an invitation to sit on the secondary PGCE committee at the School of Education, a role which then developed into a one-day-a-week job teaching on the university's MEd course. Both Kevan and Helle also recommend developing expertise in a field that is under-researched but important to education. As a specialist in communication, language and literacy development, Helle discovered that there was surprisingly little academic literature on picture books. She decided to create a niche for herself by researching the role of the picture book in children's learning and went on to use her research as the basis for running continuing professional development courses and writing for early years publications. Similarly, ten years ago Kevan tapped into the then virgin territory of boys' underachievement. He organised and directed a joint university–school research partnership that resulted in one of the first practitioner-based books to be published in this area.

Why?

Working in the field of teacher training gives you plenty of opportunity to analyse, explore and research the theory and practice of education. Helle particularly enjoys this aspect of her work: *'It's not that I didn't get the chance when I was a teacher – there was just so little time to explore something in detail. As a lecturer, it is an integral part of my job to keep up to date and pursue my research. I am also surrounded by colleagues who are as keen as I am to discuss "the great phonics debate" or the role of "real books" in learning to read.'* She also enjoys observing students in schools and helping them to analyse their successes and what they need to do to improve their practice.

In Kevan's case, a part-time lecturing role took him out of school at a time when he was starting to feel a bit stale. It gave him a new intellectual challenge and the opportunity to meet people in a different branch of education. For all these reasons, Kevan recommends seizing the opportunity to spend some time teaching in higher education. There are, however, disadvantages. As he points out, primary and secondary school teaching offers better pay and promotion prospects and is currently more secure than higher education. If you want to keep a foot in both doors, as he has done, you may end up cramming a full-time teaching job into a three- or four-day week. Helle also emphasises that you can quickly lose touch with what is happening at the 'chalk face' if you do not continue a part-time teaching job. Some members of the teaching profession are quick to dismiss the university lecturer as 'all theory and no practice', and you have to work hard at keeping up to date if you are to maintain your credibility.

Overall, however, it is a job well worth considering for those with the right career background. Teacher training is the foundation of the entire education system, and the universities will always need experienced and committed professionals to train, nurture and support the next generation of teachers.

Other opportunities

Assessing overseas-trained teachers (OTTs)

Although overseas-trained teachers can work in the United Kingdom for up to four years without Qualified Teacher Status (QTS), it is advisable for them to gain QTS as it increases their opportunities. Assessment programmes for OTTs are run through designated recommending bodies such as a university or a consortium attached to a local authority. The assessment takes place in school, with an assessor visiting the OTT to observe, offer support and decide whether the standards are being met. To find out about job opportunities as an OTT assessor, visit www.teachernet.gov.uk.

Working as a subject adviser or advisory teacher

What?

Subject advisers and advisory teachers give support, direction and training to both primary and secondary teachers within a local authority. The subject adviser's roles might include running a training course for NQTs, coaching an underperforming department, compiling a subject-related newsletter, organising conferences for heads of department in the local authority, disseminating new initiatives and troubleshooting where necessary. The role is very diverse and will vary considerably, depending on your subject and the needs of the schools in your area.

Although local authorities have different ways of organising their advisory teams, many employ both subject advisers and advisory teachers:

- **Subject adviser:** the subject adviser's role is usually non-teaching and can vary from full-time permanent posts to part-time short-term contracts. Typically, full-time permanent posts are reserved for the core subjects of literacy, numeracy, science and ICT, whereas provision for foundation subjects tends to be based

on freelance contracts of varying lengths. Many full-time permanent advisers also take on responsibility for non-subject-specific
areas such as special educational needs (SEN) or behaviour and
attendance. Job titles may vary from authority to authority,
particularly for freelance roles. If you are checking adverts in the
education press, look out for terms such as Associate Consultant
or Consultant Adviser. If in doubt, ring up the authority and
ask for a job description before either dismissing a job or going
ahead with an application.

- **Advisory teacher**: the advisory teacher is a current practitioner
  who is either released for a set number of days per year, or
  seconded for a term. If you feel you have expertise to share with
  colleagues beyond your own school, but do not want to give up
  teaching, the advisory teacher's role may be worth exploring.

Where?

As a subject adviser, you will have a nominal base at your local
authority offices. This will include a local authority e-mail address
and administrative support. In practice, however, most of your time
will be spent visiting teachers and running meetings and training
sessions in schools and teacher centres. Depending on the size of the
authority, you may do quite a bit of travelling.

When?

Your working timetable will vary to fit in with the needs of the
schools in your area. Although you will mostly be working within
school hours, you may be required to organise and run some twilight
sessions and meetings. Most full-time advisers have thirty days'
holiday a year, which should not normally be taken during term-time.

Who?

To become a subject adviser or advisory teacher, you need to have
proven expertise in the teaching of your subject, be skilled at coaching
and supporting colleagues, and be willing to keep up to date with
developments and current research. You also need a degree of resili-
ence when faced with those teachers who may be reluctant to accept
external support. The most successful advisers are realistic about the
challenges faced by teachers, empathetic to the demands of the job
and able to base their advice on a solid foundation of good practice.

Although it is not necessarily an essential requirement, in practice most advisers and advisory teachers have experience as heads of department or subject leaders.

How?

Look out for adverts in the education press, both locally and nationally. It is also worth contacting your local authority to find out whether there are any opportunities available. Becoming an advisory teacher can sometimes provide a stepping stone into a full-time post as a subject adviser.

Why?

Becoming a subject adviser or advisory teacher takes you out of the classroom but keeps you at the cutting edge of educational developments within your subject. It enables you to play a significant part in shaping and influencing the teaching of your subject, particularly at a local level. It also enables you to support, guide and advise colleagues across the county. If you are interested in developing your career as an educationalist, a local authority advisory role gives you access to up-to-date educational initiatives and developments. A part-time role can also make a useful addition to a portfolio career (see page 215).

Case study

From head of MFL to . . . MFL associate consultant

John was the head of a secondary modern foreign languages (MFL) department before becoming an associate consultant with a local authority in south-east England. Here, he describes what his job involves and outlines some of the advantages and disadvantages.

Q What does your job as an MFL Associate Consultant involve?
A *I provide curriculum support and advice to ten secondary schools, including two language colleges and an academy. This*

covers a wide range of roles and responsibilities, including Ofsted preparation, support for NQTs, departmental reviews and involvement in whole-school issues such as assessment for learning.

Q Do you work just in the secondary sector?

A Although secondary MFL is my main focus, I occasionally give advice and support to primary schools. I am currently involved in the Primary MFL initiative, training teachers to deliver the KS2 [Key Stage 2] MFL entitlement, and I also give support to two special schools that are keen to develop MFL programmes.

Q In what ways do you draw on your previous experience as a teacher and educationalist?

A I use my practical skills to teach lead lessons and I also participate in team teaching as part of Ofsted preparation and NQT support. I draw on my subject knowledge to lead continuing professional development sessions on topics such as GCSE grade improvement, raising boys' achievement and data interpretation. I use my understanding of the curriculum and experience as an Ofsted inspector to inform judgements on what constitutes good and excellent teaching and I try to communicate this to classroom teachers through feedback after lesson observations. I also see part of my role as interpreting government initiatives for colleagues and teasing out the implications for the teaching of MFL. And I prepare all my own resources for any event I deliver! This is not a job you can do without a sound underpinning of practical teaching experience and curriculum knowledge.

Q You obviously enjoy the work. What are the main advantages?

A The main advantage for me is the freedom to structure my work as I see fit, as long as I respond to the needs determined by the schools. I have a very open brief as far as MFL is concerned, as long as I don't do anything that runs counter to local authority priorities or policy.

continued

Q And the disadvantages?

A *The travelling! But then, I chose to take a job located some distance from where I live. It is occasionally frustrating not to be 'on the patch', as it can make communication difficult. Sometimes messages go astray; for example, you have eight people on the list for a training session and twelve turn up on the day, none of whom are the same as those on the list . . . Also, things can grind very slowly in schools and you sometimes find yourself wishing for a faster pace of change.*

Q Do you have any advice for teachers who would like to diversify into a similar role?

A *Develop your classroom practice and question it ruthlessly. To establish credibility, you need to become a vigorously self-evaluating practitioner. You also have to be willing to embrace change; it's the only constant thing in education and it needs to be interpreted and managed to your advantage. Make sure you build up twenty years of experience, rather than have one year's experience repeated twenty times. Read voraciously and widely: Ofsted and QCA websites, reports, the education press, anything from subject-specific organisations. Cultivate the 'big picture' and explore what this will mean for your subject. Most new initiatives and developments will have an impact on subject teaching and, as such, we ignore them at our peril.*

Other opportunities

Working for the Pre-school Learning Alliance (PLA)

The PLA is a national educational charity set up to support community pre-schools. It offers various job options for experienced early years practitioners; for example, pre-school development workers visit schools in an advisory capacity while sessional tutors plan and deliver training courses. For more information, visit www.pre-school.org.uk.

Working as a subject officer for an awarding body

What?

Awarding-body subject officers take responsibility for all aspects of assessment within a particular subject area. Although a subject officer's portfolio will vary, the qualifications for which they are responsible can range from entry level and GCSE to vocational qualifications and Advanced level. The subject officer's role covers a wide range of tasks and responsibilities, including the recruitment, training and management of examiners; overseeing the preparation of question papers, mark schemes and guidance material for teachers; managing support staff; writing specifications; offering advice at question paper development meetings; providing INSET sessions; responding to any queries; organising meetings with examining personnel and teachers; and liaising with regulatory authorities – bodies such as the Qualifications and Curriculum Authority (QCA) (England), the Department for Education, Lifelong Learning and Skills (DELLS) (Wales), the Scottish Qualifications Authority (SQA) (Scotland) and the Council for Curriculum, Examinations and Assessment (CCEA) (Northern Ireland).

Where?

The subject officer's role is mostly office based, although you will also have to attend meetings and conferences. School INSET events and training sessions for examiners usually take place at a hotel or conference centre and they can be located anywhere within the country.

When?

Although much of the job takes place during office hours, there are regular 'crunch' times throughout the year. May, June and July are typically busy months within the examination industry and there is no flexibility over meeting deadlines for tasks such as writing question papers, organising training sessions for examiners or completing and proof-reading mark schemes. Many examiners' meetings and conferences are scheduled to take place outside school hours, so you may also be required to carry out some evening and weekend work.

Who?

To become a subject officer for an awarding body, you need to have both an interest in and extensive knowledge of your subject in relation to the examination system. You also need effective communication skills, ICT proficiency, good standards of written English and the ability to edit accurately. On a personal level, you need to be flexible and have the ability to work within a team and stay calm under pressure. For example, if on the day of the exam it is discovered that two pages have been missed out of some of the papers, you are the one who will have to sort out the problem.

Although it is not regarded as essential by every awarding body, in practice many subject officers are ex-subject heads with previous examining experience.

How?

Look out for advertisements in the education press and check the awarding body websites. It is useful to gain some inside experience of the examining system by becoming an examiner, and this may also lead to further opportunities in the awarding body with which you are associated.

Why?

Becoming an awarding-body subject officer enables you to leave the classroom but stay within your subject area and maintain contact with teachers in a support and advisory role. It is a responsible job that offers the opportunity to affect the education of pupils across the country, and play a major part in shaping the future development of assessment within your particular subject. The job also enables you to have a closer working relationship with colleagues than tends to be the case in teaching.

Case study

From head of MFL to . . . subject officer at the Welsh Joint Education Committee (WJEC)

After twenty-three years as a classroom practitioner and head of modern languages, Jean was ready for a new challenge. When she saw an advertisement for a WJEC subject officer to take responsibility for French, German, Spanish and Japanese qualifications, she decided to apply. Here she describes what attracted her to the post and its many advantages:

Although I enjoyed my roles as a teacher and head of department, after spending so many years in school I had a strong desire for a change in working lifestyle and I started looking at other options. When I spotted an advert for a subject officer at WJEC, it seemed perfect; the intellectual challenge of organising everything connected with the successful delivery of language examinations was just what I was looking for, and I decided to apply.

My application involved the usual route of filling in a form with a covering letter and going through a series of interviews – much the same as an application for a teaching post. I was delighted when I was offered the job, and I have not been disappointed. I enjoy working closely with a wide range of professionals, from WJEC colleagues to examiners, teachers and personnel at outside bodies such as QCA and the DELLS. I also enjoy the flexibility of the working hours (no more jumping to bells!) and the greater independence of my new working life.

Although the job takes me out of the classroom, it is still firmly rooted within the field of education, and I have plenty of opportunity to draw on my years of teaching experience. I constantly use my communication and presentation skills through talking to teachers, examiners and PGCE students – to name but a few. I also rely on my experience and understanding of a teacher's needs, for example the different pressures that crop up throughout the school year, the demands of devising assessments and understanding the attainment levels of pupils. My years of teaching

continued

have helped considerably in my understanding of examination demands, and my curriculum knowledge has, inevitably, been essential in the development of new specifications.

For me, there are few downsides to the job, other than having to attend a number of Saturday meetings, and I would recommend it to anyone with appropriate interests and expertise. The one piece of advice I would give is to start off by learning all you can about the examination system and how it operates. Awarding bodies regularly advertise for examiners, and this is a straightforward but effective way of gaining assessment experience from the examiner's viewpoint.

Examining and moderating

What?

The examination industry is run by a small number of awarding bodies, which employ an army of teachers and educationalists to set, mark and moderate question papers and coursework. Although the greatest number of opportunities are available in the core subjects of maths, English, science and ICT, examiners are needed for just about any subject that is examined. As a result, there should be opportunities available to everyone, including those whose subjects have a lower number of entries. Examiners are also needed at a variety of different levels. Whether you want to mark A2 scripts, moderate coursework at GCSE level or become involved in examining vocational qualifications, the scope is enormous.

Examining work falls into two main areas:

- **Marking scripts**: the awarding bodies are structured organisations, and your role and responsibilities as a marker will vary depending on the position you hold. As a general rule, the senior, principal or chief examiner sets the paper while the examiners (often called 'assistant examiners') are divided into teams, usually led by a team leader. In preparation for the marking, each assistant examiner is sent a copy of the paper, the mark scheme and some scripts. They then attend a one-day group meeting with their chief examiner, principal examiner or team leader, during which they have a practice run at marking the scripts. From this point on, assistant examiners mark scripts for their allocated centres independently, although they are required to send samples of their marking to their team leader at different stages throughout the marking process. Although this adds to your administrative load as an assistant examiner, it is comforting to know that you are being closely monitored throughout what is a crucial – and, for many students, life-changing – procedure.

- **Moderating coursework**: moderating is a different process from marking scripts, although it is an equally important part of the examination system as it currently stands. Moderators are required for any part of an examination that is internally assessed, for example language orals, drama performances, subject coursework and design and technology (DT) projects. For more information and a description of the moderator's role, see the next case study.

Where?

The security of the examination system is important, and something that the awarding bodies take very seriously. Markers are not allowed to mark in a public place, which means working from home. Unlike most home-based jobs, you can't make use of a train journey or a wait for an appointment by marking a few more scripts. Nor can you slip in the odd hour's work during a free period, as your school counts as a 'public place.' As a moderator, you will often work at the centre you are assessing; this is particularly the case with subjects such as art and DT, which generate a large quantity of often bulky coursework. If, however, you are moderating taped French GCSE orals or geography projects, you will usually work from home.

Whether you are an assistant examiner, a moderator, a team leader or a chief examiner, you will be required to attend examiners' meetings based at or near the awarding body's HQ. As this may involve you in travelling, location is worth bearing in mind when deciding which awarding bodies to approach (although any travel expenses, meal allowances and accommodation expenses will be paid).

When?

Traditionally, you could expect to be marking or moderating during the early summer months and in January. Now that many courses are modular, you may be offered work at any time throughout the year. From start to finish, you can expect to be working for approximately three to four weeks. While this is a relatively short period of time, the workload can be intense. You have to meet both the final deadlines and a series of milestones where you are required to send samples to your team leader. Setting yourself a strict timetable and keeping to it, no matter what, is essential – even when a batch of scripts takes you much longer to complete than planned. If there is any delay in your team leader getting back to you, it can halt the whole process, so you may also have to be flexible over timings and able to catch up where necessary.

Your overall workload will depend on how many scripts you are allocated and, to some extent, how quickly you can work without affecting the accuracy of your marking. The number of meetings you have to attend will depend on the level at which you are working. Although assistant examiners usually attend just the one meeting, senior examiners may have meetings scheduled throughout the year.

Who?

To become an assistant examiner or moderator, you need to be educated to degree level, have appropriate subject knowledge and be IT literate. To become a chief examiner, in addition to the above you need to have experience of managing a team of professionals and appropriate experience of the examination system. You also need to be well organised, disciplined and focused. Imagine marking a GCSE class multiplied by ten, all in the space of three weeks. If you don't feel you can face the prospect, this may not be the job for you. Many examiners teach part time or are recently retired. You can take on the job as a full-time teacher (and many do), but it adds a considerable number of hours to your working day. Some teachers are able to cope with summer examining work because their own GCSE and A-level workload reduces towards the end of the academic year.

How?

Approach different awarding bodies to find out what jobs are available and how to apply. Check for advertisements in the education press and visit the vacancies section of the National Assessment Agency website (www.naa.org.uk). As long as you can meet the awarding body's criteria, you should not have too much difficulty finding work.

Why?

Examining and moderating work provide a useful income boost, often at key times of the year such as post-Christmas and just prior to the summer holidays. Although the work period is intensive, it is short lived and does not end up dominating your free time throughout the year. Marking scores of papers can become rather repetitive, but it is interesting to get an insight into how the examination system works, and your own teaching can be greatly improved through your increased understanding of what the examiner is looking for, the grading criteria for coursework and the typical mistakes that candidates make.

From a career development point of view, examining makes a good addition to your CV. Working as an assistant examiner or moderator can lead to other roles such as a full-time position with an awarding body (see page 73) or a role as a team leader or chief examiner. It can also be combined with other jobs to make up a portfolio career (see page 215), and if you are looking to develop your career in areas such as consultancy or advisory work, part-time examining can add considerably to your educational credibility, knowledge and expertise.

Case study

From geography teacher to . . . GCSE coursework moderator

Julia wanted to explore other job options within the world of education without giving up her position as a geography teacher, and she decided to look into examining work. Here, she describes how she ended up becoming a coursework moderator, what her role involves and its many advantages.

Q How easy was it to find examining work?
A *As it turned out, very easy! I telephoned one of the awarding bodies to ask if there were any vacancies and was immediately passed on to the subject officer. I was offered a choice of marking papers or moderating GCSE coursework. Although I*

continued

originally had marking in mind, the prospect of moderating coursework appealed to me and I ended up with the job of GCSE Geography Coursework Moderator.

Q What does the work involve?

A *Before the moderation process begins, I have to attend a moderators' meeting at which the coursework grade criteria are explained. I then use the criteria to judge whether a teacher's marking is fair and accurate, and whether it is in line with the awarding body's grade descriptions. If I feel that a centre's marks are too high or too low and outside the tolerances, I adjust the marks accordingly. Occasionally I am asked to take on a re-moderation, following an appeal from a centre. This process is similar to the first moderation, but I also have to prepare a detailed report on the initial moderation and the marking of the centre.*

Q How does the awarding body moderate your work?

A *Like all examiners, I am closely monitored. My team leader gives me criteria for the samples I have to send in – usually a centre whose marking I agree with and centres where I have raised and lowered the marks. Sampling continues throughout the whole process, and if a centre's marks are way beyond the tolerances, I can also refer the scripts to the team leader.*

Q What are the advantages of the job?

A *Once I have got to grips with the assessment and grading criteria, I find the work quite similar to the assessing I have to do throughout the year. I also get a fascinating insight into how different schools approach GCSE coursework, what is required for each grade and the kinds of errors that students typically make. Even after five years, I still get great pleasure from reading a particularly well-researched piece of work – and I'm equally encouraged to see the effort put in by less able pupils and their teachers.*

Q And the disadvantages?

A *The pay reflects neither the level of responsibility nor the time commitment. There is a lot of administration to deal with, and throughout the early summer months my study overflows with boxes and packages. Finally getting rid of them is as much of a relief as meeting the deadline!*

Q But would you still recommend the job?

A *Yes, I would – as long as you are good at managing your time. It's one of those intriguing jobs that you can never quite let go of. At the start of every summer term, I decide that this will be the last time – and then I reach the deadline, send off the last few packages and find myself agreeing to do just one more year . . .*

Other opportunities

Becoming an external verifier

External verifiers visit centres to check NVQ candidates' portfolios of evidence and confirm that the centre is delivering qualifications to a satisfactory standard. To become an external verifier, you need relevant qualifications and experience as an assessor and verifier in an NVQ centre (for information about becoming an NVQ assessor, see page 19). You also need to be able to demonstrate competence in the occupational area for which you are applying.

Tutoring

What?

Tutoring involves helping children in any area of their learning where they need support. Tutors usually work on a one-to-one basis, although there is also the option of running small-group sessions for GCSE or A level students. Tutoring falls into two general areas:

- **Private tuition**: this is usually arranged by parents who either find a tutor themselves or use a tutoring agency. Tutees can range from primary-aged children who need extra support with literacy and numeracy to students studying for external examinations.
- **Local authority home tuition**: most local authorities run a home tuition service providing support for sick children, excluded children and/or school refusers. Unlike most private tutors, local authority home tutors are required to liaise with the pupil's school to cover a number of different subjects and plan a variety of tasks.

Where?

Tutoring usually takes place within the child's home, with the child's parent or guardian present in a separate room. Although you can arrange for pupils to come to your home, it is advisable to request that the parent stays for the duration of the session.

When?

Private tutoring tends to take place in the evening after school or occasionally at weekends. Holiday sessions can be arranged with the parents, if necessary. Local authority home tuition is organised to suit the timetable of the child, tutor and parent or guardian but must take place within school hours. Tutoring sessions usually last for no longer than an hour.

Who?

To become a private or local authority tutor, you need a teaching qualification and, preferably, some teaching experience. Tutors are required in all subjects and age groups, although the core subjects of maths, English and science tend to offer the greatest number of work opportunities. As a responsible professional, you may also want to consider whether it is appropriate for younger children to be tutored. Harriet worked as a primary school teacher before taking a career break to bring up her family. Wanting to keep her teaching skills up to date and earn some spare cash, she put a card in her local newsagent offering literacy and numeracy help to Key Stage 2 children. Soon afterwards, she received a call from a father asking for tuition for his 5-year-old, who wasn't yet reading. Although she needed the work, she explained that it would not be appropriate to tutor a 5-year-old in reading, recommended that the father played games with, and read to, his child, and sent him on his way as tactfully as possible!

How?

There are several routes into tutoring. Martin, a maths teacher, asked his head of department to recommend him to any parents who enquired about private tutoring, and he quickly ended up with more work than he could manage. Once he had built up a reputation, tutees came via word of mouth, and he often finds himself working with the younger siblings and cousins of past pupils. He suggests contacting all schools in the area as another possibility, or advertising in local newspapers and shops.

Joining a tutoring agency is useful if you do not have many contacts or are offering a subject that is less in demand than maths. Check the telephone directory and internet, and look out for advertisements in the local press. A tutoring agency saves you searching for tutees, but they will take a percentage of your earnings (usually around 10 per cent), or the first hour's fee.

If you want to work with sick or excluded children, contact your local authority and ask to be put through to the section that runs the home tuition service (bear in mind that names for this section vary from authority to authority). Jane, a retired history teacher, followed this route, as she particularly wanted to help children with difficulties. She filled in an application form, went through an interview and was added to the local authority list. She is employed on an *ad hoc* basis, similar to supply teaching, and has worked with a wide range of tutees, including children with serious illnesses, children who are confined to home with a short-term injury such as a broken leg, and excluded children.

Why?

Tutoring is a straightforward way of earning extra income. Martin describes his tutoring sessions as *'just more of the same'*, going over on a one-to-one basis what he teaches during his regular maths lessons. As a tutor, he relishes the opportunity to assess and meet a pupil's individual needs and watch that pupil grow in confidence over the year – something a teacher often misses out on with a class of thirty or more. He also feels it has made him a better teacher, particularly in his early years. As he says, *'If a tutee doesn't understand something, there's nowhere for them to hide! It's always pretty obvious if I'm not being clear, and I then have to find other, better ways of explaining what I'm trying to get across.'* When asked about the downsides, he highlights the pressures of having to teach for another one or two hours at the end of the day – although he is equally keen to point out that tutoring has been *'a life-saver'*: *'With young children and a partner who only works part-time, the money has been vital in helping to pay the bills and enabling us to have treats we couldn't otherwise afford.'*

Local authority home tutor Jane has different reasons for tutoring. After years of teaching challenging children in school, she enjoys having the time to get to know them on an individual basis. As she says, *'at last I have the chance to look beneath the surface and find out what is really going on with these children'*. She also loves the challenge of teaching a range of subjects. When she recently had to cover *Romeo and Juliet* with a disaffected Year 9 boy, she thought the task was insurmountable – until she hit upon the idea of introducing him to the Leonardo DiCaprio film version. This and other successes have rekindled her enthusiasm for teaching and reminded her of just how much these children need committed, caring and expert help.

Other opportunities

Purchasing a subject franchise

There are various courses that can be purchased as a franchise, enabling you to run your own small business teaching children outside school hours. *La Jolie Ronde*, a French course for primary-aged children, and Kumon maths and English courses are just two well-known examples.

Working for a subject association

What?

Subject associations have a mission to further and improve the teaching of their subjects and enable teachers, lecturers and students to communicate with each other. Many of the more traditional subject associations were established in the nineteenth or early twentieth centuries, and they have a long and distinguished history with a wide, and sometimes international, membership. Many subjects also have more than one association.

The work of an association varies considerably, depending on its size and its history. Most associations offer continuing professional development courses, organise conferences and publish newsletters and journals. They may also lead curriculum development projects, such as setting up ways of sharing innovative departmental leadership; develop and offer teaching and learning resources; administer a specialist library; liaise with governmental organisations such as the Department for Children, Schools and Families (DCSF), the QCA and the Training and Development Agency (TDA); run online resources such as a database of relevant publications, links and a forum; organise social events; and administer student awards and prizes. Many associations are largely dependent on membership subscriptions to fund their activities, and encouraging new membership is important both to their survival and to the development of new projects and services.

With such a wide remit, working for a subject association offers plenty of variety and, in many cases, the chance to be innovative. The vast majority of job opportunities are voluntary, with all associations run by committees requiring presidents, secretaries and treasurers. Other roles might include taking on responsibility for editing journals and newsletters, writing articles, chairing teaching committees or joining working groups. Most associations employ just one or two paid, permanent members of staff, although there may be some opportunities for short-term paid roles such as speaking at a conference, running a project, helping to set up a website or writing for an association magazine.

Where?

Each association has its own headquarters, and they can be located anywhere across the country. Some associations also have regional offices or branches. Although administrative staff tend to be based at head office, most voluntary workers and some paid employees will work from home. Depending on your role, you may also have to travel. Our case study, Alf, is the Professional Development Manager for the Historical Association. With a remit to support over 4,000 teacher members across the country, he often find himself travelling long distances and even has to organise the occasional overnight stay.

When?

In the majority of cases, full-time job opportunities are limited to administrative roles within one of the larger associations. Even part-time paid roles are few and far between, and, as with any part-time professional post, your workload may stretch beyond your official working hours. Although Alf is contracted to work three days a week, in practice he often does more. He also finds that he never works the same three days, as dates for meetings are often set by outside bodies. As a volunteer, your timetable will vary considerably, depending on your role. Many meetings, courses and social events run during weekends and evenings, so you may have to be prepared to work outside normal working hours.

Who?

Having a passion for your subject is a prerequisite for working for a subject association. As the majority of available opportunities are either voluntary or part time and short term (and less well paid than teaching), you also have to be in a position to take a salary reduction. Working voluntarily for a subject association can be an attractive option for consultants or retired teachers who want to maintain links with both their profession and their subject, for teachers who have downsized to a part-time job and for teachers who have taken a career break to bring up children.

How?

Contact relevant subject associations to find out what work is available. Although permanent job opportunities are limited, Alf points out that there are many different ways to participate and that association personnel such as himself are always looking out for reliable people to do both unpaid and paid work. From a career development point of view, it is also worth bearing in mind that subject association employees often started out as volunteers (see Alf's case study). For a comprehensive list of subject associations, visit www.subject association.org.uk.

Why?

Working for a subject association enables you to keep up to date with innovations in your subject and helps you to explore the pedagogy of your subject in a variety of different ways. Whether you take on a short-term voluntary role while still teaching, or a permanent paid job, the work will bring you into contact with like-minded professionals. If you love your subject and want to meet and learn from other excellent teachers, working for a subject association is well worth considering.

Case study

From head of history to . . . Professional Development Manager for the Historical Association

Having taught history for over twenty years, Alf was ready for a fresh challenge. As he wanted to stay within the world of history, he decided against taking the next step up the ladder to a deputy headship and started exploring other options. Here he explains how he became a Professional Development Manager for the Historical Association, describes what the job involves and explains how it has enabled him to establish a positive work–life balance:

When I was offered the job as Professional Development Manager, it was a new post. I had done some previous work for the Historical Association and they e-mailed me to ask if I would be interested in applying. I think they had trouble attracting candidates as the pay is quite a bit lower than for teaching! At the time, I was looking to diversify beyond the classroom and I was also attracted by the opportunity to shape the job and make a real impact on both the Historical Association and history teachers in general.

The job involves looking after all our 4,000 teacher members. I organise continuing professional development events and conferences for both primary and secondary teachers. I also produce

continued

the monthly newsletter for members, respond to members' calls and concerns, and attend lots of meetings with bodies such as the DCSF, the TDA and Becta [The British Educational Communications and Technology Agency]. In fact, no two days are the same. Inevitably, my teaching experience and expertise have proved to be essential. If I am to work with the primary and secondary committees, they have to be able to respect my abilities as a good history teacher above everything else. I also draw heavily on my person management skills. I spend a lot of time persuading people to do (unpaid) work for the association – not dissimilar to managing teachers in your department and subtly persuading them to do what they should be doing anyway!

For me, there are many advantage to my job. I enjoy working on a national scale and discussing curriculum developments with the QCA and the DCSF. I work with great colleagues, and love meeting and learning from fellow history teachers. I am able to propose, develop and raise funding for new projects and I also enjoy freedom from the dreaded bell and being my own boss. Although I have to operate within parameters, day-to-day time management and work priorities are mine to set as I please. This flexible working pattern suits my current personal circumstances and I can now take my children to the school bus, go to parents' meetings and help out in school if I wish.

On the downside, the pay is not very good, and meetings and CPD events often take place at weekends. You also have to deal with the limitations placed on your actions by the nature of a voluntary organisation; sometimes it's difficult to get things done as quickly as you would like because of the need to work through committees and unpaid volunteers. For me, however, these are minor disadvantages, and I would recommend any teacher who loves their subject to consider getting involved with their subject association.

You can find out more about the Historical Association and how to get involved in its work at www.history.org.uk.

Delivering talks and workshops in schools and colleges

What?

Many schools and colleges employ outside groups or individuals to supplement their teaching and learning through talks, performances and workshops. For example, theatre-in-education groups use drama to enhance and explore various aspects of the curriculum; visiting musicians give performances and run creative music workshops; sports coaches offer activities such as athletics, extra cricket training or trampolining; an 'artist in residence' might organise a whole-school project such as making a ceramic tile frieze; and personal, social and health education (PSHE) specialists are often brought in by schools to run a theme day or contribute to an assembly.

Where?

Although most groups work in schools and colleges, the venue can vary depending on what you are offering. For example, a number of sports activities require specialist facilities; some drama groups add authenticity to their workshops by using a local theatre; outdoor art or conservation projects will take place in the countryside or local community. You and/or your group may also be employed by a cluster of schools that organise their own central location.

When?

School-based sessions mostly fall within lesson times or school assemblies. Larger projects and workshops may take up a whole morning or afternoon, or you may be asked to organise a theme day. If you are invited to contribute to an out-of-school group or run a holiday activities session, you could find yourself working during evenings, weekends and holiday periods. Planning, marketing and the administrative tasks that go with running a small business may also spill over into evenings and weekends.

Who?

Apart from a knowledge of your subject and how it can be used to enhance children's learning, you need energy and enthusiasm for this kind of work. You also need to be a confident performer, able to make an impact on your audience and form positive relationships with your pupils or students in a short space of time. Our case study, arts education co-ordinator Kate, finds that a confident performance and good communication skills are almost more important than subject knowledge. Not all teachers are totally appreciative of outside groups, and, as she says, *'without the confidence to face people who are resisting your approach, you don't have a leg to stand on'*. She also points out that every visit to a school is like a first-night performance: *'When I go into school to deliver a workshop . . . I am always nervous, it is like every day is my first.'* If you know that you operate better in a familiar environment with a regular routine, this job may not be the best choice for you.

Depending on your role, you may also find yourself running a small business. Kate is always looking ahead to the next project and finding ways to generate new work. If you thrive on excitement and risk, this will be a positive factor for you. If, however, you find uncertainty unnerving or require financial security, you may need to think carefully about taking on this kind of work.

How?

Look out for adverts in the education press. Approach groups with your CV and details and ask to be kept on file even if there are no vacancies at the time. Find out what groups are available with an internet search. For example, the key words 'theatre in education' will give you links to a wide range of drama groups, as well as information about what the work involves.

Although drama, art, music, sport and PSHE are the subject areas mostly commonly covered by outside groups, there is a potential market for just about any topic. If all you have to offer is more of what the regular staff can provide themselves, they probably won't choose to spend their precious budget on you. If, however, you have expertise in something new and different, you may be able to set yourself up as a visiting speaker. Perhaps you have worked in a part of the world that tallies with the geography National Curriculum and could deliver lively and interesting talks supplemented with slide shows and artefacts; perhaps you could run a series of Latin, Mandarin or Arabic workshops as part of a school's provision for gifted linguists, or use your expertise in sugarcraft to contribute to the food technology programme. Approach subject leaders or primary headteachers with your details. If you find that there is an initial interest in what you have to offer, you can then go ahead and market yourself as a visiting speaker. (For more information on promoting yourself to schools, see pages 223–6.)

Why?

Delivering talks and workshops to schools and colleges enables you to explore your subject area in lots of different ways – with the sole purpose of inspiring the children you work with. Although you need to have a knowledge of the curriculum, you will not usually be restricted to a syllabus or have the pressure of working towards an examination. This frees you up to concentrate on inspiring your audience and introducing its members to all that your subject has to offer. If you like to 'do your own thing' and find that the structured environment of the classroom is limiting to your creative tendencies, this kind of work is well worth considering. Our case study, Kate, gives a personal description of her role as an arts education co-ordinator, explains why she enjoys the work and touches on some of the disadvantages.

Case study

From drama teacher to . . . Arts Education Co-ordinator

Q What does your role entail?

A I work for Bigfoot Arts Education as a Co-ordinator for the South-West office. We are part of a national organisation, working alongside schools to enhance the curriculum and using drama as a tool for learning. My job involves promoting the company's work in schools and local authorities, managing tutors and delivering the programmes we offer.

Q How do you promote the company?

A The promotional side involves a range of work, from marketing the programmes in schools and arranging meetings with head-teachers, to pitching the company's work through presentations at learning community meetings. I also meet with local authority

continued

*representatives for areas such as PSHE, gifted and talented,
and extended schools, whose job it is to ensure good practice
is being delivered in schools to cover all aspects of government
initiatives.*

Q And the 'school side' of your work?

A *Bigfoot largely works in primary schools, including out-of-school
activities, supply and PPA [planning, preparation and assess-
ment] cover. We offer curriculum workshops such as Creative
Literacy or Living History, and bespoke projects written
specifically for a school.*

Q How many children do you usually work with?

A *It varies considerably – anything from a single class, a year
group, a key stage or the whole school, depending on the programme of work and the school's requirements. We also offer
an INSET programme designed to help teachers incorporate
drama into the everyday life of their classroom.*

Q What first attracted you to the post, and how does it suit
your needs?

A *The post appealed to me because it allows me to use all my
creative skills and focus on what I believe to be an essential
part of children's education. I like having variety in my work
and being able to see the immediate impact drama can have
in a number of different school environments.*

Q How did you hear of it, and what was the selection
procedure like?

A *I heard about Bigfoot through a friend who knew I was looking
for a change of direction. The selection procedure involved
an informal interview, followed by a practical workshop.
Successful candidates then had to attend a London-based
training programme.*

Q You worked as a drama teacher before joining Bigfoot.
How important are your teaching skills in your day-to-day
role?

A *My teaching skills come into play every day. It was a steep learning curve at the start as I had to adapt my skills as a secondary-trained teacher to a (mostly) primary setting. I do, however, believe that once you have the basics of teaching, they can be applied to any age group – from young children to adults. My knowledge of the primary curriculum has grown enormously, but as most of what we do is drama orientated, it is my training in theatre that stands as the cornerstone to my work.*

Q So what are the advantages of the post for you?

A *Variety – and being your own boss. I had felt a bit trapped going to the same place of work every day. By contrast, this work involves meeting new people in new settings every day and keeps my outlook far fresher. No two days are the same. I also avoid much of the bureaucracy of teaching. In this job, we get to do all the good stuff without having to justify ourselves on paper!*

Q And the disadvantages?

A *I miss the sense of belonging to a school and that unconscious 'knowing' of how a school runs. I also miss getting to know the students, seeing them progress through the school and, in most cases, the end result. In this job, it's also not so easy to separate personal and professional life, particularly as I work partly from home. I miss the Friday night feeling of having reached the end of the week and really deserving that glass of wine – and the wonderfully liberating feeling of the summer vacation and knowing you have six whole weeks off!*

Q So would you recommend the job to others?

A *Oh yes, definitely. You may feel that you are taking a huge risk, but nothing is more risky than being trapped in a situation where you are unable to fulfil your potential!*

Working as a distance learning tutor

What?

'Distance learning' is a generic term covering any course that enables a student to study at home. Increasingly, distance learning courses incorporate blended learning into their delivery, combining techniques such as correspondence courses, DVDs, videoconferencing, web-based tutorials and seminars, computer-marked assignments, e-mail contact with a tutor, and occasional face-to-face tutorials and summer schools.

The United Kingdom's Open University is one of the earliest and best-known distance learning organisations. Students start at various levels, depending on their background and how much time they have available. Gareth has worked as an Open University maths tutor for over thirty years, delivering courses that range from exploring maths in everyday life to looking at the construction, recognition and classification of geometric entities. Although the courses are based on self-study, they are supported by exercise booklets, video tapes, computer packages, course handbooks, course material, and tutor- and computer-marked assignments. As a tutor, Gareth also has to make himself available to provide telephone and online help and advice for his students.

Delivering courses via videoconferencing techniques is another option if you are looking to teach outside the classroom. Videoconferencing technology is increasingly being used to offer students a wider range of GCSE, AS and A2 choices, and typical subjects include Latin, electronics, accounting and Spanish. Students are set units of work and they then have a weekly videoconferencing tutorial with their online tutor. They are also supported by online resources and may have occasional visits from their tutor.

Not all distance learning courses are either academic or designed for school-age pupils. There are a number of practical language courses, online professional development courses covering areas such as IT, business, management and marketing, 'skills for life' courses and courses based on crafts, hobbies and leisure pursuits. If you can't find a suitable course to teach, you always have the option of starting your own. Sian was a lecturer in textiles, teaching at a college in south-west England. When one of her students moved abroad mid-year, she developed a correspondence course to enable the student to complete her City & Guilds certificate. This proved so successful that she decided to offer the course to other students, and it has now evolved into 'Distant Stitch' (www.distantstitch.co.uk), an online correspondence course with between fifty and seventy students on its books at any one time.

Where?

As a distance learning tutor you will mostly be based at home, although you could be required to make occasional trips to schools, colleges and learning centres to give face-to-face tutorials. Some courses may also include summer schools. As part of her Distant Stitch programme, Sian runs a residential course every summer. She bases the course in a country house so that she can give her students a relaxing break, as well as the chance to meet up and develop their embroidery skills.

For many distance learning tutors, e-mail and the telephone are an important means of communicating with students, as is the webcam if you are using videoconferencing technology. Although video-conferencing may seem an ideal part-time job option for those with young children, in practice you will probably have to arrange childcare (and even pet care) for the hours you are teaching, as you cannot afford any disturbances during a lesson.

When?

Your working timetable will vary considerably, depending on the course you are teaching. In many cases, the hours will be flexible. As with any teaching role, you can fit preparation and marking into your working hours to suit yourself, as long as you meet the necessary deadlines. Unlike most teachers, however, you could find yourself on call outside normal working hours, and Gareth points out that you have to be sympathetic to the telephone or e-mail demands of students who need regular support.

Allowing each student to work at their own pace is another important part of the distance learning tutor's role. At the same time, you need to monitor your students' progress and be ready to help them keep on top of their assignments. Sian encourages her students to work to a regular rhythm with a series of 'sending-in' dates – something they themselves requested, to help them fit their working routines around their domestic responsibilities. She also sets aside mornings to answer e-mails and gives priority to assessing any work she is sent – with the result that some students express disappointment at having their work returned so quickly, just when they were anticipating a break!

With the Open University and other, similar organisations, timetabled tutorials will often take place during the evenings or weekends, to fit in with the working hours of your students. If you decide to work as a videoconferencing tutor, you will be allocated regular weekly sessions to fit in with school hours. Bear in mind that you may not have much say over the timings for these sessions. If, for example, you are scheduled to give an hour-long lesson at 12.00 p.m. every Wednesday, you need to consider the effect that this one hour's commitment will have on the rest of your working day.

Who?

With such a wide range of distance learning courses to choose from, any teacher with relevant training, skills and experience should be able to find a suitable role. In many respects, a distance learning course is similar to any teaching job – except that the method of delivery is different. As Gareth points out, you need to be versatile as a teacher and able to use a variety of teaching techniques. If you work on a course that offers personal tutor support, you also need to be comfortable with e-mail and the telephone as forms of communication. With many of us becoming more adept at using e-mail, instant messaging and chat forums as a means of social contact, the distance learning format does not preclude forming a positive relationship with your pupils. In spite of never actually meeting many of her students 'in the flesh', Sian gets to know them well. Hearing all their news and sharing in their successes, is one of the most enjoyable aspects of her online contact. Nevertheless, for those who particularly enjoy the face-to-face contact of teaching, a traditional role may in the end be more suitable.

Teaching via videoconferencing technology or running online seminars does demand a particular style of teaching. If you are an energetic practitioner who bounds around the classroom and relies on your outgoing personality to engage with your pupils, you may find the webcam a little restrictive. A calm, clear, structured delivery based on thorough forward planning is often the most successful style of teaching for online and webcam sessions.

How?

Check the education press for adverts. If you want to look into tutoring for the Open University, visit the 'jobs' section on their website (www.open.ac.uk). For courses with a more vocational leaning, try the Open College (www.opencollege.info). Nelson Thornes is a major provider of distance learning courses for schools and colleges, and it has a 'current vacancies' section on www.nelson thornes.com. You can also find out about a huge variety of distance learning courses at learndirect (www.learndirect.co.uk). Even if there are no jobs available at the time, ask an organisation to keep your details on file in case of future opportunities.

Why?

Being able to operate from home and having a (mostly) flexible timetable are perhaps the two main advantages of distance tutoring. If you are doing other jobs or based at home owing to family commitments, the work can also keep your teaching skills current and up to date. This is certainly one of the advantages for Gareth, whose daytime role in FE management leaves him with little opportunity to teach or interact with the students at his college. Distance learning has opened up the field of education to a huge number of people who might otherwise have missed out – and the work will bring you into contact with a wide range of self-motivated individuals from a variety of different backgrounds. As Gareth says, working as an Open University tutor enables you to offer educational access to a large demographic group whose talents would otherwise be greatly underused.

Contributing to an education website

What?

There has been a proliferation of online resources in recent years – and with the DCSF encouraging all UK schools to set up their own virtual learning environments, this looks set to continue. The nature and content of education websites vary considerably. Some sites are devoted to GCSE and A level revision, others are linked to a specific subject such as history, or offer resources and activities for a variety of different subjects. Sites are also available in every sector, from primary to further education. A site may be run by an education company or by a single individual with teaching expertise in their subject or field (see the next case study). Although sites vary in what they offer, a typical menu might include online lessons, free downloadables, interactive quizzes, revision diagrams and exercises, chat forums, news stories and links to relevant sites, awarding bodies and subject associations.

In many respects, contributing to an education website is not dissimilar to writing for education magazines, journals and supplements (see page 101). You will, however, have access to computer technology, with all that it has to offer (interactive elements, slide shows, relevant links, downloadable graphics and diagrams – the options are endless). If you have enough time, energy and ICT knowledge, you could also consider starting your own website. This can be a project that you run alongside your teaching job or a full-time commitment, as with our case study, Catherine.

Where?

Whether you are running your own website or just making the occasional contribution, you will be based at home and working mostly on your computer.

When?

If you are contributing to a website, you can fit the work around your other commitments, as long as you meet any deadlines set by the website editor. For our case study, Catherine, running her own MFL sites is a full-time job and she often finds herself at her computer during evenings and weekends.

Who?

As with educational writing (see page 101), you need to have teaching expertise in your subject area, along with a range of up-to-date, creative and practical ideas. A working knowledge of ICT and how your activities can be presented online is also useful – although you can always ask for support from a computer-literate friend or relative if your own skills are not very advanced.

How?

Keeping a website current and offering relevant new material is a major task, and a number of editors welcome contributions. To find appropriate sites, check the education press for adverts and do a computer search, for example for 'GCSE maths revision' or 'early years websites'. Most websites give contact details so that you can get in touch, as well as including links to other relevant sites. A few of the sites run by larger organisations also have a jobs section.

If your ultimate aim is to set up your own site, contributing to someone else's site makes a useful starting point. Apart from giving you experience of creating online resources, it will get your name known in your particular circle. Catherine also recommends becoming involved in ICT at school, perhaps as the ICT co-ordinator for your subject. This is one of the best ways to get an in-depth knowledge of how school networks operate and what actually works for both teachers and pupils.

Another important part of your preparation is to research the resources that are already out there. As with any new business, if your site is to be successful, it will need to be different from, or more exhaustive than, what is currently available.

Why?

If you enjoy the planning and preparation side of teaching, contributing to a website gives you the additional option of using online resources to present your activities. As with writing education articles for paper publication, you also have the satisfaction of sharing your ideas and expertise with colleagues across the country. Running your own website gives you editorial control over your output and helps you to explore all aspects of your subject and its teaching. It also makes an impressive addition to your CV.

Case study

From MFL teacher to . . . running an MFL education website

Catherine had been teaching for ten years when she set up her first MFL website, Zut! She describes how the website

continued

developed into a full-time commitment, her experiences of running an education website and the difference it has made to her working life:

As an MFL teacher, I had always been interested in the use of ICT in language teaching and I regularly designed computer-based resources for my own classes. My online exercises were usually well received by my pupils and I started sharing them with colleagues, eventually putting them on a website for people to access as and when they needed. In 2002, I developed my website into 'Zut!' (www.zut.org.uk), a live online resource available for all teachers and pupils. A year later, I was able to draw an income from the site by charging subscriptions, and I have since added German, Welsh and Spanish sites to my portfolio. At this point, the sites were proving to be such a commitment that I had to give up teaching and run them full time.

With two young children, I like the flexibility of running my own business. I also enjoy the variety: dealing with administration, creating new material for the site, organising the recording of native speakers, liaising with the IT company who look after the design and technical side of the sites, and responding to clients' queries and problems. On the business side, going from teaching to self-employment was a huge leap. I swiftly had to find out about taxes, VAT, PAYE and so on, and was very grateful to have a good accountant!

As with any job, there are disadvantages. Working from home means that I have to be disciplined and manage my time carefully. I'm never far away from my computer, and as I never know when my customers will need help, I even take the laptop on holiday. Being self-employed also means a constant concern about money and whether I will have enough subscriptions each month to pay the bills. As a school-linked business, I do particularly well from September to March (the end of the schools' financial year) and June and July, when departments have their new budgets. August is quiet, and I have to budget accordingly. Overall, however, the pluses far outweigh the minuses, and I have never regretted my career shift. If the idea of running your own website appeals, you can set it up alongside your teaching job and 'dip a toe in the water' before deciding whether to take the plunge into a full-time commitment.

Writing education books and articles

What?

- **Magazines and education supplements**: there are numerous educational publications on the market, and they all need experienced professionals to contribute features and articles. Whether you are an early years teacher or a lecturer in maths at a sixth-form college, you should be able to find magazines, journals and newspaper supplements catering for your particular subject or sector. Activities and ideas for lessons make up a large part of many publications, although there are also opportunities to write 'think pieces' about aspects of your teaching experience, report on new initiatives, education shows, conferences and courses, or review books and resources.
- **Education books**: writing education books is another option. Subject matter is hugely wide-ranging and includes student textbooks, revision booklets, collections of lesson plans aimed at both primary and secondary school teachers, books introducing practitioners to the theory of education and new initiatives, and photocopiable or computer-based games, activities and resources.

Where?

Most freelance writers work from home, although you will need to draw on your teaching experience and keep your practice up to date, either through your daytime teaching job or by visiting schools on a regular basis. In recent years, the internet has become an invaluable means of research. Depending on the level at which you are writing, there may also be times when you will need access to a good library.

When?

Flexibility is one of the great advantages of writing. As long as you meet the publisher's deadlines, it doesn't matter when you write, and you can even combine writing with a full-time teaching job if you don't mind its eating into your leisure time. Early years specialist and freelance writer Helena finds that most magazine editors will allow a couple of days' flexibility with deadlines if she gets behind, although she emphasises the importance of keeping them informed and waiting until you have a reputation for reliability before asking for an extension. If you are writing a book, the deadlines tend to be more rigid. This is particularly the case with the larger publishers, which follow a tight timetable leading up to the book's publication date.

Who?

The first prerequisite is to be an experienced teacher with good ideas and/or an unusual and interesting perspective on your job. Apart from experience, you also have to be able to write well, meet deadlines and show attention to detail. It makes an editor's job much easier if your writing is accurate and well researched. Many magazines provide writers' guidelines so that you can fit in with their house style, and although editors will expect to edit you, you probably won't be given any further commissions if your article requires *too* much editorial input.

How?

You can find a comprehensive list of publishers and publications in the *Writers' and Artists' Yearbook* and/or *Willings Press Guide* (reference copies should be available in your local library). Once you have a list of relevant magazines and newspapers, try to get hold of some copies so that you can check the nature of their style and content. If you want to write a book, order some publishers' catalogues or have a look at their websites to get some idea of the kinds of topics they cover and identify gaps in the market. Many publishers specialise in a particular sector, subject matter or aspect of education such as special educational needs (SEN) or pastoral support.

The next step is to come up with some interesting ideas. Although there is always room for clear, well-written features on the basics of teaching, most editors are constantly on the lookout for something fresh. It is also worth making the most of any new initiatives that are relevant to your skills and experiences. Helena had been writing for a year or so when the 2000 Curriculum Guidance for the Foundation Stage was introduced. This triggered a mini publishing boom in the sector, and Helena was commissioned to write a number of books and articles demonstrating how the new curriculum could be put into practice within the early years setting. Publishers and editors need to keep abreast of new developments and they will be particularly open to your ideas if you have expertise relating to the latest initiative.

Getting a foot on the bottom rung of the ladder is often the hardest. Once you have an article in print, it enables you to show an editor your work (and evidence that someone else saw fit to publish you always goes in your favour!). If you have difficulty getting a commission, look into writing for no fee as a first step. Free local magazines and papers are often glad to publish a piece, especially from a community-based professional such as a teacher. Other possibilities include writing for the school magazine, a local National Childbirth Trust publication or even the parish magazine – anything to get your work in print and show editors that you can write.

Helena also recommends keeping a constant eye out for writing opportunities. Apart from contributing to most early years publications, she has also compiled a booklist for a well-known children's publisher, writes regularly for a couple of magazines aimed at nannies and childminders, and has the occasional article accepted by teaching union magazines. The next stage of her career development plan is to investigate writing for early years websites and start contributing to parenting magazines – although she suspects that it will prove more difficult to get commissions in this sector, as she will be competing with a much wider field of journalists.

If you want to write a book, visit educational publishers' websites and follow their instructions for submitting a proposal. Unlike many kinds of publishers, educational publishers usually welcome proposals, and you won't need to go through an agent. In most cases, submitting a proposal involves filling in a proposal form, writing a sample chapter and organising referees. The process can be quite time-consuming, and you may prefer to ring a publisher to find out if they are interested in the sound of your idea, before going to the trouble of writing up your proposal.

Why?

People's reasons for writing vary considerably. You may simply love writing and want to share your expertise with your colleagues. Having run a highly successful nursery school for thirty years, Sarah had decided to retire. Her daughters suggested that she should make a record of her career, and she came up with a plan for a practical, ideas-based book on running an early years setting. A publisher was immediately interested and, on the basis of her proposal and sample chapter, gave her a commission. For Sarah, the book provided a fascinating opportunity to review her career and analyse how her practice, and the early years sector as a whole, had developed over the years. The resulting book has been well received, and although she will not make much money from it, she regards it as a fitting swansong to a long and successful teaching career.

Matthew's motivation for writing is somewhat different from Sarah's. He has spent the past fifteen years as head of a highly success-ful science department in a large comprehensive school. Five years ago, he reached the point where he wanted to develop his career and increase his earnings, but did not wish to take on a deputy headship or find a job that took him out of the classroom. When the opportunity to write Key Stage 3 and 4 textbooks arose, it seemed ideal. He knew that his particular strengths lay in helping pupils towards examination success, and he was confident that he had the expertise to write a useful series of textbooks. Unlike Sarah, he makes a healthy additional income from his writing. When an early years setting decides to buys Sarah's book, it buys one copy; when a secondary school decides to buy Matthew's book, it buys fifty copies or more and continually replaces its stock as the books become lost or damaged.

Being able to list your books and articles adds gravitas to your CV. Your publications will give you credibility as a conference speaker or trainer and act as a form of networking (authors and writers are often invited to contribute to events on the back of their published work). Writing a book or article also requires detailed research and helps you to focus on your subject matter. It is probably not, how-ever, a recommended career choice if you need to earn a living wage. Only a relatively small percentage of freelance writers and even fewer authors are able to survive solely on their fees or royalties. Educational writing is probably best regarded as a fascinating supplement to your teaching job or a means of adding value to your profile as an educational consultant.

Other opportunities

Working in educational publishing

See pages 155–6 for a survey of how to break into the field of education publishing, the various job opportunities and what the work involves.

Other opportunities

Reviewing book proposals

When a book proposal is submitted to an educational publisher, the commissioning editor will often ask practitioners to review the proposal to help establish whether or not the book might have a market. Although the work is not particularly well paid, it is interesting and gives you an insight into the early stages of a book's publication. Contact the larger educational publishers to find out if they have any available opportunities.

Chapter 3

Effectively transferring . . . your leadership and management skills

Leadership takes place at all levels within a school or college. From students leading their own learning through ICT to support staff introducing a new administrative software package, the most effective schools look to nurture leadership opportunities for everyone. Nevertheless, schools and colleges are highly structured organisations with a wide variety of middle and senior leadership and management opportunities. Any teacher who has held a leadership or management position will possess a wide range of skills, and has a number of different job options beyond the school or college setting. If you do not have a clear idea of the direction you want to follow, it can be useful to analyse what makes a leader, what makes a manager and the various positions within the wider field of education that might suit your particular skills, interests and experience.

Leadership and/or management?

What is the difference between 'leadership' and 'management'? Although there is a strong overlap between the two roles, there is also a distinct philosophical contrast. Whereas a leader makes decisions about *what* to do, a manager's task is to bring those decisions to fruition. An effective leader has vision and aspirations, a sense of purpose, the ability to inspire, motivate, create effective teams and act as a role model. An effective manager has the ability to develop practical strategies, organise resources and finances, monitor pupil and staff performance, and implement self-evaluation systems.

Of course, a good leader should also have strong management skills and vice versa. However inspirational your latest strategic idea might be, it is of little use if you cannot also judge whether or not it is workable on a practical level. Similarly, when a manager has to implement a new initiative or monitor performance, it helps if they have the capacity to inspire and enthuse their team. It is also useful to be able to recognise what your leadership and management role actually involves and where your strengths and weaknesses lie. As a leader, you may be fantastically inspirational and charismatic, but not good at day-to-day planning. If this is the case, identify where you need to improve, work at it and delegate certain tasks to individuals who *do* have the skills that you lack. As a manager, you may be very good at taking a logical, clear-sighted approach to curriculum planning, but not great at 'selling' your ideas to your staff. Again, you need to identify and play to your strengths; many teachers appreciate a clear, logical presentation every bit as much as an entertaining performance, particularly when they are the ones who have to put your ideas into practice!

If you are considering moving from your school- or college-based leadership and management role, identifying where your strengths lie can also help you decide which direction to follow. For example, if you know that you are more of a leader than a manager, choose a role where you can give full rein to your visionary qualities – working at the cutting edge of educational development within the DCSF or QCA, for example (see page 112). If you know that you are a charismatic speaker and enjoy having an audience, go for a role such as School Improvement Adviser (see page 126), where you will be required to inspire and communicate with a wide range of different people. If, however, you know that your strengths lie in your planning and organisational skills, choose a role such as working for an awarding body, where your skills will be pivotal in ensuring the development and smooth running of the examination system.

Interpersonal skills

Regardless of whether you see yourself as predominantly a leader or a manager, your interpersonal skills are crucial to your effectiveness. You need to get things done, and in many cases you have to take ultimate responsibility for what happens within your curriculum area, year group, key stage or school. It is down to you to ensure that all personnel are fulfilling their roles and pulling in the same direction, and you have to be able to motivate and support your staff, deliver sometimes difficult messages in a constructive manner, and delegate appropriately.

An effective leader or manager treats every staff member as an individual. To encourage your colleagues to work at full capacity, you have to be able to read someone's frame of mind and work out how best to approach each situation. For example, supporting a newly qualified teacher who has not yet understood the full extent of their responsibilities is very different from working with a staff member who is exhausted, disillusioned or nearing retirement. You also have to make judgements over what you *ought* to address, what you *must* address and what to leave well alone. When should you be understanding and supportive (the 'carrot' approach), when should you be firm (the 'stick' approach), and, most difficult of all, can you be firm without causing so much resentment that the original problem is only exacerbated? As a leader or manager, you won't be accorded respect from the people you manage just because of your position. You have to earn it.

Apart from requiring all your interpersonal skills, a leadership and management role within a school or college can place you in some delicate situations. Teaching is largely a graduate profession, and you may find yourself promoted above individuals who are more highly qualified than you. It is also not uncommon for a subject leader or year head to step down, and you can end up managing the person who held the position before you, or even your ex-boss! Most teachers spend much of their working day managing their own classroom, and not all teachers are particularly open to 'outside interference' in the form of new initiatives, being observed or having to undertake additional training. As a senior leader, you will also find yourself giving support across a very wide range of issues, including difficulties with discipline, classroom management, the curriculum and learning issues, implementing new initiatives, observing and assessing your colleagues, and even dealing with personal problems.

All this gives you plenty of opportunity to hone your interpersonal skills within the sphere of leadership and management. If you have held a leadership and management role in a school or college, you will certainly have plenty of experience in managing people! How you then go on to use these skills will depend on the position you wish to take up. In many roles within the wider field of education, you will not have such regular contact with your staff as you did in school. For example, if you are co-ordinating a team of freelance consultants to work on a short-term project or appointing and briefing trainers to contribute to a course, much of your initial contact will be via the phone or e-mail. Without the opportunity to build up long-term relationships with staff, every communication has to count, and you will need to draw on all your charm and motivational skills to make a swift impact on the people you are leading. Whenever you are in situations where you have limited exposure to your team, your extensive experience of reading people and making accurate judgements on how best to handle them will prove to be invaluable.

Intrapersonal skills

Whereas your interpersonal skills involve your relationship with others, your intrapersonal skills are all about your relationship with yourself. Are you able to remain calm and present a professional front even when you are feeling tired, demoralised or unwell? Can you judge when you need to act and when it is better to let go? Do you know when to have an open door policy and when to set boundaries? Do you understand the difference between self-worth and arrogance, and never allow the two to overlap? Can you recognise your achievements and use them to build up your self-esteem? Can you assess your weaknesses and work on improving them, without at the same time feeling inadequate? Accepting that you will be challenged and not taking things personally is a significant aspect of coping with leadership and management (see Chapter 6 for some tips on handling work-based stress). Gone are the days when you can grumble about 'the management'. Once you become 'the management', you must be positive and convincing even if you don't agree with the latest initiative or directive that you are having to put in place. This is particularly the case within senior leadership, which can sometimes feel a lonely place to be.

A leadership and management role in a school or college will give you endless opportunities for personal development, all of which can be transferred to management roles within the wider field of education. Whether you are having to stay calm in the face of a pressing deadline as an educational publisher (see page 152), support and encourage a nervous speaker as a conference organiser (see page 148) or maintain your self-belief when faced with a challenging headteacher as an Ofsted inspector (see page 120), school leadership will give you plenty of experience to draw upon. As a successful subject, key stage or senior leader, you should have developed more than enough intrapersonal skills to cope with the generic pressures of management within any other workplace or setting.

Troubleshooting

A school or college populated with hundreds of students is bound to generate endless situations that simply can't be left until later, and all leadership and management roles involve a degree of trouble-shooting. Although any teacher has to deal with crises, as a manager you are regularly required to step in and give immediate support to your colleagues. Whether the site manager has gone sick and you need to find cover, an incident in the playground demands an immediate response or the school has not been supplied with enough Standard Attainment Tests (SATS) papers for a year group, it is down to you to find the answer.

One of the most challenging aspects of troubleshooting is having to make an immediate response. There are arguably very few jobs that demand quite so much on-the-spot crisis management as teaching, and this is something for which you cannot prepare. Most teachers have someone they can turn to in a crisis, but when that someone is you, you have to remain calm and know what to do, even if you are not always certain that your response will turn out to be the right one. And if, as is inevitable, you sometimes make the wrong call, you have to be able to analyse the situation in hindsight, learn from your mistakes and move on.

The majority of crisis management scenarios also demand a degree of sensitivity, particularly when someone is asking you to intervene in a situation with a pupil. As a manager, you are expected to take charge, but at the same time you have to be sensitive to a colleague's wishes and take care not undermine their authority, especially in public. Occasionally your assessment of a situation can be quite different from that of your colleague, and you need to have confidence in both your judgement and your right to handle things as you see fit. This can cause friction with some individuals, and in these instances you have to be able to take charge without making your colleague feel belittled or unsupported.

Making an immediate response and taking charge in a crisis are not the only elements of troubleshooting. Once a situation has been dealt with, you then have to ensure that you follow things up wherever necessary. For example, if the crisis involves a confrontation with a student, once you have dealt with the immediate incident you need to decide what strategies should be put in place and ensure that they are followed through to their conclusion. You also need to record each event appropriately and, where necessary, inform the relevant personnel of what you have done and any further action required. As a manager, you take ultimate responsibility, and it is essential that that you cover yourself.

A school or college is a highly complex organisation, and any individual who has held a management role within one of these settings should be an expert at troubleshooting and handling crises. As a subject, key stage or senior leader, you will have had endless opportunities to adopt a flexible approach to your working day and develop the ability to assess a crisis swiftly, act appropriately, respond with sensitivity and good humour, and analyse a situation after the event. These are highly transferable management skills that will stand you in good stead whether you are moving to a leadership and management role within education or making a complete change of career.

Strategic and operational leadership and management

Once you take on a leadership and management role in a school or college, you have to start looking at 'the bigger picture' within the context of developing your vision for the future and carrying it through. Whether you are operating at a middle or senior level, this involves taking into account a huge number of factors, including personnel, resources, curriculum requirements, finance, external demands, local needs and pupil voice – to mention just a few. You need to be able to identify key issues and develop appropriate strategies, plan for both the short term and the long term and modify your planning where necessary to fit in with regular changes in government policy, budget cuts and even increases in funding. There is a growing culture of self-evaluation within schools, with all leaders and managers constantly having to assess where they are at, where they want to be in the short, medium and long term, and how to bring their plans to fruition. As a leader or manager, you are also required to collate a body of evidence to support any evaluation you might make.

A school or college leadership and management role will give you essential experience in all aspects of strategic and operational planning, and a set of skills that transfer well to any workplace. Apart from developing your generic planning and organisational abilities, school leadership requires you to develop an in-depth knowledge, understanding and experience of how schools function, what is required for your own particular school to develop, and the impact of new initiatives on teaching and learning. This is a set of skills and knowledge that are highly desirable, and in some cases essential, for any of the jobs surveyed within this chapter.

SO WHAT'S OUT THERE? . . . JOB OPPORTUNITIES

Working for a government, or government-funded, organisation

What?

There are many different government or government-funded organisations within the field of education, all of which offer various management opportunities. For example:

- **The Department for Children, Schools and Families (DCSF):** the DfES is the UK government department responsible for all aspects of educational policy, ranging from establishing strategies at every stage of the educational process to reviewing the school leaving age or agreeing conditions of service within schools. Typical management opportunities include becoming a 14–19 Adviser with a remit to support the delivery of strategies for young people, or a regional Children's Services Adviser working to the Every Child Matters agenda and developing partnerships between different children's services. Both roles require experience at senior management level.
- **The Qualifications and Curriculum Authority (QCA):** the QCA is a non-departmental body responsible for maintaining the National Curriculum, ensuring consistency across the awarding bodies, and monitoring qualifications in schools, colleges and the workplace. Although there is a relationship between the DCSF and the QCA, as a general rule the former is orientated towards setting policy while the latter focuses more on developing and publishing the curriculum. Typical management opportunities include becoming a Programme Manager, which involves leading the provision of team-specific programmes, or becoming a board member. The QCA also appoints consultants and practitioners to sit on panels examining key educational issues.

   The QCA was established to serve education within England. The equivalent organisations throughout the rest of the United Kingdom are the Scottish Qualifications Authority (SQA), the

Northern Ireland Council for the Curriculum and Examinations and Assessment (CCEA) and the Welsh Department for Education, Lifelong Learning and Skills (DELLS).

- **The Learning and Skills Council (LSC):** the LSC is a non-departmental public organisation with responsibility for the planning and funding of post-16 education and training in England. The overall purpose of the LSC is to improve provision for this age group and give the necessary support to ensure a world-class workforce for the future. Typical management opportunities include becoming an Adult Support Policy Director, which involves developing financial strategies to support the training needs of vulnerable adult learners, or a Policy and Planning Manager with a remit to implement initiatives and meet local learning needs.

Where?

The majority of DCSF and QCA jobs are based in London (although the QCA is relocating to Coventry in 2008). The SQA (Scotland), the CCEA (Northern Ireland and DELLS (Wales) are located in Glasgow, Belfast and Cardiff respectively. The LSC also has regional locations. If you wish to work for the LSC, you will probably be able to find an office within reasonable commuting distance of your home, although you may at times be required to travel beyond the usual work base.

Whether you are office based, able to work from home, travelling up to London a few times a year or visiting educational institutions will depend on the nature of your job. As a representative for the DCSF or QCA, you may be required to contribute to conferences across the country.

When?

Your working hours will depend on whether you are full time, part time or employed on a freelance basis. If you have a full-time post, you will mostly work office hours and organise any school- or college-based meetings during school hours. You are unlikely to get school holidays. Taking on the position of a QCA board member requires a commitment of approximately fifteen days throughout the year, while participating in a project for the DCSF or QCA will last for the duration of the project, with meetings arranged periodically. If you are a practising teacher, you will need agreement from your headteacher and/or governing body so that you can be released to attend term-time meetings.

Who?

For any management role in a government or government-funded organisation, a leadership and management background is necessary. Whether you need middle or senior management experience will depend on the position for which you are applying. For example, to become a board member for the QCA, you would need to be the practising head of a successful school or college. If a role is specifically connected with the curriculum, you will have to demonstrate subject knowledge and understanding and experience of pedagogy, curriculum and assessment in relation to your subject. If you wish to work for the LSC, you will need to have knowledge and experience of post-16 education and/or training. Depending on your role, you may also require specific skills such as expertise in IT or research methodology.

The majority of managerial roles within the DCSF, QCA or LSC revolve around the development of educational policy and strategies. To carry out this kind of work, you have to be prepared to read weighty documents in some detail, able to synthesise information from a variety of different sources and able to distil key messages from your research and translate them into practitioner-friendly language. You also need to have a strong interest in the policies and theories that inform and underpin teaching practice and provision.

How?

Check the education press for vacancies. Organisations with regional offices, such as the LSC, may also advertise in the local press. It is also worth checking websites for vacancies. Visit:

> DCSF www.dcsf.gov.uk (click on V for vacancies in the site
>   A to Z)
> QCA (England) www.qca.org.uk
> SQA (Scotland) www.sqa.org.uk
> CCEA (Northern Ireland) www.ccea.org.uk
> DELLS (Wales) http://new.wales.gov.uk/about/departments/
>   dells
> LSC www.lsc.gov.uk

Why?

If you are interested in education policy, a management role in a government-funded organisation will give you access to the cutting edge of current thinking, as well as the opportunity to help shape the future of education within your field of expertise. If you wish to develop your career as an educationalist, working for a government organisation in a research and consultancy role will also bring you into contact with some of the leading figures in education and make an impressive addition to your CV.

Case study

From lead teacher to . . . Regional Adviser for the Secondary National Strategy

Moira taught secondary maths and worked as an adviser with her local authority before becoming Regional Adviser for the Secondary National Strategy. Here she describes her career development, what her current role involves and why she finds her job so interesting.

I always scan the jobs section of the education press to see what is available, even if I am not particularly looking to make a move. When I spotted an advertisement for a Regional Adviser working with the SNS [Secondary National Strategy], I thought it looked interesting. As a core subject specialist and local authority adviser, I had enjoyed working with the SNS and was ready to move to the next level, both regionally and nationally. I decided to apply, and after a short but challenging interview which tested my presentation skills and knowledge of whole-school issues, I was offered the job.

My particular area of responsibility is whole-school initiatives (WSIs). This includes Assessment for Learning (AfL), Literacy and Learning (LaL), Leading in Learning (LiL), Pedagogy, and Practice and Coaching, with the main focus on AfL. My role is to help local authorities develop WSIs in the schools they support. I work

continued

alongside consultants, developing leadership roles in schools to support the progression of WSI, modelling processes for consultants and helping to devise systems to monitor and evaluate progress. We also spend a lot of time considering how schools can evaluate the effect of WSIs on pupil learning. This is a challenge, as it can be difficult to identify causal links between improvements in teaching and learning and their impact on standards.

I am passionate about the role that WSIs have to play in improving provision within schools, and my job with the SNS has turned out to be everything I hoped for. Apart from the opportunity to promote an important area of education, I enjoy the variety of the work. One day I can be visiting a school to assess the impact of AfL on pupil learning; the next day I can be working with lead consultants; the next day I might be updating ITT [initial teacher training] providers on developments in the strategy; and the next, writing material for presentations either locally or nationally. The salary is also attractive when compared to what I could hope to achieve in school, and I feel that my non-standard background is better appreciated than is sometimes the case within the more rigid structure of a school.

For anyone who wants to follow a similar path, I would recommend gaining as wide a range of experience as possible. You never know where something might lead; I believe I can trace my current position right back to becoming a lead teacher in my local authority. Although this was an unpaid role, it was a major factor in my gaining employment as a local authority adviser, which in turn led on to my role with the SNS. You also have to be prepared to take some risks. When I left teaching, I left behind job security and I constantly have to move beyond my comfort zone. However, for me, the excitement of my new role has been well worth the risks, and I would recommend a similar career progression to anyone who wants fresh challenges within education.

Other opportunities

Management roles in UK government-funded careers services

There are government-funded regional careers services throughout the United Kingdom, providing support, advice and career guidance to young people between the ages of 13 and 19. Although the majority of positions are for careers advisers, there are also opportunities for leadership roles such as becoming a team leader or performance manager. For more information, visit:

England: Connexions www.connexions.gov.uk
Wales: Careers Wales www.careerswales.com
Scotland: Careers Scotland www.careers-scotland.org.uk
Northern Ireland: Careers Service NI www.careers
  serviceni.com

Working as a manager in an awarding body

What?

Awarding bodies are responsible for implementing the examination system in UK schools and colleges. Apart from examining and moderating (see page 76) or working as a subject officer (see page 73), awarding bodies also employ personnel to undertake a wide range of management and administrative roles. Some management opportunities are linked to the examination system itself: for example, taking responsibility for a particular specification such as entry-level qualifications, overseeing quality assurance, developing a syllabus or carrying out research. Other roles are more generic; as with any business, awarding bodies require staff to manage and administer areas such as customer services, finance, IT, marketing and business development.

Where?

The larger awarding bodies have several offices across the country, and as a manager, you will be based at one of these locations. You may also be required to visit centres, lead or contribute to INSET training and attend conferences as a speaker or delegate.

When?

The majority of management positions are full time, particularly if you take on a more senior role. You will mostly work during office hours, apart from occasional one-off events such as attending conferences. There may be restrictions over when you can take holidays and time off; for example, May, June and July are particularly busy months in the examination industry.

Who?

The examination system is forever shifting in response to government initiatives and changing trends. To thrive in this job, you need to be willing to face constant new challenges and ready to adjust and adapt your working systems to meet whatever initiatives are introduced.

The majority of management roles require you to have recent teaching, management and examining experience and a demonstrable knowledge of the education and examination system as a whole. Specific jobs will also have specialist requirements; for example, to work as a research officer, you will need to have knowledge of research methodology and statistical analysis, along with experience of assessment and measurement.

How?

To find out what opportunities are available, visit the 'jobs' sections on the awarding body websites. Vacancies are also advertised in the education press. If you are already working for an awarding body, it might be worth approaching your line manager to discuss your options, as opportunities for internal promotion can sometimes arise.

Why?

Awarding bodies are at the cutting edge of UK education, and taking on a management role enables you to make a real impact on the future development of the examination system. If you have a particular interest and experience in examining, a management role will also enable you to utilise your specialist educational skills within what is essentially a business environment.

Case study

From head of year to . . . Assistant Director (Communications) at the Welsh Joint Education Committee

After nearly twenty-five years in teaching, Brian left his job as a head of year at a large mixed comprehensive to take on a management role at the Welsh Joint Education Committee (WJEC). He has recently retired from his final post as Assistant Director with responsibility for communications.

Q Describe your career development at WJEC.

A *In my first post at WJEC, I was responsible for entry-level qualifications. This involved a great deal of marketing and training, as well as the long-term implementation of access arrangements. My final post, as Assistant Director responsible for communications, was partly an extension of my previous work and partly a chance to experience and address new challenges. It was an internal appointment, although I had to go through the usual application process.*

Q What did the post involve?

A *I had a variety of responsibilities, including all aspects of service to centres, overall responsibility for access arrangements and special consideration, managing the INSET unit and the training of all the centres' examination officers in Wales. I was also Marketing Director for the Examinations Section, Publicity Officer, and Liaison Officer with responsibility for the modernisation programme and links with the NAA in England.*

Q It sounds as though you had a wide range of roles and responsibilities. Did you enjoy the job?

continued

A *Very much so! I had a lot of freedom to plough my own furrow, as it were. I was able to be proactive in terms of marketing and developing new initiatives, as well as instrumental in taking the organisation forward in a number of ways. On the downside, management, at whatever level and in whatever context, can be a lonely position. You sometimes find yourself faced with a great deal of opposition, and as a manager you are often left to 'carry the can'.*

Q Do you have any advice for teachers who want to follow a similar path?

A *Make the most of your teaching and leadership experience and remember just how many transferable skills you possess. Communication, presentation and organisational skills, marketing, managing people, using your initiative and being proactive, working as a team, adaptability, diplomacy – these are just some of the skills that we develop in our teaching careers, all of which prepare us for the range of challenges and contexts that come into a job such as mine. You also need to be prepared for a 'culture shock' when you first make the switch. Initially, I found it really hard to leave teaching after twenty-four years. On the other hand, I went on to enjoy a further nineteen years of employment, thanks to a change of direction and a set of fresh challenges and new experiences. In career terms, switching jobs gave me a new lease of life!*

Inspecting schools

What?

School inspectors are required to visit all maintained and some independent schools in the United Kingdom to monitor and report on the effectiveness, efficiency and inclusivity of a school's educational provision. There are four inspection bodies, covering England, Scotland, Wales and Northern Ireland. Although the inspection structure and standards will vary depending on where you work, the fundamental process is similar across the United Kingdom. Throughout this section, we will profile the English organisation, Ofsted. If you want to look into working as an inspector in Scotland, Wales or Northern Ireland, see contact details under 'How?', below.

Within Ofsted, inspection teams are made up of 'additional inspectors' and led by a 'lead inspector' or an HMI (Her Majesty's Inspector). As an additional inspector for Ofsted, you could be involved in three different types of inspection:

- **Standard school inspections**: all schools are currently inspected at least every three years. During a standard inspection, the team gathers evidence and makes an informed and objective judgement about a school's performance.
- **Subject surveys**: Ofsted and the DCSF collaborate in the organisation of annual national surveys. These surveys are carried out by both additional inspectors and HMIs, and they focus on a specific subject, an area of learning or an educational issue such as the performance and achievement of EAL students.
- **Schools causing concern**: if a school is placed in special measures or given notice to improve, an Ofsted team will monitor their progress at regular points throughout the improvement process.

Inspections are overseen by regional inspection service providers (RISPs). Each RISP is responsible for appointing inspectors and organising inspection teams for their geographical area.

Where?

Inspections are held at schools throughout the United Kingdom. Once you have decided where in the country you want to work, you then register with the relevant RISP. You can register with as many RISPs as you wish, depending on how much you want to work and how far you are willing to travel.

When a team of inspectors arrive at a school, they are usually provided with a base room from which to work, although much of the working day is spent inspecting lessons and holding meetings with staff and students. On rare occasions, a team will go off-site to inspect a school's provision at a local college or other institution. Depending on how far you have to travel, you may be required to stay overnight. Hotel accommodation is something that you organise yourself and pay for out of your flat-rate inspection fee, although you can offset any expenses against tax.

When?

The majority of additional inspectors work on a part-time, freelance basis, but there are also full-time, employed posts available. As a freelance inspector, the number of inspections you carry out will vary depending on how many RISPs you register with, how many contracts you are offered and how much work you want to take on. As a full-time employee, you will be expected to carry out a set number of inspections through the year.

Inspections for larger schools often last for two days, whereas those for smaller schools usually take just one day. The inspection team is often in school by 8.00 a.m. and does not leave before 5.30 or 6.00 p.m. Most inspectors will then spend the evening reading documentation and digesting the evidence they have gathered during the day. Although schools only receive three working days' notice, as an inspector you will usually be contracted on to a team a couple of months in advance of the inspection date. Occasionally you will be telephoned by an RISP and offered a last-minute vacancy.

Who?

To become an additional inspector for Ofsted, you need to have up-to-date knowledge of whole-school issues and competence in IT. You must be educated to degree level, have a recognised teaching qualification, a minimum of five years' recent teaching experience and two years' substantial management experience. It is also possible to work part time as an additional inspector, alongside holding a leadership position in a school. You will, however, need agreement from your headteacher and/or governing body, as you will have to be released for a certain number of days throughout the school year.

On a personal and professional level, you need to be thorough and incisive, with the ability to interpret accurately a wide range of evidence within a short space of time. You need to be a good team player and able to form positive working relationships with people you will usually not have met prior to the inspection. You also need to be personable and able to deliver feedback in a constructive and supportive manner, even if the message you are giving is not particularly palatable.

How?

If you are interested in becoming an additional inspector for Ofsted, apply to your nearest RISP (to find out contact details, visit www. ofsted.gov.uk). If you are selected, you will then undergo a training process organised and conducted by the service provider. This includes attending taught days, distance learning modules, placement on inspections and assessments. Trainee inspectors vary as to how long they take, but most will complete the course within a few months.

For information about working in Wales, Scotland or Northern Ireland, visit:

Wales www.estyn.gov.uk
Scotland www.hmie.gov.uk
Northern Ireland www.etini.gov.uk

Why?

The Ofsted training is rigorous and helps you to develop both a mindset and a set of skills that are useful in many aspects of education: for example, observing and assessing colleagues; identifying appropriate evidence for any judgements you make and building a watertight case; working quickly, efficiently and accurately; and meeting tight deadlines. The work is also quite well paid and makes an impressive addition both to your status as an educationalist and to your CV. If you operate as a freelance additional inspector, you will also have a degree of flexibility over when you work – although, as with any freelance jobs, the offers may start to dry up if you turn down too many contracts.

Case study

From deputy head to . . . additional inspector

Karen had left her job as a deputy head and was working as a consultant and adviser when she decided to add school inspection to her portfolio of jobs. Here she describes her role as an additional inspector for Ofsted and explains why she finds the job such an interesting challenge.

continued

Q Describe a 'day in the life' of an additional inspector.

A *Before the inspection begins, I am contacted by the lead inspector and informed of the whole-school areas that I will be inspecting. Each inspector in the team usually takes responsibility for a couple of areas, ranging from Personal Development and Wellbeing, Teaching and Learning, and Curriculum to Leadership and Management and Overall Effectiveness. My role is to gather evidence for my areas in order to make a provisional judgement based on that evidence. Evidence includes documentation, the school's self-evaluation form, observing lessons and interviewing staff and students. Once all the evidence has been gathered, the team of inspectors meet to discuss their findings, agree on their judgements for each area and make an overall judgement: is the school outstanding, good, satisfactory or in need of improvement? I then write a paragraph summing up my findings for each area within my portfolio of responsibility, and the team finish up by meeting with senior leadership staff to give feedback on the inspection findings.*

Q It sounds a responsible job.

A *It is very responsible – and challenging! You have to be thorough in gathering evidence and take great care with your interpretation and judgement. As with any professional dialogue, you may at times be challenged by both your fellow inspectors and the schools you are inspecting. You need to feel secure in your judgements so that you can explain and defend them if necessary. The Ofsted inspection is a powerful process. A judgement made on a school can have far-reaching effects on the future of that school and it is a process that needs to be taken very seriously by all involved. Schools also have a lot of comeback, and any complaints about the inspection team are, quite rightly, taken seriously.*

Q What are the advantages of the job?

A *It is fascinating, stimulating and keeps you up to date with educational developments and initiatives. It is also a privilege to* witness so many examples of good practice in schools across the country, and meet so many colleagues. Every school is different, every inspection is different and you do not have a moment of boredom from start to finish.

Q And the disadvantages?

A *It can be hard when you have to make tough decisions and deliver messages that people would rather not hear. A number of the schools I inspect are also a long way from home and I have to stay overnight. After a while, yet another characterless hotel room can start to pall! Staying away from home also adds to the intensity of the working period; you live and breathe the inspection for those two days. I do enjoy 'getting stuck in', but it can be a little disorientating when the inspection is over and you have to return to your everyday life. It is also quite a pressurised role. We have to cover a huge amount in the two-day period, as well as being sensitive and supportive to those staff who find the whole inspection process difficult.*

Q Do you have any tips for those who would like to diversify into a similar role?

A *Think carefully about the challenges of the role. Are you a confident practitioner? Are you a good team player? Are you sensitive to the needs and feelings of others? Can you think on your feet? Can you work quickly and efficiently and cope with a heavy workload in a short period of time? If the answer to all these questions is 'yes', then get in touch with your nearest RISP and go for it!*

Other opportunities

*   **Becoming an HMI**: HMIs are mostly full-time, permanent Ofsted employees with a broader remit than the additional inspector. Although they may head up an inspection, the HMI role also includes research, policy

continued

making and procedural reviews. To find out about job opportunities, check the education press and the Ofsted website.

- **Quality assurance roles**: once an inspection report has been completed, it is checked for wording, inaccuracies and contradictions. To become a quality assurance reader, you must be a trained and experienced inspector. Contact the various RISPs to find out what opportunities are available.

- **Training the inspectorate**: experienced inspectors are constantly required to run continuing professional development courses for both serving school leadership teams and inspectors. Contact Ofsted or the Wales, Scotland or Northern Ireland inspectorates to find out what is available. In England, the RISPs also organise and implement training.

- **Independent schools inspections**: most independent schools are inspected by teams of serving senior leaders. In order to train as an Independent Schools Inspectorate (ISI) team inspector, you must have at least four years' experience in a school belonging to an Independent Schools Council (ISC) association, and at least three years' experience as a member of the senior management team or equivalent position. For more information, visit the ISI website: www.isinspect.org.uk.

- **Inspecting HE and FE institutions**: there are also opportunities to work as an additional inspector, inspecting colleges and work-based training providers. For more information, visit the Ofsted website.

Working as a school improvement adviser

What?

School improvement advisers offer support, guidance and statutory advice to schools on issues such as whole-school assessment, standards and achievement, NQT induction, and the role and responsibilities of the leadership and management team. As a school improvement adviser, you will be employed by the local authority to work as part of an advisory team along with subject advisers or consultants and advisory teachers, and in many cases you will act as line manager for a group of advisers. Unlike the subject adviser or consultant, you will, however, be looking at the 'bigger picture' rather than a specific subject area. Many local authorities also employ secondary strategy consultants for English, maths, science, ICT, and behaviour and attendance. Although these consultants have a whole-school improvement brief, they focus exclusively on strand-related issues.

Your overall purpose as a school improvement adviser is to ensure that leadership teams are empowered to drive up standards, and you will liaise mostly with headteachers and senior leadership staff. You may also be required to speak at headteachers' conferences and take part in the appointment of headteachers within your local authority.

Where?

As with subject advisers (see p. 68), school improvement advisers are nominally based at their local authority offices, although a number of advisers operate mainly from home. The greater part of the working day is spent visiting schools and various venues for meetings, conferences and training sessions. As a result, the job involves a considerable amount of travelling, although this is mostly within the confines of the local authority.

When?

Your working timetable will vary to fit in with the needs of the schools in your authority. Although you will mostly be working within school hours, there may be a small amount of evening work, for example attending governors' meetings, interviewing headteachers and contributing to conferences. Most full-time advisers are allotted thirty days' holiday a year, which should not be taken during term-time.

Who?

To become a school improvement adviser, you need to be innovative and willing to keep up to date with developments and current research. Previous leadership and management experience is an essential requirement, and you need to be skilled at coaching, supporting and managing colleagues. As you will mostly be working with senior leadership teams, you have to be confident enough to advise professionals who may have gone further up the leadership ladder than you did yourself. Are you willing to challenge and be challenged, and ready to cope with some rigorous professional dialogues? Your answer to this question needs to be a confident 'yes' if you are to feel comfortable in this role.

How?

Check the education press and visit your local authority website to find out whether there are any vacancies. If you leave teaching to take on a role within your local authority, it is well worth looking out for new opportunities once you are established. As with our case study, Peter, many school improvement advisers started out as local authority subject advisers or advisory teachers.

Why?

For those who wish to continue developing their professional expertise, becoming a school improvement adviser offers access to up-to-date information and training. It has the potential to be an interesting job, bringing you into contact with a wide range of whole-school issues and giving you the opportunity to shape the future development of education in your area. If you are interested in education as a whole, the job also enables you to witness and learn about good practice within a variety of different schools, and to share your knowledge and expertise. For a personal description of the role, its advantages and some of the disadvantages, see our case study.

Case study

From head of science to . . . school improvement adviser

Peter was a head of science before taking up a position with his local authority as a science adviser. Over the years, his role has developed and he is now a school improvement adviser. Here he explains what his job involves, how he uses his teaching and management background and the advantages and disadvantages of the role.

When I first left teaching, I worked for the local authority as a teaching and learning consultant in science. Over the years, my role has gradually evolved into that of school improvement adviser and I now have a range of different responsibilities. I am the Assessment Co-ordinator for the county, which involves giving statutory advice and training on assessment and visiting schools to monitor arrangements for National Curriculum tests. I act as line manager for two secondary strategy science consultants and I am also the NQT Induction Co-ordinator.

I particularly enjoy my assessment role. It gives me the opportunity to use the data analysis skills that I developed over the years as a head of science. I also draw on my experience as a departmental head when it comes to co-ordinating induction, although I do find that working with NQTs at risk of not meeting the standards demands all my interpersonal skills! Some skills I have developed and built upon since leaving teaching, for example lesson observation and training colleagues. It is also important to be able to keep in contact and liaise with national bodies such as the NAA [National Assessment Agency], the DCSF and the TDA. Overall, I enjoy the variety and flexibility of the work, with no day turning out to be the same as the next. I also enjoy the opportunity to visit and work within a range of different schools.

On the downside, the role can be quite solitary. As my office is based at home, I am never quite sure when the working day has stopped, and I have to be disciplined about bringing my work to a close. I also find the sheer quantities of paper rather a headache. It all has to be stored, and when it is no longer required, any confidential material has to be shredded and disposed of (and without secretarial support at home, this time-consuming task falls to me!). However, I would recommend the job to anyone with the right background, skills and expertise. It is certainly an interesting and fulfilling way to use your management and teaching experience beyond the classroom. The one thing to consider is whether you will miss contact with pupils. Although you are maintaining your links with a variety of schools, bear in mind that you will mostly be working with adults rather than children.

Other opportunities

Working as a school improvement partner

By early 2008, all schools in both the secondary and primary sectors should have been allocated a local authority school improvement partner (SIP), although many schools are already working with their SIP. The majority of SIPs will either be practising headteachers, experienced school improvement advisers or independent consultants. To become a SIP, you need to have proven experience of school leadership and understand the realities of school improvement. You will also be required to undergo training and become qualified and accredited according to national standards. A SIP will work for approximately five days a year with each allocated school. The role involves helping a school to improve through a process of both challenge and support, focusing on pupil progress and attainment, advising the school in planning its future development, analysing evidence in order to assess the school's current performance, and identifying areas and strategies for improvement. SIPs will also advise governing bodies on the headteacher's performance management, although governors will retain overall responsibility for appraisal of their headteacher. For more information about becoming a SIP, visit www.ncsl.org.uk.

Other opportunities

Supporting home education

Supporting families who have chosen to home-educate offers a potentially unique set of experiences, as our case study, Mac, explains.

Q Describe your role as a part-time home education officer.

A *I have a number of different roles and responsibilities, including visiting homes and preparing reports outlining the areas of educational provision; making judgements about the standard of provision; supporting start-up programmes; advising about resources and other learning aids; and acting as a supporter, mentor, counsellor and adviser.*

Q What attracted you to the post?

A *I have always held the belief that autonomous learning has many benefits. The work offered me the opportunity to become involved in a different aspect of education, and one that could be developed away from the constraints of the school setting.*

Q How do you use your teaching skills?

A *Although I am now working in a completely different environment, I use most of the skills I honed as a teacher and headteacher. I have to deal with a range of different families, assess their varying needs and decide how best to respond. I have to switch from adviser to inspector as required, manage my time and motivate myself to keep on top of all the follow-up paperwork.*

Q What are the advantages and disadvantages of the role?

A *I love the freedom and relative autonomy of my new working life. I also enjoy meeting the challenges that some families present and the satisfaction of being able to help. On the downside, it can be frustrating not being able to offer more support – in the form of financial help, for example.*

continued

> **Q** Any tips for other teachers who are interested in similar work?
>
> **A** *Opportunities differ from authority to authority. There are a relatively high number of home educators in my area, but this will vary depending on your location – as will the support that a local authority chooses to offer. You need to keep a lookout for adverts and grab any opportunities quickly, as they can be few and far between.*

Working as an education consultant

What?

Education consultants work with schools and colleges in a support and advisory capacity. Education consultancy offers opportunities to give guidance in just about any aspect of school or college life, and most education consultants also offer specialist expertise in specific areas. Typical consultancy projects might include assisting a school with strategic management, delivering governor information sessions, reviewing a particular aspect of whole-school provision, giving advice on the setting up of a new curriculum or working with an under-performing department. Depending on your area of expertise, you could find yourself liaising with staff at any level, from the leadership team and governing body to NQTs and support personnel.

The majority of education consultants work in a self-employed, freelance capacity, although some consultants are employed by education companies. Local authorities also buy in the services of an education consultant if the consultant's area of expertise matches what is required by a school in the authority. For example, if a drama department needs support with post-16 teaching and none of the local authority advisers have relevant expertise, the authority may employ a specialist consultant for a set number of days. In many respects, the role is not dissimilar to that of an adviser or advisory teacher (see page 68), except that the education consultant works independently.

Where?

Much of the education consultant's working life is based in schools or colleges. If you are self-employed, you can choose to work wherever you wish, but you may have to be willing to travel widely in order to earn a substantial salary. A self-employed consultant will need to have a home-based office, whereas a consultant employed by an education company will often be based at the company's offices, with the flexibility of some home working.

When?

Your working hours will vary depending on how many contracts you have and the nature of a particular contract. As a self-employed consultant, you can take on as many or as few contracts as you wish, although your timetable is to some extent governed by how much work you are offered. The core of your work will take place during school hours, but you may also have to attend after-school meetings and training sessions, and set aside time for paperwork. The time you spend on work generated by a contract needs to be factored into your fee, as does the cost of your travel. There will also be little work available during school holidays. If you are self-employed, you will have to budget accordingly and plan tasks such as developing your marketing strategies, carrying out research and catching up on administration.

Who?

Although it is not essential, in practice most education consultants have a senior leadership background. Management experience helps to give a consultant credibility and adds 'leadership and management' to their areas of expertise. As with any freelance role, you also have to be confident, outgoing and willing to market yourself. Paul is a freelance education consultant with fifteen years' experience. He emphasises that a wide professional network is essential, and recommends making good use of your own contacts in order to keep up with educational developments and find contracts.

How?

To become a self-employed freelance education consultant, you will need to market yourself and work at establishing a client base. Get in touch with schools, colleges, local authorities, education companies and any personal contacts who may require your services. Some education companies also act as agencies for consultants and trainers.

Although a percentage of your client's fee will go to the agency, agencies have access to a wide range of schools and colleges, and they can also be useful if your areas of expertise are not mainstream. For more on becoming self employed, see Chapter 5.

To find work as an employed education consultant, contact the larger education companies to discuss possible opportunities. Carry out an internet search for 'education companies' and check the adverts in the education press. It is also well worth setting up your own website with links to other relevant sites. If employment is your preferred option and you are not keen on extended travel, consider looking into becoming a local authority employed adviser or advisory teacher (see page 68).

Many education consultants include consultancy as part of a portfolio career. If you have several strands to your income, this can remove the pressure to fill your days with consultancy contracts. Both freelance work and part-time employment as a consultant can be combined with other jobs such as training, speaking at conferences, inspecting, writing and part-time teaching or lecturing. Many part-time consultants also find that their consultancy work supports and informs their other roles, and vice versa. For more on developing a portfolio career, see page 215.

Why?

Education consultancy allows you to use your experience and expertise to support your colleagues in a professional capacity. If you want to escape the limits of the classroom but do not wish to abandon working in schools or colleges altogether, education consultancy gives you the best of both worlds. Paul also enjoys being his own boss and what he describes as the 'non-parochial' nature of the work. Tasks and responsibilities vary considerably from one week to the next, and you will meet and work with a wide variety of people. If you are interested in both the current state of education and its future development, educational consultancy requires you to stay at the cutting edge and gives you access to lots of different networks – although Paul does point out that you have to work at keeping in touch, as you no longer have the teacher's free access to official information and resources.

On the downside, the job can be insecure, particularly if you choose to work freelance. As Paul says, there is considerable competition, you are appraised at every turn and if you do not perform, further work will be difficult to acquire. Unlike a teacher, you also have to live with the constant pressure of finding sufficient contracts to cover next month's expenses. Paul recommends thinking carefully and realistically about how many days' work you need in order to make a living. As he says, *'£400 a day sounds great, but you may only be able to get four days' work per week for thirty weeks in the school year. Once you take off expenses such as running your car and your office, fees for attending courses, hotel accommodation, insurance and pension payments, your £400 fee quickly reduces to £200. In actual terms, this gives you an annual income of not much more than £24,000 – which is subject to tax.'* Like many education consultants, he supplements his income with other education-related work.

As with most jobs, education consultancy has its minuses as well as its pluses, and Paul admits that he sometimes longs for the security of working for a single institution. If, however, you have reached a stage in your working life where you can take a bit of a risk, and you want to 'spread your wings', education consultancy could be just what you are looking for.

Other opportunities

Working for the National College of School Leadership

The National College of School Leadership (NCSL) serves the needs of school leaders, with the goal of furthering children's welfare and educational development through supporting school leadership. The college offers programmes and courses for both experienced and newly appointed leaders, along with an online learning environment. It is also involved in strategic initiatives and research linked to leadership development. There are various job opportunities for individuals with school leadership and management experience; for example, working as a senior operations manager or a research officer with a remit to help manage and carry out various projects. For more information about the NCSL and a list of vacancies, visit www.ncsl.org.uk.

Other opportunities

Working for the Specialist Schools and Academies Trust (SSAT)

The SSAT aims to improve educational provision for young people through building networks, enabling schools to share their practice and providing support. It offers a variety of opportunities for individuals with a leadership, management and administrative background, for example, working as a project officer, business development manager or information and data analyst. For more information about the Trust and its work, and details of vacancies, visit www.ssatcareers.co.uk.

Other opportunities

Working as an NPQH assessor

All headteachers appointed since April 2004 are required to hold the National Professional Qualification for Headship (NPQH). If you have substantial school leadership experience, hold the qualification and are interested in becoming an NPQH assessor, visit www.teachernet.gov.uk or the National College of School Leadership website, www.ncsl.org.uk, for more information.

Managing outdoor education, field and study centres

What?

Managing an outdoor education, field or study centre is a demanding job with a wide range of tasks and responsibilities. In some respects, the breadth and diversity of the role are not dissimilar to those of a headteacher's role. As a manager, you will be concerned with staff recruitment, planning and marketing the courses, handling the budget and overseeing all aspects of the centre's operations. (For more information on what the job involves, see the next case study.)

Most centres provide residential courses, and they fall into a range of different categories; for example:

- **Residential field centres**: offering fieldwork-based courses for students studying subjects such as geography, geology, biology and environmental sciences.
- **Residential centres for outdoor pursuits**: offering activities such as canoeing, abseiling and climbing, and/or Duke of Edinburgh expeditions and explorations.
- **Permanent camps**: offering organised activities and 'the camping experience', often used by schools for their annual summer camp expeditions.
- **Local authority residential education centres**: offering a wide range of residential extension courses, including activities for the gifted and talented, Outward Bound courses, team-building activities and holiday courses. Many local authorities also run residential centres for professional development, adult education and the arts.

Where?

Outdoor education, field and study centres are located across the country. Although the location will depend on what a centre has to offer, they can usually be found in rural areas and places of geographical, geological and environmental interest. For example, a centre that organises Duke of Edinburgh expeditions might be located in the Brecon Beacons or on Dartmoor. The centre manager's role is often residential, and accommodation is provided as part of the job package.

When?

As a centre manager, you have a duty of care to the residents that lasts day and night, for the entire duration of their stay. Even when you are not on duty, the final responsibility for any serious problems will rest with you. You will often work evenings and weekends, and you will not get school holidays. For many people, the role becomes as much a way of life as a job.

Who?

In order to take on this role, you need management experience, and many centres also require a relevant teaching background. For most jobs, you will need to be an 'outdoor type' and have the energy to cope with long and sometimes erratic hours. As with any management role, you also need to be able to deal with lots of different people, ranging from pupils, teachers and staff to a variety of outside agencies. If you are combining your career with bringing up a family, think carefully about whether the work will leave you with enough time and energy to give to your own children.

How?

Look out for adverts in the national and local press as well as the education press. Our case study, Chris, also recommends getting as much relevant additional experience as possible while you are still teaching, for example examining, writing resources, taking on pastoral roles, training and extra-curricular work such as running the Duke of Edinburgh scheme or teaching at a centre as a part-time tutor. The role of a centre manager is very diverse, and the wider your CV, the more attractive it will appear to a prospective employer. She also suggests contacting a centre before making an application to check that your background and experience are suitable.

As with management roles in education, the recruitment process is usually quite rigorous. In order to win her post as head of a residential fieldwork centre, Chris underwent a two-day interview procedure that included two presentations, a formal interview and a lot of social interaction.

Why?

If you feel that you can cope with the responsibility, the long hours and the commitment that this job demands, it has a lot to offer. Many positions include accommodation, and you are likely to be located in a beautiful part of the country. You will meet and work with a steady stream of visitors to your centre, and the variety of roles and responsibilities means that you are unlikely to get bored. Our case study, Chris, describes what her role involves and explains why she has never regretted taking on the job.

Case study

From head of science to . . . head of a residential fieldwork centre

Chris was a subject leader for science and head of sixth form before leaving teaching to work at a botanic garden. This proved to be a stepping stone to her current role as head of a residential fieldwork centre.

Q What does your job involve?

A *As head of the centre, I have a wide range of tasks. I manage a budget of £700,000 a year and I take responsibility for everything, from catering and housekeeping to providing curriculum-linked education for the students and ensuring their welfare and safety both in the centre and out on fieldwork. I have certainly learned a lot of new skills.*

Q It sounds like a great deal of responsibility. How has your teaching background helped?

A *As an ex-head of science, I understand the curriculum and I know what will appeal to teachers. I also know what teachers need from a visit and the issues they tend to worry about; I can talk the same language! Being able to teach gives me credibility with visiting teachers and centre staff, and I am used to dealing with groups of students, both in a teaching capacity and when it comes to sorting out problems. I also have the teacher's ability to keep going throughout the day with very few breaks!*

Q What about your management background?

A *Apart from managing staff and a budget, I draw on my experience of planning the curriculum, preparing resources and buying equipment. I also have to focus on 'whole-centre' issues such as ICT development and Investors in People – not dissimilar from working on whole-school initiatives with other departments. I don't, however, think I could have gone straight from my post as head of science to this job. My interim role as*

continued

head of education at a botanic garden proved to be an invaluable stepping stone between teaching and taking on responsibility for heading up and running a whole centre.

Q So you enjoy the job?

A *Very much so. I have lots of autonomy and I am never bored. I love being able to spend at least some of my time outdoors and I enjoy working with adults as well as children. I am also very glad to be able to use my curriculum knowledge and expertise, as well as my actual teaching experience. I still teach, but not all day every day, and I am never as exhausted as I used to be at the end of term. I also get to live in a beautiful part of Wales!*

Q Are there any disadvantages?

A *No job is without some disadvantages. The hours are very long and can be unsociable, with a lot of evening and weekend work. As the job is residential, I never get to 'go home'. There is also a great deal of responsibility, as I manage all aspects of the centre and its operations – although I do get a lot of support from head office. Overall, though, the advantages far outweigh the disadvantages.*

Q Do you have any tips for teachers who would like to follow a similar path?

A *Never assume that a lack of obvious qualifications will stop you from getting a job. As long as you have expertise in a general area, you don't necessarily have to have a geology degree to run a geology field centre. If you can demonstrate that you are a competent professional, enthusiastic and willing to learn, that is the most important thing. I would also recommend anyone to think long and hard about whether this kind of work is right for them. Always bear in mind that it's a lifestyle, not just a job!*

Other opportunities

Houseparenting in the independent sector

Running a boarding house at an independent school is another job possibility for those who are interested in residential work. The role is largely pastoral, with the houseparent acting *in loco parentis*. As a houseparent, you will also be responsible for housekeeping, organising meals, weekend trips and entertainment, homework supervision and managing domestic staff. Most houseparents combine their role with teaching at the school, although there may be opportunities for couples to share the work, with one or both houseparents also working as teachers. The majority of boarding houses are for secondary-aged pupils and sixth-formers, although a few schools offer boarding facilities for the seven-plus age group. To find out what job vacancies are available, check the local, national and education press, and contact any boarding schools in the area where you would like to work.

Working as a manager in a vocational training company

What?

Vocational training companies manage the assessment and verification of vocational qualifications in the workplace, for example NVQs, apprenticeships and other certificated courses such as 'Food Hygiene' or 'First Aid'. Apart from employing NVQ assessors (see page 19), training companies also need managers to co-ordinate teams of freelance assessors and verifiers; liaise with employers, candidates and awarding bodies; organise training sessions for candidates and prospective assessors; take responsibility for business development; and manage office staff.

Where?

As a manager, you will mostly be based at the company's offices, although there will also be occasions when you will travel to work-places to meet employers and candidates. Many companies specialise in a particular occupational area such as childcare or construction, and the workplaces you visit will vary accordingly.

When?

Your working timetable will usually be standard office hours. Unlike NVQ assessors, most managers are full-time employees, although some companies may be willing to negotiate a part-time contract.

Who?

To take on a management role in a vocational training company, you will need to have some knowledge and experience of the sector. For an ex-teacher, this could include involvement in school- or college-based vocational education. You will also need some management experience, as you will be required to liaise with, support and manage a wide range of individuals, set up and organise systems, and play a major part in the overall running and ongoing development of the company.

How?

Look out for advertisements in the local and education press and on the internet. You can also approach vocational training providers in your area to discuss whether they have any opportunities available. If you already have links with a company as an assessor, let them know that you are interested in a management role should a vacancy arise.

Why?

Working as a manager within a vocational training company enables you to use your experience of vocational education within the sphere of management. The role is worth considering if you enjoy organising and managing an office, setting up and maintaining systems, and working with a wide range of people. In many cases, you should also get the opportunity to be creative and help develop and expand the company as a business. Our case study, Karen, describes her job as an operations manager for a small training company and talks about some of the advantages and disadvantages.

Case study

From deputy head to . . . Operations Manager for an NVQ training company

Karen had left her job as a deputy head in a large comprehensive to relocate to a new area with her husband. After taking a year out to organise their house move, she decided to change direction and started exploring her options. Initially, she responded to an advertisement from a company looking for NVQ assessors and offering free training to successful candidates. After an application and interview, the company appointed her, and she had only just started her training when the position of Operations Manager became vacant due to a maternity leave. Knowing that she had had school-based management experience, the company director offered her the job and she decided to accept. Here she describes what the work involved and how she drew on her leadership and management experience.

I was surprised but delighted to be offered the post of Operations Manager, as I consider management skills to be one of my strengths. There was only one snag: the post was full time and I wanted to continue with my training as an NVQ assessor. Fortunately, the company director was willing to cover some of the administrative tasks herself and we negotiated a three-day week.

The job was varied and I drew considerably on my teaching and management experience. I liaised with a wide range of people, including office staff, assessors and verifiers, candidates, employers and awarding body personnel. This was something I found quite straightforward, given my experience of managing and/or working with teachers, support staff, pupils, parents, governors and local authority personnel. My general organisational

continued

and time-management skills also came in useful. I have always said that a competent schoolteacher is the most organised person on the planet, and efficiency is certainly a necessity in the world of vocational qualifications! I have to follow a number of set procedures – but this is not a problem for anyone who has coped with the National Curriculum, implemented the literacy and numeracy strategies or taught to a GCSE syllabus. I also loved the nine-to-five day and being able to forget all about work when I left the office.

For me, there were very few disadvantages to the job, as I worked well with the director of the company and had a loyal and conscientious office staff; in fact, I was quite sorry to give it up when the permanent manager returned from her maternity leave. The only real disadvantage was the pay, which did not equate to that for a school-based management position. This was not a problem for me, as I was able to take a salary cut, but it's something to think about if you need to maintain a certain level of income. For anyone interested in a similar role, I would strongly recommend training as an NVQ assessor if you have not already done so. Although not strictly necessary, having an in-depth knowledge of the sector gives you credibility, enables you to 'speak the language' and helps you to gain the respect of those at the coalface – something that is crucial to being an effective manager.

Managing business, vocational and enterprise education

What?

Business, vocational and enterprise education is an increasingly important part of school provision and there are a growing number of groups, organisations and companies offering support in this area. The following job profiles and case studies cover just a few of the opportunities available:

- **Education Business Links Adviser for the Education Business Partnership (EBP):** Roy lectured in agriculture at a college of FE before taking up a position as Education Business Links Adviser with the EBP. His role includes organising professional development placements for teachers, FE lecturers and Connexions personal advisers in industrial and business organisations. He works with a number of schools on their enterprise and work-related learning curricular requirements, and he also recruits business advisers to support school-based events organised by the EBP.

- **Local co-ordinator for a vocational education support organisation**: Alison was a secondary school assistant head-teacher before leaving teaching to develop her career as an education consultant and trainer. Always on the look out for new possibilities, she was delighted to be offered a freelance contract with a national organisation providing support in vocational education to schools, colleges and work-based training institutions. She describes her role as being similar to that of a project manager, with responsibility for co-ordinating six networks (groups of employers, careers advisers and institutions providing vocational education) and overseeing their projects. A typical network project includes developing a co-ordinated approach to initial assessment forms, monitoring documents and exit forms for vocational provision. She also targets schools that might be in need of support with their vocational qualifications, identifies training needs and organises appropriate training programmes.

- **Regional co-ordinator for the 14–19 diplomas support programme**: Zia was the Vocational Curriculum Manager at a large comprehensive school before being employed by Nord Anglia as a Regional Co-ordinator delivering the 14–19 diplomas support programme on behalf of the Quality Improvement Agency (QIA). Her remit is to work with the co-ordinator for specialist schools in her region, supporting consortia who are seeking endorsement to deliver the new diplomas. The role also involves supporting, guiding and advising consortia who have already successfully gone through the gateway.

Where?

With such a wide range of different opportunities, your place of work will depend on the nature of your job and the organisation that is employing you. For example, as an Education Business Links Adviser, Roy is based at the regional EBP offices, whereas local activities co-ordinator Alison works mostly from home. Regardless of the particular nature of your role, you will probably spend much of your working life liaising with and/or visiting schools, colleges, work-based training providers, employers and careers advisers. Many of these jobs are, however, regionally based, so you are unlikely to undertake much travelling beyond your local area.

When?

Your working hours will depend on whether you are full time, part time or employed on a freelance basis. If you have a full-time post, you will mostly work office hours and organise meetings, training sessions and other appointments with educational institutions during school hours. School holiday periods are useful for making links with employers, writing training materials and catching up on paperwork. As a part-time freelance consultant, you will be contracted to work a certain number of days a year and your timetable will vary according to what you are working on at any one time.

Who?

To take on a management role in an organisation offering support within the field of vocational education, ideally you need to have experience of delivering or managing vocational qualifications and dealing with employers; for example, while Zia was still in teaching, her responsibilities as a vocational curriculum manager included organising and overseeing work placements for her pupils and monitoring a range of vocational qualifications in her school. For many roles, some form of business experience and understanding is also useful; in between teaching and working for the EBP, Roy was employed by a private education company to organise courses and conferences, which involved researching and meeting the demands of the market, keeping within a budget and making a profit. Most positions necessitate management experience, as you will probably be required to undertake management-based tasks such as implementing new curricula, monitoring and assessing the quality of vocational teaching, identifying appropriate qualifications and training needs for a particular school, liaising with employers and educational institutions, and, in many cases, managing staff.

How?

Check both the education press and local newspapers for advertised jobs and be prepared to read advertisements carefully and contact companies to discuss what a job involves. If you have a background in vocational education, management and/or business, you may find that you are qualified for a far wider range of jobs within this field than you might think. If you currently deliver or manage vocational qualifications, you can also try approaching the companies you use for publications, training and support to ask if they have any vacancies available. If you are in a position to take on a part-time, temporary post, you may find that it develops into something full time. Roy began his career with the EBP working freelance alongside his part-time job as a conference organiser. When a full-time fixed-term contract became available, he was interviewed and given the post, which ultimately developed into the permanent position he holds today.

Why?

Working within this field is a fulfilling role if you are committed to vocational and business education and want to help industry and education to co-operate and work together. Most jobs will enable you to maintain your links with schools and colleges, alongside gaining access to the wider world of work-based training providers, employers and a range of different workplaces – giving you the best of both worlds. Roy also points out the rewards of going into schools and providing teachers with the support and information they need to enhance their provision of business and vocational education. He usually finds that the pupils enjoy a break from the regular timetable and respond well to his theme days, and he particularly enjoys introducing an 'entrepreneurial spin' into the otherwise structured routine of the school day.

Other opportunities

If you have the appropriate expertise and background, you can choose to specialise in business, vocational and enterprise-related education as:

---

continued

- an independent education consultant (see page 132);
- a writer contributing to educational magazines and text-books (see page 101);
- a freelance trainer or conference speaker (see page 51);
- an NVQ assessor for a training company or college (see page 19).

Planning and directing education courses and conferences

What?

Most education conferences and courses are run by private commercial companies. Apart from requiring speakers and trainers to contribute to their events, companies also employ conference and course directors. Every event takes a huge amount of planning, and the conference director's role is diverse, with tasks and responsibilities ranging from researching current issues to liaising with speakers and evaluating feedback from delegates.

Courses and conferences cover all sectors of education, from early years to further education. There are, however, more job opportunities for secondary specialists, as secondary schools tend to be better placed both to fund the course fee and to arrange cover for a teacher attending an event.

For more information about education courses and conferences and becoming a speaker or trainer, see page 51.

Where?

Conference directors are mostly based at their company's offices, although there may be opportunities to work from home, either as an employee or in a freelance capacity. As a conference director, you do not always have to attend the events themselves unless you are acting as an event manager (see 'From deputy head to . . . working as an events manager', page 180). In practice, however, if one of your courses is being run for the first time, many companies insist that you are present in order to evaluate the event.

When?

Many conference and course directors work as full-time employees. There are also opportunities for part-time work, and some companies buy in freelance support on an *ad hoc* basis. For freelances and part-time employees, the role tends to be quite piecemeal and it can be difficult to fit the work into specific days. For example, speakers are not always easy to contact and you may have to make and receive telephone calls and e-mails at any time throughout your working week. You also have to meet deadlines for each stage of the planning process, regardless of how difficult it might be to chase up trainers, get hold of a vital piece of research or keep on top of marketing and mailshots.

Most conferences and courses take place during weekdays, as they are regarded as part of the delegates' working week. Some events last for two days, and if you are attending in a quality control or event management capacity, you may have an overnight stay in a hotel. (Expenses are usually paid by the company.)

Who?

Although it is not essential, as an education conference and course director you will ideally have an educational background and experience of management. As with any management role, you need to be a good organiser with up-to-date knowledge of your sector and the ability to 'think outside the box'. What developments are on the horizon? What will appeal to teachers and what will their senior leadership team be prepared to pay for? How might a new initiative affect schools and what conferences or courses could be provided to give teachers the information and support they need? If you can get in at the start of a new trend and offer what schools are looking for, your course or conference is much more likely to be successful. Unlike teaching, organising events is a money-making business, and you constantly have to keep an eye on both your budget and the saleability of what you are offering.

You also need to have good 'people skills'. Some potential speakers require a degree of persuasion, and you have to form judgments about whether a practitioner will make an effective speaker, regardless of their success in the classroom. At the other end of the scale, conferences usually feature a keynote speaker, and you may have to liaise with some high-profile professionals who are leaders in their field.

How?

As companies are dependent on advertising to market their events, you shouldn't have much difficulty getting hold of contact details. Check out adverts in the education press, gather up all the flyers that are sent to your school and approach a few companies to find out what opportunities are available. Have some ideas up your sleeve to demonstrate to a company that you are aware of the market, and ask for your details to be kept on file even if there are no opportunities available at the time.

Another option is to look into organising conferences alongside a part-time, or even a full-time, teaching job. Companies are often glad to have a current practitioner working for them, and you can negotiate a contract to organise as many or as few events as you feel you can manage. This can be a good way of finding out whether the job might suit you as a full-time option.

Why?

Organising conferences is a flexible role with a huge amount of variety. It takes you out of the classroom but keeps you at the cutting edge of educational developments and brings you into contact with people from many different backgrounds and settings. It also enables you to make good use of both your creative and your organisational skills. Our case study, Karen, gives a personal account of her experiences as a course and conference director and explains what makes it such an enjoyable and interesting job.

Case study

From deputy head to . . . conference director

Karen had given up her deputy headship to move to a new area with her husband. Although she wanted to remain within education, she decided to look for work outside the classroom and she started exploring her options:

My husband had attended a training course and came home with the company's leaflet, suggesting that I contact them to offer my services as a speaker. Although the most I was hoping for was the odd day's work, to my surprise they offered me a permanent job as a training director. The original post was full time, but as I had several other 'irons in the fire' I wanted to keep my options open and the company agreed to a part-time contract.

The work is full of variety, which is probably what I enjoy the most. Initially, I have to research current educational issues which may translate into a course or conference, for example 'Using Data in Special Schools', 'Behaviour Management for NQTs' or 'Primary Modern Foreign Languages'. The next stage is the creative bit. Having decided which area to focus on, I liaise with my speakers and trainers, and design the event itself, constantly keeping an eye on what teachers and managers 'at the chalkface' will actually find useful. I also have to book the speakers, negotiate their fees and expenses, and explain what I need them to do. I am constantly on the lookout for new people and I also work hard at maintaining positive relationships with established speakers. A good speaker is key to the success of your event and like gold dust for a conference organiser! Once the course content has been decided and the speakers and/or trainers booked, I write the marketing blurb to send out to schools. After the event is over, I also evaluate the feedback from the delegates and deal with any issues that might arise.

There are many advantages to the job. I am pleased to be able to utilise so many aspects of my teaching and management experience, even though I no longer teach. I love meeting such a wide range of people, including some impressive practitioners and figures of national importance in the education world. I also enjoy having almost complete control over the planning and organisation of my events.

On the downside, there is a lot of pressure to make money. The education conference business can only survive if the events attract delegates, and you are under constant scrutiny from your employer. This aspect of the job is quite different from teaching and it comes as rather a culture shock. Although teachers have to get results, your job is unlikely to be at risk if your performance

continued

is not as good as it should be. In the business world, you could find yourself 'eased out' if you persistently fail to deliver. It can also get a bit boring if you keep churning out the same old events. You need to keep one step ahead all the time and be ready to try out new ideas. These are, however, minor grumbles. Overall, the job is interesting and fulfilling – and unlike many education-related roles, the salary equates to that of a middle management teaching post. I would recommend it to anyone who thinks it might offer what they are looking for.

Working in educational publishing

What?

There is a huge market for educational publications, with a potential readership ranging from pupils of all ages to teachers in every sector and subject, as well as leadership and management personnel. There are various ways of becoming involved in educational publishing, apart from writing (see page 101). The following job profiles and case studies cover just a few examples of the many different possibilities:

- **Working for an educational publishing company**: educational publishers offer various different career opportunities, for example:
  - *Commissioning editor*: a commissioning editor is responsible for assessing the market, commissioning and supporting authors, and seeing a project through every stage of publication. Usually a commissioning editor has previous experience as an editorial assistant, although individuals with a specialist background may occasionally be employed directly into the role of commissioning editor.
  - *Assistant editor*: an assistant editor supports the commissioning editor in all aspects of the job, with responsibilities often developing as expertise grows. Becoming an assistant editor is a good way to gain experience in publishing. With the larger publishers, an assistant editor may be able to progress up the career ladder without having to move to a different company.

- *Copy editor*: a copy editor checks copy prior to publication to ensure that it is well written, uses a consistent style and is factually correct. If you are employed as a copy editor by a publishing company, you will receive training in the workplace. If you want to work as a freelance, you will need to undergo training delivered by a professional body. An increasing number of copy editors work for a range of different companies.
- *Proof-reader*: a proof-reader checks copy for grammatical, spelling and typographical errors. Many copy editors perform a proof-reading function alongside copy editing. As with copy editors, an increasing number of proof-readers undergo training with a professional body and work freelance for different publishing companies. As a copy editor and/or proof-reader, you can work on magazines, journals and publicity material, as well as books.

- **Director of Schools Publishing at an education company**: Geoff was a senior teacher before leaving teaching to develop his interest in training, examining, and writing design and technology textbooks. Initially, he worked as a training director for one of the large education companies before developing the publishing side of the company, and he now leads a team of editors and commissioning managers in the design and production of resource files and materials for both teachers and support staff. His many tasks and responsibilities include visiting schools, teachers and potential writers, and researching education fully in order to identify resource needs within schools and colleges. He also has to prepare an annual business plan and budget for the company, and work with the managing director to appraise quarterly performance against key performance indicators.
- **Independent publisher**: Steven had written several maths textbooks for a large educational publisher when he decided to start his own publishing company. Although setting up a business involved a degree of risk, he wanted to have more control over what he wrote, and he downsized to a part-time teaching job to provide an income while he became established. After five years, he was able to give up teaching altogether and concentrate solely on running the business. As a small independent publisher, he covers most aspects of the publishing process himself. His first task is to commission and brief his writers, all of whom are practising teachers. He then edits their work, finds

a typesetter who is able to cope with the special requirements of maths textbooks, liaises with the printer and markets the finished product, including direct mailing to more than 5,000 secondary schools and 22,000 primary schools.

- **Self-publishing support material**: Dave is a behaviour consultant and trainer, working throughout the United Kingdom with teachers, lecturers, senior management teams and support staff. Although he has written a number of education books for the larger publishing companies, he also publishes his own support material in the form of leaflets and booklets. This involves writing the material, planning the design, format and layout, organising a local printer to produce the material, and selling it at the various conferences and training events he attends. He also runs his own website and sells his publications through mail order (for more information, visit www.behaviour-solutions.com and www.yourdesignsolutions.co.uk).

Where?

Depending on the nature of your job and your employer, you will either be office based or work from home. If you are involved in researching and identifying teachers' requirements, you may need to visit schools and other educational establishments. Marketing your books or those of your company could also involve you in attending education shows and other events such as conferences and courses. If you want to work for a UK publisher, the majority of job opportunities are in or around London, although some companies are based in large regional centres or cities with a strong publishing tradition, such as Oxford.

When?

Your working hours will vary depending on the nature of your role and whether you are employed full time or part time, or are self-employed. Steven works as and when necessary to maintain his business, and his workload varies depending on the particular stage a project has reached. Co-ordinating the different elements of the publishing process and meeting deadlines can result in a high level of work pressure at certain times. If, however, you run your own business or, like Geoff, are able to work from home, you will also have a degree of flexibility. As he says, '*Working from home requires discipline but it also provides enormous freedom. There is a job to do, but how you do it and when you do it is very much up to you. . . . I have to prioritise, but I can do things in the order I want to do them.'*

Who?

Although a teaching background is not essential for a job in educational publishing, as an ex-teacher you may be given preference over candidates without specialist experience. There is no doubt that your instincts for what teachers require (and will buy), your ability to 'speak the language' and your many contacts in the educational world will prove useful. All three of our case studies were teachers before moving into publishing, and they constantly draw on their experience to identify developments within education and ascertain what will work in the classroom.

On a personal level, you need to be well organised and able to meet strict deadlines and cope with working under pressure. Proficiency in IT and the ability to write clearly and succinctly are other important skills within the publishing world. Preparing information for brochures and advertisements, coming up with the blurb for the back of the book and editing copy all demand good written communication skills – something that most teachers practise regularly throughout their careers with tasks such as writing reports and Universities and Colleges Admissions Service (UCAS) references.

How?

Although your educational background may give you a head start for a small number of specialist roles within educational publishing, overall this can be a difficult field to break into. Jobs in publishing are often not widely advertised, and although some of the larger publishing houses run graduate training schemes, they are heavily oversubscribed. The specialist press is the best place to look for advertisements (check the *Writers' and Artists' Yearbook* or *Willings Press Guide* in the reference section of your library for a list of specialist magazines and journals). To become a commissioning editor, you will usually have to start off at a more junior level, typically as an editorial assistant. Even to get on to the bottom rung of the ladder, you may have to work at making contacts and be prepared to take on unpaid work experience. Writing educational books (see page 101) will help you to network and also give you some experience of the publishing process; each of our three case studies was a published writer before taking on a publishing role themselves.

Following in Steven's footsteps and starting your own company can be even more of a challenge. You need to have the initial capital and be aware that you run the risk of losing it. As a published writer, Steven had some knowledge of the market and perceived that the risk was worth taking, although he gave himself a safety net by continuing to teach part time. There is a lot of competition within the world of educational publishing, and if you want to start your own company, you need to find a niche opportunity, keep up to date with market requirements and be ready to adapt as necessary. Very occasionally, independent publishing companies are put up for sale, offering another option for a would-be publisher who wishes to run his or her own business.

Why?

Educational publishing takes you out of the classroom but keeps you at the cutting edge of what is happening within education. There is also plenty of opportunity to be creative and 'think outside the box'. What kinds of resources do teachers want, and what are they likely to buy? How can you match your publications to the ever-changing face of education and what might be the next new initiative, strategy or innovation? If you enjoy taking risks, educational publishing will offer you plenty of excitement and variety, as well as the satisfaction of seeing a project through from start to finish. If you are able to run your own company, you also have the freedom to control your working timetable and develop your business in whatever way you choose.

On the downside, as with any sales-driven business you will not necessarily have job security, and you will also be under constant pressure to make money. As Geoff says, *'Private companies make people redundant, with companies like mine driven by the bottom line. In schools, the bottom line is results, whereas in the private sector, very often it's pounds.'* He also points out that you lose access to long holidays and a very good pension scheme when you leave teaching. Overall, however, he recommends that teachers should not feel tied to the security of teaching, and he is adamant that any teacher who wants a fresh challenge has more than enough experience, skills and qualifications for a new role. As he puts it, *'Have degree – have teaching skills – will travel!'*

Chapter 4

Effectively transferring . . . beyond education

Although there are many jobs within the general field of education, making a complete career change is another option. Perhaps you have decided that education is not for you. You may have a burning ambition to act, or become an engineer, or go into medicine; you may want to translate a hobby or interest into paid employment, or run your own business; you may be retired and looking for work to supplement your pension and fill your time. If any of these scenarios describes you, a complete change of career could be the answer.

This chapter is divided into three sections:

- professional roles;
- running your own business;
- retirement opportunities.

The case studies within each section profile teachers who have chosen to transfer into a wide variety of different jobs. Each individual explains what their job involves, why they chose to make their move, how they went about it and, perhaps most important of all, how they use their teaching skills and experience in their new working lives.

Professional roles

The term 'professional' is widely used within the jobs market. As a broad definition, it refers to anyone with a paid occupation and it is usually taken to indicate an individual with training and qualifications. As a teacher, you already count as a professional, although a move from teaching into a different profession may involve you in further training. For the 'traditional' professions such as law or medicine, you will have to retrain in preparation for your new career.

For many other roles, it is often possible to carry out any necessary training once you are in the job.

The professions we profile in this section include law, management consultancy, business development roles and librarianship. They represent just a small number of options for those willing to consider further training and take on a level of commitment and responsibility compatible with teaching. If you are relatively early on in your career and prepared to retrain, other possibilities might include accountancy and bookkeeping, medicine, dentistry, optometry, engineering, architecture, social work, journalism, working as a careers adviser or becoming involved in scientific research. If you are in any doubt about which career path to follow, visit a careers adviser to discuss your options. You can also sign up with a recruitment consultant, who will be able to identify your skills, qualifications and experience and match you with possible employers.

Case study

From science teacher to . . . management consultant

Theresa had been teaching science and IT for nearly twenty years when she decided to apply for a local authority vacancy as an IT advisory teacher. After she had been four years in the job, the local authority funding began to dry up and she started exploring other options.

Q Describe your career path since you left teaching, and explain how you ended up working as a management consultant.

A *My job as an IT advisory teacher had become insecure, and although I was happy to go back into the classroom, I decided to 'test the water' by sending my CV to a recruitment agency. Within a fortnight, I was offered a job as a training strategist for a small consultancy company. The company specialised in helping businesses to improve their communications and they wanted to develop the training side of the operation – which is* *where I came in. During the fourteen years I spent with the company, it was taken over several times and my role continually changed and developed. By the time I retired two years ago, my job profile had evolved into management consultancy, and the small organisation I joined had become part of a company with a workforce of over 90,000!*

Q What did your work as a training strategist involve?

A *Initially, I was involved in the development of training programmes for staff in both private and public sector organisations. My very first project was helping to implement a new coding and classification system of diseases for hospital doctors, followed by a project to improve workflow for forensic scientists and another long project to radically change the way a building society operated and was managed.*

Q So how did your role as a training strategist develop into management consultancy?

A *For me, the move up the hierarchy started during the three-year-long project with the building society. For the last year of the project, I moved into a role that involved making strategic decisions, as well as supporting the society's staff during the process of developing and delivering an intensive training programme. A formal management consultancy was set up within our parent company and I was gradually included in teams of general management consultants. This led on to a role as team leader with responsibility for the development and well-being of around ten consultants. I was then trusted to manage project teams as well as helping to put together proposals for multi-million-pound projects. After I had been with the company for five years, I was promoted several times in quick succession, becoming a member of the UK Consulting Management Team, head of our Management of Change service and responsible for consultant development across Europe.*

Q In what ways did you use your teaching skills and experience?

A *Teaching encompasses such a broad range of skills, and they all*

continued

came in useful: dealing with people; being able to work on your own and as part of a team; good organisational and time-management skills; flexibility, adaptability and creativity; being prepared to 'go the extra mile'; the ability to multi-task and think on your feet . . . Just like teaching, much of my job involved working with people and motivating them to do things differently. In the early days, I also took on many of the most important presentations, as I had much more experience of public speaking than my colleagues (twenty years of taking assemblies came in useful after all!). Even my subject skills stood me in good stead. The 'techies' often didn't expect a woman to know what they were talking about, and it was sometimes nice to surprise them!

Q So what are the advantages of the role?

A *Management consultancy is a very satisfying job, certainly on a par with teaching. It is a privilege to be invited into the heart of an organisation, observe and challenge what they do, warts and all, and then help them to move forward. Every project is different, every day brings new challenges and, as with teaching, it is great to see organisations and their people grow. In many ways, the role is addictive and you can't wait to start the next project – although inevitably, you will sometimes get 'the project from hell'. Other advantages include the chance to work with some very capable colleagues in a meritocracy, along with excellent levels of pay.*

Q And the disadvantages?

A *I missed the school holidays! I thought I worked long hours as a teacher, but this was even more demanding. You can also be away from early Monday morning to late on Friday night, depending on the project and where it is located. You do need to think about whether your home life and relationships can stand the strain of your long absences. I certainly couldn't have taken on the role before my children were well into their teens.*

Q Do you have any tips or advice for those who are thinking of following a similar path?

A *To anyone who feels the role offers what they are looking for, I would say be brave and go for it. The organisation I worked for employed several ex-teachers and we all did well (those people skills you acquire as a teacher are in short supply in the business world!). After I had been a consultant for about three years, one of my bosses commented, 'I find it amazing that there are people like you hidden away in education'. Apart from what this suggests about attitudes to education within business, it demonstrates that teachers have to sell themselves to the outside world; they aren't expected to be any good!*

Q No regrets, then?

A *None whatsoever. Having now worked for more than forty organisations in a consultancy role, I'm sure I would be a better educationalist if I were to go back into the classroom. Maybe we should be sending prospective headteachers into the business world to find out what is expected of young people?*

Case study

From history teacher to . . . operations director in the printing industry

Although Richard enjoyed teaching history, he couldn't foresee it becoming a lifelong career and he decided to explore other options while he was still in his twenties. He explains how he ended up working in the printing industry, what his job involves and how he has utilised his teaching skills and expertise:

Q Describe what you did when you first left teaching.

A *My decision to leave teaching coincided with the computer boom, and as all the newspapers were suggesting that this was a growth area, I started looking for opportunities within the*

continued

computer industry. A large software company was advertising for arts graduates with good communication skills to write manuals for their business programs, and they employed me as a 'technical writer'.

Q How did the role develop?

A *Part of my job involved buying in design and print services. I became interested in the design and print process, and after five years as a technical writer I accepted a job from one of the printing companies I had worked with. I set up a design and reprographics function for them, and three years later helped to start a new company offering a similar service. This was eventually merged with the main print business and I was appointed Operations Director.*

Q What does your job involve?

A *As a board director and shareholder, I am involved in all aspects of developing and running the business. I am responsible for equipment, workflows, staffing and business direction, and I also manage the client services function, sales and sales support. Another key responsibility involves managing a design and graphics business, which runs as a facilities management operation in a large corporate account. I was instrumental in winning this business and in setting up the operation. Over an eight-year period, the business has grown from a turnover of £750,000 with ten employees to a £6 million business with sixty staff.*

Q Bringing about that kind of growth must have involved a lot of hard work!

A *Yes, the hours are long and the stress levels can be high. Printing has become quite a difficult industry, with over-capacity and low margins. It is also hard to escape from the job, even when on holiday.*

Q So what are the positive sides of your job?

A *I enjoy being involved in the whole process, from winning the* *business contract to overseeing production, and I get a great deal of satisfaction from finally seeing all our plans reach fruition. The salary and benefits are also good, particularly compared with teaching!*

Q Do you have any advice for teachers who want to follow a similar path?

A *Look beyond your subject area, and bear in mind that your main skills are likely to be communication based. Many small and medium-sized companies are good at their core business, but poor at peripheral areas such as marketing and client services. As these areas mostly involve communication, presentation and 'people skills', the trained and experienced teacher has a lot to offer to the business world.*

Case study

From English and drama teacher to . . . criminal defence solicitor

Catherine had been teaching English and drama for ten years when she decided that she was ready for a change. Although she was looking for a new intellectual challenge, she still wanted to work in an environment that provided a service, and a career in the legal profession seemed to offer just what she needed.

Q What was it about becoming a criminal defence solicitor that appealed to you?

A *When I first decided to change careers, I had a session with a careers adviser. As part of the consultation, I filled in a questionnaire which flagged up law as a profession that matched my skills and interests. The prospect of becoming a solicitor certainly appealed to me. I had always been fascinated by the*

continued

drama of legal 'stuff', and, in hindsight, I think my decision had something to do with the draw of the stories involved – the English and drama connection!

Q Describe your job and what it involves.

A *As a criminal defence solicitor, my clients are mainly defendants in criminal proceedings, ranging from minor driving offences to serious crown court matters. At the start of a new case, my first contact is usually with the police. I get as much information as I can from them and then visit the arrested person in the detention block of the police station. I give advice over legal rights and likely procedures, listen to their explanation of what happened and then explain the legal elements of the crime for which they are being detained. I also check that the police are meeting any special needs, in the case of a juvenile detainee for example, and conducting their detention of the person within the confines of the law.*

Q So do you have to attend court?

A *Yes – if the person is charged, I make arrangements to represent them in court and give advice about plea, trials and possible sentences. If it's a more serious case destined for the crown court, I deal with the early hearings in the magistrate's court and then instruct a barrister to take on the case for the crown court trial.*

Q There must be a lot of preparation and paperwork.

A *There certainly is! Apart from advising clients, a substantial amount of work involves preparing for advocacy in the magistrates court – for example, applications for bail or a plea in mitigation in a sentencing hearing. Although many applications are straightforward, it's important that you are accurate with the facts. If a barrister is briefed for a crown court case, it is my job to draft the brief and organise copies of all documents. Once a case is under way, I have to obtain disclosure from the police and Crown Prosecution Service of as much material as possible, investigate the defence, interview witnesses, take* *statements, take photographs, find and instruct expert witnesses, and supply them with copies of all the evidence – the list can seem endless.*

Q It sounds hard work!

A *It is! You do have some secretarial help with typing and filing, and computer technology has certainly made a difference, but there is still a huge administrative load, and many solicitors are expected to do much of it for themselves. As I often have up to eighty cases 'on the go' at any one time, the paperwork can be a burden!*

Q In what ways do you use your teaching skills?

A *I spend a lot of my time explaining complex legal arguments to teenagers and vulnerable adults. My teaching experience can be very useful in helping me to find an appropriate level of language and build a rapport with some difficult characters. My classroom teaching skills, especially the ability to speak clearly, authoritatively and audibly, are a distinct asset when it comes to court advocacy work. When I did my advocacy training, the comment on my assessment sheet was: 'This candidate is a qualified drama teacher – and it shows!'*

Q So what would you describe as the advantages of the job?

A *There's never a dull moment. No two cases are the same, there are constant new challenges and you never know how the day is going to pan out. You get to work with some interesting, intelligent and dedicated people in a variety of different fields of expertise, and you also get out of the office on a daily basis.*

Q And the disadvantages?

A *Be warned – criminal defence work is poorly paid compared with other branches of the legal profession. Believe it or not, I earned more as a teacher. Another disadvantage is the intense pressure. If you make an inadvertent mistake, you can be slammed by the judge – which plays havoc with your self-confidence. The hours are also irregular, and difficult to*

continued

organise around family life. After years of teaching, the loss of the school holidays comes as a bit of a shock!

Q Any tips for teachers who would like to follow a similar path?

A *Be sure that you have the staying power, both for the work itself and the training. I did a part-time CPE [Common Professional Examination] and legal practice course, and over the four years I had to learn masses of information and take over twenty exams. You also have to be in a position to fund your training. I ended up taking out a business development loan, which then took me five years to repay. However, I was able to combine the training with looking after young children and a small amount of part-time teaching. Overall, I would say that, although not an easy option, practising as a criminal defence solicitor is an endlessly fascinating and worthwhile job for anyone with the appropriate skills and stamina.*

If you would like to follow a similar path to Catherine and do not have a law degree, you will have to enrol on a law conversion course. For information about training options and eligibility, visit www.lawsociety.org.uk.

Case study

From maths teacher to . . . Head of Strategic Planning for a healthcare agency

After completing his maths degree, Carwyn decided to follow his father's career path and train as a teacher. Although he enjoyed teaching, he quickly realised that his (non-teaching) university friends were working shorter hours and earning more money than he was, and he decided to explore other job options. When an opportunity arose within the world of pharmaceuticals, he decided to go for it, and he is now the Head of Strategic Planning for a healthcare agency.

Q Describe your current role within the healthcare agency.

A *The agency I work for provides a service for a number of pharmaceutical companies and I am responsible for developing and implementing the marketing strategy for various healthcare brands. This involves creating sales aids such as brochures, examining the position of different brands within the minds of potential purchasers, preparing advertising briefs for the creative team, presenting strategic thoughts to clients in the form of marketing plans, and running workshops. All the agency's departments integrate with Strategic Planning, and I also have to liaise with advertising, PR and medical education personnel.*

Q What is it about the job that appeals to you?

A *I have quite a lot of autonomy. I can do my own thing and make every day a little different. The role is exceptionally fast-moving and can change by the hour, depending on client needs. There is also the opportunity to travel across the globe – and it is well paid!*

Q How does it compare with teaching?

A *I miss not having responsibility for educating children, and the feeling that your work is making a real difference every day. I miss the staffroom – there is less camaraderie with colleagues in my current job. I also miss the holidays!*

Q Do you feel your teaching experience helps you in your role?

A *Yes – very much so. Interestingly, I talk about being an ex-teacher quite often, probably because I enjoyed it and it generated some good stories. Teaching develops and uses a lot of transferable skills. For me, the key ones are:*

- ***Presentation skills****: it's crucial to be able to engage and connect with your audience, understand their needs and convince them that you know what you are talking about!*

continued

- **Communication skills**: *helping individuals to solve problems and being able to explain things clearly are classic teaching skills that I constantly utilise.*
- **Time management**: *not a favourite of mine, but teaching did help me to become a 'just in time' protagonist!*
- **Analytical skills**: *marketing is based on customer insight. My ability to assimilate information about customer requirements and apply it to solve a problem is what teaching is all about.*
- **Project management**: *even as a mainscale teacher, you are continually in a leadership position. Interestingly, in business there is a significant amount of 'buck passing' and poor accountability. As a teacher, you have nowhere to hide, and this willingness to accept accountability translates itself as strong leadership in the business world.*

Q Any tips for others who would like to follow suit?

A *You can't leave it too late in your career if you want to change tack completely, as I did. The business world offers a different philosophy and working environment from teaching, and you need time to adapt and retrain. Once you have decided to make the move, be confident in the many skills you have learned as a teacher. They may not be formal business qualifications, but they will still be invaluable.*

Case study

From geogaphy teacher to . . . school librarian

Janet taught geography before giving up teaching to start a family. As her husband was also a teacher, they decided that they could not run two full-time teaching careers alongside a young family, and she started looking for something a little less demanding.

Q How did you come across your job as a school librarian and did you need to retrain?

A *I saw the job advertised in the local press. I did not need to retrain before applying for the job, although in some schools the job is given a higher profile and they may ask for chartered librarians. I have been fortunate, as my school is very supportive over training and development. I attended a course for school librarians at my local FE college and I have also been able to attend a wide variety of courses run by the School Library Association, some organised by our local branch and some by the national association.*

Q Describe your job as a school librarian.

A *For the last five years, I have had full responsibility for managing the learning resource centre at the school where I work, and I report directly to a member of the senior management team. Apart from the day-to-day running of the library, I liaise with departments to develop resource-based learning and information literacy skills; research, order and catalogue new books; set up displays and open evenings; organise author visits; promote events such as World Book Day; and manage a substantial budget.*

Q Do you have much contact with the students?

A *Yes – apart from running events and book groups, I supervise students during break and lunchtime. I also run library induction and information skills courses, as well as supervising and giving support to students working independently in the library.*

Q So your teaching skills and experience come in useful?

A *They certainly do! I have a personal understanding of a teacher's needs, which helps when it comes to communicating with and supporting the teaching staff. I appreciate how resources will be used within the curriculum, which informs the selections and evaluations that I make when ordering new materials for the library. Running induction courses and supervising students is yet another very important part of the job, and I constantly use*

continued

the teaching and behaviour management skills I learned in the classroom.

Q It sounds a fascinating job! Has it turned out to be what you were hoping for?

A Very much so. I can fit the work around family life, leaving evenings, weekends and school holidays free, while still utilising the many skills I developed as a teacher. The job is interesting, varied and gives me ample opportunity to be creative, alongside all the administrative tasks. Most of the time, it is also much less stressful than teaching.

Q Any downsides?

A The salary – which is only about 50 per cent of what I would now be earning had I stayed in teaching!

Q Do you have any tips or advice for teachers who would like to follow a similar path?

A School library provision and associated roles vary from authority to authority, so you will need to look out for jobs in the local press. It is also worth checking the 'support staff' section of your local authority bulletin. Although I would recommend the job to anyone who can afford the cut in salary, bear in mind that there may be aspects of teaching that you will miss; nothing is more rewarding than a class of pupils who are truly enthused by the work they are doing. On the plus side, you still get plenty of contact with young people, without running the risk of becoming totally stressed or burned out. I have certainly never regretted my decision to change career paths!

Running your own business

Running your own business gives you considerably more autonomy over your working life than you had as a teacher, as well as the opportunity to utilise your skills, interests and expertise. On the downside, it also brings with it the pressure of having to find customers, clients and contracts, and keep up to date with the financial and administrative side of the business. The majority of teachers who leave teaching to work for themselves end up operating as sole traders or running a small business with just a few employees. The businesses we profile in this section range from selling handmade greetings cards for 'pocket money' to earning a substantial living through running a café. For more information on the financial implications and practicalities of becoming self-employed, see Chapter 5.

Case study

From MFL teacher to . . . aromatherapist

Karen had always been interested in complementary therapies, and she made the decision to train as an aromatherapist while she was still an MFL teacher. Although it wasn't her original intention to leave teaching, she found it difficult to combine the two careers, and eventually she decided to give up teaching to concentrate solely on her work in aromatherapy.

Q What is it about aromatherapy that appeals to you?

A *My personal interest in aromatherapy is long-standing. Although I probably wouldn't be allowed to do it today, in the early years of my teaching career I put lavender on the classroom radiators to create a calming atmosphere. The difference it made to the behaviour of challenging pupils was remarkable, and I decided to explore the other benefits of aromatherapy. Apart from its healing potential, working as an aromatherapist enables me to give quality time to my clients. Complementary therapies embrace an empathetic approach, and there is also plenty of opportunity to offer advice and guidance – not dissimilar from the pastoral side of teaching.*

Q In what other ways does your teaching background help you as an aromatherapist?

A *You have to be able to read people. Some clients are sceptical, and you need to pick up on this and help them to accept the therapy – much the same as nurturing a reluctant pupil. Ten years of teaching gave me the confidence to deal with people*

continued

from all walks of life, and there are times when I know that my teaching experience has helped me to avert potentially difficult situations. My teaching background has also opened doors into various training posts.

Q How did you go about getting work as a trainer, and what does it involve?

A *It was a case of being in the right place at the right time. The aromatherapy college I trained with knew that I had a teaching background and they contacted me when they needed to fill a vacancy. I also answered a job advertisement and taught an adult education course in aromatherapy at a college of FE. Most aromatherapy tutors don't have a teaching background, so I was at a distinct advantage. Apart from drawing on my general experience in education, I use techniques from the classroom to help me teach anatomy and physiology – flash cards and sorting activities always go down well! I am now in the process of starting my own training company, 'karita', with my business partner.*

Q Are you still able to combine teaching aromatherapy with working as a practitioner?

A *Yes, I have a client base that I keep small so that I can continue with my teaching. I practise from home, although some practitioners work in clinics or beauty salons, while others visit clients in their own homes. Because I can only manage a small number of clients at the moment, I don't advertise, relying instead on word of mouth.*

Q What are the advantages and disadvantages of the job?

A *As a freelance practitioner, you are able to choose where and when to work. The hours are extremely flexible and there are opportunities for weekend and evening work as well as daytime hours. It is also a very satisfying job. Most people find aromatherapy beneficial and it is good to know that you are helping your clients with the stresses and strains of their lives. On the downside, the work can be irregular. You can never quite be* *sure how much work you will have from one week to the next, and until you build up a sound client base, your income can be variable.*

Q Do you have any tips for others who would like to follow a similar path?

A *Get the best possible training you can find and research courses to make sure that yours is recognised nationally. At the moment, therapists are not regulated, but this is going to change, and practitioners with insufficient qualifications will have to upgrade. If you want to build up your business, it can be worth training in other therapies such as reflexology and Indian head massage so that you can offer clients a broad range of choices. Apart from getting the business side of your new role organised [see Chapter 5], you must also have good insurance. When you are dealing with people's health and well-being, you can't be too careful!*

Case study

From PE teacher to . . . running a gardening and painting and decorating business

Steve was in his mid-fifties when he took early retirement from his job as a PE teacher. Although his wife was still teaching full time, he had young children and needed to make a contribution to the family income. He had always enjoyed gardening and DIY, and he decided to set up a small business as a gardener, painter and decorator.

Q Why did you decide to set up your own gardening and decorating business?

A *There is always a market for gardening and decorating, and it was something I could fit around my family commitments and the odd day's supply teaching.*

continued

Q What does the work involve?

A *Anything and everything: general garden maintenance, landscaping and any odd jobs that people want doing around the house, from decorating a room to fixing cupboards.*

Q In what ways do you use your teaching skills?

A *The communication skills I developed during years of teaching are probably the most important. Whenever someone wants a job done, I have to discuss what the job involves, ask the right questions and interpret the answers so that I can work out what the customer actually wants me to do. I also use my planning and organisational skills, and I have to research certain projects in quite some depth. For example, I was recently asked to create a boules park at a local hostel. Ordering the materials, arranging deliveries and timetabling the construction of the park proved to be quite complex, and I had to do my research to make sure I was using the right dimensions and including the correct features.*

Q What are advantages of your new working life?

A *I like being able to set my own agenda and having the freedom to manage my time accordingly. After years of teaching, I also enjoy not being managed, and, overall, my working life is much less stressful.*

Q And the disadvantages?

A *I miss daily contact with young people, and I miss teaching sport. My working life no longer has the same structure on a day-to-day basis – something to watch if you are self-employed, as you have to create your own structure. My income is also variable and I have to work hard at getting contracts. The jobs market is not always very vibrant for the over-fifties, particularly in a rural area such as mine.*

Q Do you have any tips for people who would like to follow a similar path?

A *Check your basic finances before making any decisions, and* *research all aspects of running your own business before you go ahead. It's a good idea to organise some contracts before you finish work so that you can get going straight away. Once you have done all that – just follow your heart!*

Case study

From EBD teacher to . . . running a café

After working in a school for pupils with emotional and behavioural difficulties (EBD) for several years, Sarah decided it was time for a change. When she and a partner from a similar teaching background were presented with the opportunity to run The Coffee Pot in the Somerset village of Martock, they jumped at the chance. Here she explains why they went ahead with a career move, the many advantages of their new working life and a few of the disadvantages.

Q Why did you decide to leave teaching?

A *Working in an EBD setting can be very stressful. Teachers are regularly exposed to abuse, both verbal and physical, and situations can occasionally turn quite dangerous. The paperwork burden was also becoming too much, and we decided it was time for a change.*

Q So what was it about running a café that appealed?

A *We wanted to become more involved with the community and offer a service to all ages. We also wanted greater control over our working hours and to be our own bosses. Running a café in the local village seemed to tick all the boxes.*

Q Describe what the job involves.

A *We design menus; order and buy produce; prepare, cook and serve the food; keep up to date with accounts, banking and other administration; maintain records for the Environment*

continued

and Health inspectorate; and organise staff training to make sure we are up to date with food hygiene regulations.

Q How do you use your teaching experience?

A In many different ways! We constantly use all our organisational skills and the ability to plan both short term (what we want to achieve within the year) and long term (where we want to be within three years). Most teachers have a natural interest in people, and this also comes in useful. Social skills are very important, as is the ability to read a situation. Dealing with awkward customers is sometimes reminiscent of dealing with challenging pupils! A teacher also has to be aware of everything that is going on in the room – useful when it comes to scanning the café and spotting that a customer needs your service.

Q What would you describe as the advantages of the job?

A Being your own boss is great after the restrictions of teaching. As long as we plan staffing, we can both regulate the hours we wish to work and leave work behind when we close the door of the café; it is much less stressful than teaching and there are very few external pressures. We also have a better lifestyle. Because we are working in the community where we live, we feel much more a part of things and have virtually no travelling to contend with.

Q And the downsides?

A Customers and a set income are never guaranteed. We are also open six days a week, and the work is physically quite tiring.

Q Do you have any tips for teachers who would like to follow a similar path?

A Bear in mind that any new business is always a gamble. If you want to start your own café from scratch, look at how much you think it will cost and then double it. Things always work out more expensive than you expect, and if you open up having gone over budget, it can take a long time to straighten out your *finances. Work at treating every customer as special: for example, being willing to make a particular cake if a regular customer requests it. Be aware that everyone has their own individual needs and be prepared to talk to people on different levels. This is what will bring people back in (apart from the food, of course!). Otherwise, if the job appeals, go for it. Although running a café is hard work, it's a hugely rewarding way to earn your living.*

Case study

From art teacher to . . . handmade greetings card designer

Laura was in her mid-fifties when she decided to take early retirement from her job as an art teacher. With her pension to fall back on, she did not need an income, but she wanted to fill her time with something constructive. She had always enjoyed working with paper and she decided to set up a small business designing, making and selling her own greetings cards.

Q What was it about making and selling greetings cards that appealed to you?

A *As an artist, I had always dreamed of people buying my creations. It is, however, very difficult to find a market, and only a tiny proportion of artists make a living from selling their work. As I was retired and had my pension, I decided to give it a go by selling my cards.*

Q What does your job involve?

A *First of all, I plan a design and source the materials to create the design. I then experiment with the design and get the card just as I want it. Apart from creating new cards, I continue making up my old designs to restock my current outlets and try*

continued

out in new outlets. I also have to keep my records up to date: for example, how many of each card I have sold, which outlet has sold which cards, invoicing and payments . . . There is quite a lot of paperwork if you are going to do it properly.

Q What are the advantages of the job for you?

A That's an easy one – I can spend all day, every day being creative. Selling my cards also pays for the materials and it does give me a bit of extra pocket money. Unlike larger pieces of art, you can sell lots of cards, and I get a real kick from knowing that people across the country are buying and enjoying my work.

Q And the disadvantages?

A The money! To make a handmade card business viable, you have to come up with designs that are quick to produce. I will not compromise on my designs; if a card is complicated and takes forever to make, so be it. People don't always appreciate the time it takes to make a card, and some customers won't pay a premium for handmade items. I also don't particularly enjoy dealing with certain shop personnel. Buyers and shop owners are often inundated with people like me, and you can get rather short shrift from some of them.

Q How do you use your teaching skills?

A I don't particularly use my teaching skills, but I do use my subject knowledge. After years of experience as an art teacher, I am adept at design, colour co-ordination and composition. I also have a steady hand and a good eye. I never cease to be amazed at how many card makers cannot actually cut straight or handle glue. Not that this is a problem if you are just making cards for pleasure, but if you want to sell them, they do have to be well crafted.

Q Any tips for others who would like to follow suit?

A First of all, decide why you want to sell your cards. If it is just to fund your hobby and earn a few pennies, that's fine. If it is *to make more serious money, you will need to plan carefully and have a back-up income in case things don't work out. Make sure your designs are original, and create cards to suit different outlets. For example, my range of baby and children's birthday cards sell well at my sister's nursery school, whereas my standard floral designs are popular with the elderly clientele at my friend's tea shop.*

Q How do you find outlets?

A *You need to be constantly on the lookout for possible outlets. Ask friends to take a box to their workplace, try craft and gift shops, local post offices, farm shops and tea shops. Hold 'card parties', rent a stall at a craft fair and try internet selling, either through your own website or through one of the sites that act as agents for handmade card makers. One word of warning: some shop owners are put off by the term 'handmade card'. Try to get an appointment so that a buyer can at least look at your work and see its quality before dismissing it.*

Q Do you have to register with the Inland Revenue?

A *Yes – if you are earning money, you must regard the project as a small business and register with the Inland Revenue. You probably won't make enough to pay tax on your card sales alone, but the Inland Revenue still likes to be informed, and if you have any other income, then your card sales will be taxable. I would recommend checking out the craft websites on the internet; many of them offer sound advice about the business side of selling your cards. There is also a huge internet community of card makers on the website forums. They are an extremely supportive group who are endlessly willing to give advice on anything from handling a heat gun to the ins and outs of selling. The internet is also useful for sourcing items you cannot find in your local craft shops.*

Q So would you recommend making and selling cards to others in your position?

continued

A *I would certainly recommend anyone who is 'crafty' to give it a try. At the very least, you should recoup the cost of your materials, and you will never be short of something to fill your time!*

Retirement opportunities

Teaching is not a job that is easy to sustain in the later years of your working life, and many teachers choose to take early retirement. If you are still relatively young and/or energetic when you retire, you will suddenly have lots of free time to fill. If you have had to take an actuarially reduced pension, you may also want to supplement your income with part-time work. In many respects, once you have retired, your horizons could well appear wider than at any other time in your life. Most people will have sorted out major financial burdens such as mortgages, you will probably be more or less free from dependants, and the urge to climb the career ladder should now be long gone. Perhaps it is time to explore a low-key but enjoyable job such as working in a bar, or give your time voluntarily to a charity. Perhaps you would like to follow the example of one of our case studies, Peter, and develop a whole portfolio of diverse and unusual roles. Whatever direction you want to follow, the great thing about 'retirement' is that you need never actually retire!

Case study

From deputy headteacher to . . . events manager

Although Chris had retired from her job as a deputy head-teacher, she wanted to remain active and, if possible, supplement her pension. Event management offered a complete job change, and the *ad hoc* nature of the work enabled her to fit it around her other retirement pursuits and hobbies. Here she describes what her job involves, explains how she draws on her many years of teaching experience and gives some tips to teachers who would like to follow suit.

Q Explain what your job involves.

A *Most event managers work freelance and are employed by companies on an ad hoc basis. Event management is an organisational role, with the event manager taking overall responsibility for the smooth running of a course, conference or exhibition. The job is very varied: for example, managing a typical event can include liaising with venue staff, checking that the room is ready and that any materials have arrived, setting up the room as the company has requested, putting out delegates' folders, arranging refreshment breaks, liaising with speakers, registering delegates, double-checking that all equipment is working . . . the list is endless! Any problems that arise fall into the lap of the event manager, and the job can involve quite a bit of troubleshooting.*

Q It sounds as though you have to be very well organised – and very diplomatic!

A *Yes – it is essential to stay on top of things and handle situations sensitively. Some events can get quite fraught, particularly when you are dependent upon others to do their bit. People skills are also important. Apart from interacting with everyone involved in the event, I have to soothe anxious speakers and give whatever support is required by delegates – from ordering taxis to directing them to the first aid facilities. I also have to deal with any complaints.*

Q Apart from your interpersonal skills, how else do you draw on your teaching experience?

A *You have to be able to oversee the smooth running of the event and handle crises – very similar to classroom management, in fact! Good timing is also important. I have to get everything ready for the start of the event, and I also have to make sure that speakers do not overrun their 'slot', or the whole event can be knocked out of kilter. The teacher's ability to be motivational is yet another useful weapon in my armoury, particularly when a speaker is nervous or inexperienced.*

continued

Q What are the advantages of the role?

A *The job certainly keeps me on my toes, and I meet a lot of interesting people, some of whom are quite high profile. As many of the events I manage are within the field of education, it helps me to keep abreast of what is going on – although this may not be regarded as an advantage by everyone! The level of pay is also reasonable, with fees equating to those of supply teaching, plus expenses.*

Q And the disadvantages?

A *It can be a bit of a nightmare when speakers, equipment or folders don't turn up – the buck stops with me when it comes to sorting it all out! Dealing with difficult delegates can also be unpleasant. If you are not keen on overnight stays away from home and long, intensive working hours, this counts as another disadvantage. Typically, you arrive at the hotel the night before the event and are up early the next day to check that every-thing is in place. You are then on duty until the event is well and truly over and everything has been 'wrapped up'.*

Q Any tips for those who would like to follow suit?

A *Find out about companies that run events and approach them with your details. There are plenty of education companies around, but you don't have to stay within the field of education just because you are an ex-teacher. Look into other sectors such as law, health, business and commerce. I would also advise thinking about finances. If you need to earn a substantial living, you may not be able to do so with event management alone. It does, however, make a great supplementary income, as well as being a job that you can fit around your other pursuits. I would certainly recommend the role to anyone with the appropriate organisational and people skills. There is nothing to beat the sense of satisfaction when an event has run like clockwork, and you know that it is all down to your careful planning and management!*

Case study

From primary school teacher to . . . domestic cleaner

Following a period of ill health, Rachel was forced to take early retirement from her job as a primary school teacher. Once she had recovered, she needed to supplement her pension but did not want to take on anything too stressful or pressured. She had always enjoyed housework, and when a friend mentioned that he must get himself a cleaner, she decided to offer her services.

Q What was it about domestic cleaning that appealed to you?

A *Towards the end of my career, the stress of teaching was really starting to affect me and I took early retirement so that I could focus on regaining my health. Once I was back on my feet, I needed to earn a bit of money and I wanted to do something to get me out of the house. I didn't, however, want to take on anything that really 'mattered'. Domestic cleaning seemed to be the answer.*

Q What does your job involve?

A *I mostly work for friends or friends of friends, although I have occasionally answered ads in the local press. I do whatever is needed: vacuuming, polishing, ironing. Some jobs are two hours a week, some three. It's a very casual role. If I'm going through a bad patch health-wise, I will hand in my notice and then take on a new job once I feel better. I can also take on extra work for a while if I need to increase my earnings.*

Q What are the advantages of the job for you?

A *For me it has been a life-saver. It gives me a routine and it keeps me physically active. Most people's houses make a very pleasant workplace and there is a sense of satisfaction in creating order out of chaos. I also find it calming and thera-peutic. I listen to the radio or think while I polish away – there*

continued

is absolutely no pressure whatsoever and you are mostly left to yourself. As it is casual work, you also have a surprising amount of control over who you choose to work for. Woe betide anyone who starts treating me as a drudge! If they do, I just leave (tactfully, of course) and find another job. This is a rare occurrence, though; as long as you are reliable, most employers will treat you with the greatest respect and courtesy.

Q And the disadvantages?

A *For me, not many! The wages aren't great, particularly if you earn enough to pay tax. My employers don't cover sick pay or holiday pay, although I think that is gradually changing, particularly if you work for city-based professionals. It can get a bit boring at times, something you can either put up with or not, depending on your personality. You also have to deal with other people's reactions to what you do. We are all very much defined by our jobs, and some people can be quite snobbish, or even confused that a graduate teacher has chosen to become a cleaner. At the same time, it's interesting to discover how many people envy your decision to opt out.*

Q How do you use your teaching skills?

A *I don't, really, other than using general work-related skills such as time management, assessing what needs to be done and attention to detail.*

Q Any tips for others who would like to follow suit?

A *If you think the job offers what you are looking for, give it a go and ignore any negative reactions you might get. You can always use it as a stop-gap or a means of earning a basic core income while you do other things. Check the local press and cards in shop windows, and let all your friends know you are available. 'Word of mouth' tends to be the best source of employment, and people often don't realise they need a cleaner until you put the idea in their heads.*

Case study

From headteacher to . . . RSPCA animal centre manager

Sally was an acting headteacher at a Welsh comprehensive school when she decided to retire from teaching. She had been involved in the work of the RSPCA for some time and was delighted to be able to step into a more active role once she had finished teaching.

Q Describe how your work with the RSPCA developed into your current managerial role.

A *I was elected chair of the Llys Nini Branch while I was still teaching, and I juggled both roles until I decided to retire. At the time of my retirement, the animal centre was experiencing financial difficulties and needed someone to take on an active managerial role. With time on my hands and my experience of school management, I was well placed to fill the position.*

Q What does the work involve?

A *I oversee the animal centre manager, the part-time fund-raiser, the finance manager and five shop managers. This involves implementing financial controls over spending, budgeting, fund-raising and, along with my fellow trustees, deciding policy and development plans. I am also responsible for a project to develop a 'green visitors' attraction at the animal centre, I act as a volunteer education officer and I make applications for grants and draft strategic and development plans.*

Q It sounds like a full-time and very demanding job!

A *It is, although as it is a voluntary, unpaid role I don't have to do it, which lifts some of the pressure. My school was closed due to falling numbers and I was able to retire while still young enough to take on another active role. I felt I had had a good career and was ready for a different 'profession' – but, thanks to my pension, I am able to work as a volunteer.*

continued

Q So what are the advantages of the role?

A *As I've already mentioned, the voluntary nature of the role gives me quite a degree of freedom. I manage my own time, plan my own working days and take holidays during term-time. It is also great to know that I am supporting a charity I care about.*

Q And the disadvantages?

A *As a small and financially challenged charity, there is no administrative support. In many ways, the role is like that of a headteacher, except that you also have to do your own typing, photocopying, and so on. I also miss having a senior management team with whom to share ideas and develop strategy.*

Q Would you recommend the role to others, and do you have any tips?

A *Oh yes, it is extremely rewarding and worthwhile. You could not, however, do something like this alongside a paid job. If you want to make a significant voluntary contribution to a charity, make sure you do not need to earn an income. In many respects, the role is ideal for a retired teacher who wants to remain active, use their management expertise to make a difference and does not need to supplement a pension.*

Llys Nini Animal Centre

Llys Nini Animal Centre in Swansea is a local charity caring for hundreds of animals each year. It receives none of its running costs from the national RSPCA and relies on local donations to care for the rescued animals. To join the Safe Haven Scheme, visit www.llysnini-rspca.org.uk. You can also register with www.everyclick.com and pick RSPCA Llys Nini as your charity. Every search or click you then make will earn cash for the animals.

Case study

From assistant head to . . . barman in a village pub

Ed had taken early retirement from his position as assistant head of a large comprehensive. With time on his hands, he was looking out for part-time work to supplement his pension when he noticed an advertisement for bar staff at his local pub:

Q What made you decide to work in a pub?

A *Although I wanted to supplement my pension, I was not looking to start a new career or take on anything particularly demanding. The pub was in the village where I live, so I didn't have any travel expenses and I enjoyed being able to walk to work. The hours also suited me. I only worked for three-hour shifts over four lunchtimes, so the rest of the week was mine to do with as I wished.*

Q What did the work involve?

A *What you'd expect, really: serving behind the bar, taking customers' food orders, serving meals and clearing tables, writing bills and taking payments. The job offered quite a lot of variety and social contact. You are always busy, mostly on your feet and never bored!*

Q Did you use any of your teaching skills?

A *I was surprised at how useful my interpersonal skills turned out to be. As an assistant head, I had dealt with all sorts of people and a range of different situations. Although a pub in a sleepy village does not generate a lot of problems, there were occasions when I had to draw on my ability to handle tricky situations in a calm, controlled manner. The other teaching-related skill that came in useful was my awareness of people's needs. Like all teachers, I have a sixth sense for what is happening throughout the room, and I could always spot that*

continued

a customer was waiting to be served or that tables needed to be cleared.

Q Any disadvantages?

A *Only the pay! It was barely above the minimum wage, so you would struggle to survive on your earnings alone, even if you worked full time.*

Q You have moved on from the job now. Would you recommend it to others?

A *Although I enjoyed my time as a barman, I wanted to try other pursuits. However, I would definitely recommend the job to anyone who enjoys being sociable and is happy to deal with the general public on a day-to-day basis. If you have taken early retirement and moved to a new area, it's also a great way to get to know people – whether you need the money or not.*

Case study

From head of drama to . . . tour guide, civil celebrant, TV extra, film maker, theatre treasurer . . .

Having run a drama department in a large comprehensive school for nearly thirty years, Peter had had enough of the management and administration side of teaching and he decided to take early retirement. He did not, however, go for the option of a quiet retirement, and over the past couple of years he has built up a wide portfolio of both paid and unpaid work.

Q You seem to be just as busy now as when you were teaching full time. Describe your various jobs.

A *It makes quite a long list! I work as a tour guide for Casterbridge Tours, guiding parties of US students around*

London, Scotland and France; I conduct naming and partnership ceremonies for a civil celebrant company; I am working in conjunction with an ex-colleague, filming a series of pro-grammes based on 'Maths in the Community' for use in schools; I work as an extra for film and TV companies; I am currently providing technical support with the lighting for a newly com-missioned opera and directing a one-man play, prior to its UK tour; and I am also the treasurer for a Bristol-based theatre company and an executive member and treasurer of National Drama, a teacher association.

Q Working as a tour guide sounds interesting. How did you come across that job and what does it involve?

A *An advert in one of the local papers put me in touch with Casterbridge Tours and I trained with them as a tour guide. I have now run several tours for them, stayed in some great hotels, seen places I haven't been to for years and met some terrific staff and students from American schools. Some of the tours are with choral groups, so I have also attended some wonderful concerts in churches and cathedrals across the UK.*

Q . . . and conducting naming and partnership ceremonies?

A *A civil celebrant company was advertising for celebrants in my area. Having previously arranged my granddaughter's naming ceremony, and enjoyed both the preparation and the day itself, the role appealed to me. The initial training was a straight-forward 'hands-on' process, with the opportunity to work through a number of prepared ceremonies. The business side of things has also turned out to be very straightforward. The company sends me details of the event, I have a brief meeting with everyone involved and then spend a very pleasant couple of hours surrounded by happy families of all generations.*

Q . . . and your work as a film and TV extra?

A *This partly came about through a former student, who was directing a film in my home town and asked me to be a part of it. However, the bulk of my work comes through a local agency*

continued

who provide extras for various television dramas. Although the shoots are sometimes held at night, the hours are long and it is often cold and wet, overall, working as an extra is great fun. The food is good, you get to meet some really interesting people (including well-known actors) and you have your eleven seconds of fame!

Q Do all these different roles and responsibilities generate a lot of administrative work?

A Yes – just organising my diary is quite a task in itself. I also have to keep on top of accounts, invoices and tax returns, and some of my jobs involve additional home-based work such as preparing notes for tour guides, editing film for the maths project and reading reports and papers in connection with my voluntary roles.

Q What are the advantages of your new working life, compared with teaching?

A With very few exceptions, I can do what I want when I want – without being governed by a bell! Sometime I might simply choose to go for a walk, just because the sun is out. I also enjoy meeting and working with lots of people who say, 'yes, that's interesting' rather than an instinctive 'no'.

Q And the disadvantages?

A Unlike teaching, the income is not constant – although that is not such a problem if you have reached the point where you can draw your pension. Chasing up invoices is a nuisance, and working alone can sometimes seem strange after being in a school for thirty years.

Q How did you go about developing such a wide portfolio of jobs and do you have any tips for those who would like to follow a similar path?

A I have been struck by the fact that there are so many opportunities out there that one is unable to discover or pursue while teaching full time. You need to keep a constant lookout for possibilities and read all the job adverts, including the local 'throwaway' newspapers. Let everyone know what you are doing and that you are open to offers. Working on the maths project came about because an ex-colleague knew that I had filming and editing experience, and that I was available to help out. My advice to anyone who wants to follow a similar path is to go ahead, take the plunge . . . and network!

Chapter 5

Effectively developing your career . . . the practical implications

Making a career move is a major life change that involves a large amount of planning. This chapter covers the practicalities of taking your career in a new direction, and explores the following areas:

- auditing and planning your finances to help you through a job change;
- looking into the effects a career change might have on your pension;
- making choices about the right direction for you;
- working as a freelance, becoming self-employed and running a small business;
- the different mindset required to work in a setting other than a school or college.

Auditing your finances

Working out your financial situation is an essential part of making a career change. How much do you need to earn? Can you allow yourself a period of reduced income? How will changing jobs affect your pension?

As a starting point, make a list of all your outgoings alongside any income (apart from the job you are vacating). This will enable you to work out how much you need to earn in order to function. Tables 1 and 2 (see pages 194 and 195) may come in useful.

If you are lucky enough to make a seamless move from your teaching job to a new role with a commensurate salary, your financial planning can probably end here. If, however, it takes a while to find a new job, *or* you want to build up a portfolio career, *or* you want to downsize and accept a reduced salary, you may have to make some savings. The following suggestions cover just some of the economies you could consider:

- **Clothes**: look into cutting clothes purchases to the essentials or even managing on what you already have until you are more financially stable. (Charity shops can be a great source of cheap clothing – with the added benefit of helping the charity!)
- **Food**: explore ways of cutting down on your food bill – by eating out less often, avoiding takeaways, shopping in cut-price stores, bulk buying where possible, using supermarket 'value' products, bulk cooking and making good use of your freezer . . .
- **Entertainment**: although enjoying your leisure time is important to your well-being, there may be some painless savings you can make. Replace trips to the swimming pool with brisk walks; rent a DVD rather than going to the cinema; entertain friends at home rather than taking them out for dinner . . .
- **Mortgage breaks**: explore whether it is possible to take a brief mortgage break, making interest-only payments while you sort yourself out. Do, however, be absolutely clear about the long-term effects; as with any major financial decision, seek professional advice.
- **Changing loans**: explore the possibility of reducing monthly loan repayments by taking out a loan over a longer period of time. Although you will end up paying more interest for the duration of the loan, you may feel this is a worthwhile cost if it helps you to cut your monthly outgoings. One thing to consider: it may not be so easy to get a loan if you have already given up your job or reduced your income. Seek professional advice to discuss the pros and cons of this particular option.
- **Switching credit cards**: although 0 per cent credit card deals are no longer so easy to find, it is still worth looking out for a credit card company that offers better terms and/or a cashback scheme. Ask advice from an independent adviser or search the internet to find out what is available. Do, however, make sure that you read the small print. Added extras such as a transfer fee may soak up any advantage offered by a lower interest rate.
- **Using savings**: if you have been saving 'for a rainy day', decide whether this is it. One possible option is to use savings to reduce or even pay off your mortgage. Given that mortgage repayments make up the largest financial outgoing for many people, this can give you a sense of freedom, quite apart from helping you to balance your finances. Once again, seek professional advice.

Table 1 Listing your outgoings

Outgoings	Cost (£)
Mortgage/rent	
Loan repayments	
Credit card payments	
Utilities (e.g. gas, electricity, water)	
Council tax	
Insurances (e.g. mortgage, life, sickness, disability, house content, domestic appliances)	
Car running costs (e.g. fuel, tax, insurance, estimated repairs, membership of breakdown service)	
Other travel costs (e.g. buses, trains, taxis)	
Telephone bills (including mobile and internet)	
Healthcare costs (e.g. private health cover, dental insurance/costs, optician, prescription charges)	
Savings plans	
Children's schooling costs (e.g. school fees, school trips, extra-curricular lessons and activities, meals)	
Childcare costs	
Children's pocket money/allowances	
Pets (include food and accessories, vet's bills/insurance, kennel bills)	
Food	
Clothes (including dependants)	
Entertainment (e.g. sports-related subscriptions, eating out, theatre and cinema, TV licence, satellite TV, newspapers and magazines – include costs for dependants)	
Any other outgoings	
Any other outgoings	
Any other outgoings	
Total	£

Table 2 Listing your income

Income source	Income (£)
Pension	
Partner's income/pension	
Child benefit	
Family tax credits	
Share dividends	
Interest on savings	
Any earned income from additional sources (e.g. exam marking, tutoring)	
Any other income	
Any other income	
Any other income	
Total	£

- **Taking a lodger**: if you have your own home with a spare room, consider making use of it. Taking in a lodger may not appeal to everyone, but it can be a relatively simple way of earning extra cash when you most need it.
- **Eligibility for tax credits, allowances or grants**: check whether you are eligible for any support. For example, if you earn below a certain amount, you may be entitled to the Working Tax Credit. If you are starting a business, you may qualify for allowances or grants. For more information on tax credits, contact HM Revenue and Customs (www.hmrc.gov.uk). For information about business grants, contact Business Link (www.businesslink. gov.uk).
- **'Make do and mend'**: if you find your life balance has shifted to a 'time rich/money poor' scenario, try doing your own decorating, gardening, cleaning, ironing and DIY jobs around the house. You can also have great fun renovating the old rather than buying new. Give those bookshelves a new lease of life with a coat of paint; patch the tear in the spare-room duvet cover rather than

replacing it . . . Such thrift will make you feel very virtuous as well as saving you money!

- **Be organised**: if you tend not to keep a close eye on the 'infra-structure' of your life, try to be a little more organised. Late payment penalties, bank charges for going overdrawn, library fines and parking tickets can all add up to quite a lot of wasted cash – not something you want when you are watching every penny.
- **Selling things**: do you have some saleable items that you could quite happily live without? If you don't think you would miss Aunt Edna's silver candlesticks, find out whether a local antique dealer or auction house might be interested. Do, however, think carefully about selling sentimental possessions; it's easy to end up regretting the sale of a precious item once you are through your lean period.
- **Major downsizing**: if you are serious about downsizing your working life or taking early retirement, consider freeing up capital and/or cutting mortgage payments by moving to a less expensive house (although don't forget to factor in the costs of moving). A slightly less drastic option is to buy a cheaper car. If your current car is high maintenance, you could make quite considerable savings in petrol, insurance and repair bills by going for something smaller and more economical.

These are just a few suggestions. There may be many other savings that you can make, and every individual will differ in what they do or do not regard as essential to their lives. When you actually start planning how to economise, it can be quite exhilarating to pare down your needs and requirements to the basics. If you find it difficult to cut back, keep reminding yourself that your thrift will (hopefully) only have to be short term, and that it is helping you towards a better lifestyle.

At this stage in your planning, it is a good idea to consult an independent financial adviser – particularly when it comes to major decisions about mortgages, the best use of savings, and switching loans and credit cards. An independent adviser will still have a vested interest in selling you certain financial services, but they will not be affiliated to any particular institution, and it is in their professional interest to give you the soundest possible advice. To find a financial adviser, visit www.aifa.net. Another route is to seek personal recom-mendations from friends and acquaintances or ask your teaching union whether they have a list of approved financial advisers who can offer the kind of support you are looking for.

Once you have carried out your financial audit and sought professional advice, it may be worth thinking about the timing of your career change. Staying in your current role for a year or two longer could give you the time to put economies in place and even pay off loans, reduce your mortgage and accrue savings. Getting your finances sorted out and running smoothly will free you up to concentrate exclusively on your new career.

Checking pension provision

Checking your pension is a very important part of your financial planning. If you leave teaching altogether, how will this affect your future pension provision? Will you be in a position to make up the shortfall? Does your partner have a pension that you can count into your future planning?

If you decide to leave teaching before reaching pensionable age, there are currently four possible options:

- You may be able to transfer your pension rights to another scheme, although this is dependent on the new scheme being willing to accept them.
- You may be able to take a 'repayment of contributions', as long as you do not qualify for benefits and have been out of pensionable employment for at least a month.
- If you leave teaching temporarily, you may be able to pay both your contributions and your employer's contributions for a limited period of time.
- You can leave the benefits you have accrued in the scheme to draw as a reduced pension once you reach pensionable age. At the time of writing, this will be index-linked from the date at which you leave teaching.

If you choose to take a part-time teaching job and wish your earnings to be treated as pensionable, the onus is on you to inform the Teachers' Pension Scheme. If you want to take early retirement, you may be able to draw an actuarially reduced pension. This can be a useful option in helping you bridge the gap between full- and part-time work (at the time of writing, there was no ceiling on the amount you are allowed to earn on top of your reduced pension). You do, however, need to consider how you will manage with a reduced pension if and when you are unable to make up the shortfall through part-time work.

In planning how a job move will affect your pension, your partner's pension provision is also something to take into consideration. Do, however, find out what entitlement you will have should your partner predecease you. For example, at the time of writing, the Teachers' Pension Scheme entitles a widow or widower to half their spouse's pension – but only if they are married or have entered into a civil partnership.

Pensions can be a minefield and things are constantly changing. The above information gives some indication of the possibilities, but we cannot overemphasise the importance of checking how *any* intended career change might affect your entitlement, or whether it makes sound financial sense to draw your pension early. For up-to-date and reliable information, visit www.teacherspensions.co.uk. If you belong to one of the teaching unions, they may also be able to give you appropriate advice.

Making choices

The impetus for developing your career as an educationalist, or diversifying into a different role, will vary from person to person. Some individuals come across, or are offered, opportunities that can be taken up alongside their full-time teaching career. Others choose to take a career break, for a variety of reasons, and then look to return to a role outside the classroom. There are also many teachers who take early retirement or decide to go part time and then look for work to supplement their pension or reduced income. Whatever your circumstances, unless you are one of the lucky few who finds a new job dropping into your lap, you will need to think through your requirements and the kinds of roles that will suit your needs. As a part of this planning, try asking yourself the following questions:

HOW MUCH DO I NEED TO EARN?

This is a key question for many of us; how much do you need to earn in order to support your current lifestyle and financial commitments such as mortgages, outstanding loans and dependants (for more on financial planning, see pages 192–7). If you require an income equating to a full-time teacher's salary, decide whether you want to achieve this through a single job or whether you could do so with a portfolio career made up of part-time roles (for more on this, see 'Becoming self-employed', page 207 and 'From deputy head to . . . a portfolio career', page 215). In spite of the teaching profession's perennial complaints about pay levels, not all education-related jobs will comfortably give you an equitable salary, particularly if you have responsibility points. As another possibility, a complete change of career may give you more scope for high earnings (see Chapter 4).

For some people, income is less of a concern, either because they are retired and have a pension or because they need only to supplement a partner's income. If you are in this fortunate position, you can focus to a much greater extent on what you want to do rather than how much you have to earn. If income is of little importance, consider a voluntary role such as working for a charity (page 38). This will give you the opportunity to use a variety of skills and the chance to meet new people and contribute to the community without the financial and bureaucratic complications of taking on salaried work.

WHEN DO I WANT TO WORK?

Your reasons for changing career or diversifying into a new role will often have a direct bearing on when you can work. If you have no family commitments and lots of energy, you may feel able to take on a job with variable or unsociable hours; for example, becoming a trainer and INSET provider (see page 51) or additional inspector (see page 120) will take you the length and breadth of the country, with overnight stays and an irregular working timetable. Alternatively, if you have children or other responsibilities as a carer, you might want to consider jobs that involve an evening commitment or can be fitted around school hours. It is also worth thinking about the kind of time-table that will suit you. If you tend to be a bit of a night owl, you should have no trouble teaching evening classes or running a youth club. Alternatively, if you prefer a regular life and like to keep your evenings, weekends and holiday periods sacrosanct, check out what extra commitments a job may involve. For example, although running a Brownie pack generally takes up just one evening a week, you may have to commit to some weekend activities and summer camps.

Balancing the number of hours you work with the income you require is yet another consideration. Assuming that you have to earn a given amount, do you want to work shorter hours in a more demanding job or longer hours in a less high-powered role? For example, your fee for giving one conference speech would probably equate to a month's earnings as a teaching assistant. The question to ask yourself is whether you are willing to deal with the short-term but potentially high stress levels of public speaking, or whether you are willing to accept longer hours for the sake of less stress and responsibility.

WITH WHOM DO I WANT TO WORK?

The vast majority of education-related jobs involve working with people. To get some idea of the demographic group with whom you want to work, ask yourself which aspects of your teaching role you particularly enjoy:

- **Working with groups**: if you feel that you would miss the 'performance' element of teaching, consider jobs that involve working with groups, for example running extra-curricular clubs for children (see page 30), teaching adults (see page 41) or running a summer school (see page 35).
- **Working with individuals**: do you particularly value the (often all too rare) opportunity to work with children as individuals? If so, consider tutoring (see page 81) or mentoring (see page 10).
- **Supporting colleagues**: have you discovered a penchant for liaising with and supporting colleagues? Becoming a subject adviser (see page 68), trainer (see page 51) or education consultant would give you lots of opportunity to make the most of these skills.
- **Working with a different age group**: would you like to change age groups? Look out for roles that offer you the chance to work with your chosen age group, for example volunteering for a local youth club or Rainbow group (see page 31). This will help you find out whether you enjoy working with a particular age range. Switching from one sector to another is also an option (see page 57).
- **Teaching adults**: have you had enough of working with children altogether, but don't want to waste your years of teaching experience? If you fit into this category, adult education (see page 45) or becoming an NVQ assessor (see page 19) are two roles that are worth considering.

WHAT NATURE OF WORK AM I LOOKING FOR?

If you want to be happy in your new role, this is one of the most important questions to ask yourself. One option is to look at any possibility that comes up and then decide whether or not the job appeals. If, however, you prefer to plan in advance, it can be helpful to think about which of the many aspects of teaching you wish to continue in a new role:

* **Subject specific**: if you want to remain working within your subject area, there are many teaching opportunities outside schools. Adult education (see page 45), tutoring (see page 81) or working in summer schools (see page 35) all enable you to continue teaching your subject. If you want to use your subject knowledge in ways other than actual teaching, you could consider examining work (see pages 73 and 76), becoming an advisory teacher (see page 68), working for a subject association (see page 84), writing about your subject for educational publications (see page 101) or roles that include supporting, coaching and training colleagues (see pages 51, 68 and 132).
* **Support roles with young people**: if you have experience of working in a pastoral role and enjoy this aspect of teaching, you may want to consider a job such as mentoring disaffected students (see page 10), working in a youth club (see page 30), becoming a personal adviser for Connexions (see page 14) or even training as an educational psychologist.
* **Leisure pursuits**: if you want to encourage young people to use their leisure time in positive ways, consider working in a holiday playscheme, summer school or out-of-school club (see page 35), a youth club (see page 30) or for the Guide or Scout movement. Look out also for privately run groups where your skills as a teacher of sport, dance, music, drama or art and craft will be much appreciated (see page 30).

HOW MUCH RESPONSIBILITY DO I WANT?

Many individuals choose to take a different career direction in order to reduce their levels of stress. If you want less responsibility but still want to work with children (and can afford a cut in salary), becoming a teaching assistant (see page 15) may be worth considering. You could also look into teaching part time and supplementing your income with other, less demanding work. It is, however, essential to think clearly and honestly about the aspects of your current job that you personally find stressful. On paper, the majority of teaching assistant jobs carry less responsibility than that of the fully qualified teacher, but if you know you would find it difficult to relinquish the relative autonomy and control of the classroom teacher, you may simply end up swapping one type of stress for another. Similarly, while a portfolio career can be highly fulfilling, some people find self-employment more stressful than even the toughest demands of a regular teaching job. Try putting different aspects of your job into two columns marked 'enjoyable' and 'stressful' and analyse the results. If you can make the list as comprehensive as possible, you may be surprised at what emerges and just how much it can tell you about the kind of work you should be looking for. For an example, see the list compiled by our case study, primary school teacher Harriet (Table 3), along with an analysis of her responses (Table 4).

Table 3 Auditing your stress

Enjoyable	Stressful
I do a lot of work with children on a one-to-one basis or in small groups, helping them with their literacy – I love doing this as I can properly get to grips with their difficulties.	We have a number of children with quite severe behavioural difficulties. I find challenging behaviour hard to deal with in the context of the classroom – I'm OK one-to-one, but sometimes I find it tricky to keep on top of the whole class.
When a child opens up to me with their worries, I really value the trust they are placing in me and I take my pastoral role seriously. It's what makes the job worthwhile for me.	I worry that the quieter, less demanding children will miss out because of the time and attention I have to give to those children with difficulties. Sometimes I feel that I don't have the time or space to do anything properly.
I enjoy planning lessons, preparing resources and putting up displays. I love using my art and graphic design skills to make my classroom a stimulating and attractive learning environment – and getting the kids' input!	School trips! I hate the responsibility of taking the children into the 'big wide world'. I'm happier within the safety of my classroom where I can keep an eye on all of them.
Unlike many of my colleagues, I don't mind marking and record keeping. I also quite enjoy the challenge of getting to grips with new initiatives.	I find parents' evenings difficult. If I sense any criticism, I feel really

Table 3 continued

Enjoyable	Stressful
Most of my colleagues get frustrated with the changes and they often ask me to 'fill them in', knowing that I will probably be quite up to date. Giving presentations to colleagues and parents – I quite enjoy doing this, as long as I have time to prepare. I do get nervous, but the nerves are manageable compared with a difficult parents' evening. I love the staff camaraderie in my school. I've always found the vast majority of my colleagues to be tremendously supportive – and appreciative of the support I give to them, both as their literacy co-ordinator and as a friend. Even though I have responsibility for literacy, I love teaching the whole curriculum. I did an English degree but I think I'd have got bored just teaching English. As a primary school teacher, I've become an 'expert' in subjects such as maths, science and ICT. I get a real kick from helping a child get to grips with his sums and I understand his difficulties because I struggled with maths, too!	guilty and worry that I'm letting them and their child down. I need to learn not to take things so personally. I'm not always brilliant at making quick, on-the-spot decisions. I dealt well with a recent stealing incident because I was able to think through how to handle it – but I know I'm not always at my best when I have to handle a tricky situation there and then. I can find the sheer number of people stressful to deal with – school is a busy and teeming place! I love it when everyone's gone home and I can sort out my classroom alone and in peace!

Table 4 Analysis of Harriet's stress audit

Harriet enjoys working with individuals and small groups, but finds dealing with large numbers of pupils stressful – particularly when she also has to handle behavioural difficulties. She does, however, enjoy supporting children with problems and takes her pastoral role seriously. Tutoring individual children (page 81), or mentoring work (page 10) might be worth considering. She could also look into running extra-curricular activities with small groups (page 30), perhaps drawing on her interest in art and craft.

continued

Table 4 continued

Harriet enjoys working with colleagues. She also likes getting to grips with new initiatives and appears to be skilled at disseminating information to her colleagues. Once she has enough management experience, she could consider becoming an advisory teacher (page 68) or a trainer (page 132). Given that she can cope with the demands of public speaking, she might also consider contributing to conferences.

Harriet enjoys preparing resources and planning lessons. With her background in English and her role as literacy co-ordinator, writing for educational magazines and journals might appeal to her (page 101). As she enjoys 'time to herself', she would probably cope well with the solitary nature of writing. She could also consider a future role working on curriculum planning (page 112) or becoming an HMI (page 125).

Harriet finds 'on-the-spot' situations difficult to deal with and is nervous of taking responsibility for children in the outside world. Jobs that involve trips, camps and Outward Bound activities are probably best avoided. Although she seems to have the skills for pastoral work, she might be more comfortable working within the school environment as a learning mentor (page 10) or school counsellor, rather than less structured environments such as youth work (page 30) or holiday play schemes (page 35).

WHERE DO I WANT TO WORK?

Most teachers have little choice over their workplace. They spend by far the greater part of their day in the school that appointed them and do not usually have much say over which classroom they are allocated. Changing jobs and developing your career beyond the classroom brings with it the opportunity to think about your working environment, and make some choices:

- **Staying in schools or colleges**: if you like the buzz of a school or college, the staffroom camaraderie and the huge variety of different events all taking place within the one location, consider going for roles that keep you on school premises. If you want the chance to visit lots of different schools (which can be fascinating), look into roles such as mentoring (see page 10), or becoming a subject adviser (see page 68), an inspector (see page 123) or an education consultant (see page 204).
- **Other workplaces**: a number of teachers want to get away from educational institutions altogether. The majority of jobs within the field of education are, inevitably, based in schools or colleges. If, however, you like the prospect of visiting other types of work-

place, such as shops, offices, estate agencies, hairdressers and care homes, investigate becoming an NVQ assessor (see page 205) or getting involved in business and vocational education (see page 144). Contributing to education conferences and courses (see page 51) can also take you into the hotel-based world of corporate events – generally a more luxurious environment than the average school or college!

- **Working from home**: working from home is yet another possibility to consider. Because educational work revolves around schools and colleges, the options for home-based work are more limited. However, educational writing (see page 101) and examining work (see page 73) can both be completed at home, although you will need to keep abreast of current trends in schools and attend examiners' meetings. A number of roles also involve having a home-based office. As an inspector (see page 123), freelance trainer (see page 182) or educational consultant (see page 132), you will need to carry out preparation and paperwork at home. For more on the practicalities of home working, see page 214.

Summary

Some key questions to consider when seeking a new role:

Earnings

How much do I need to earn?
Do I need an income to equate with a full-time teacher's salary or am I aiming just to supplement a pension or partner's wage?
Can I afford to do voluntary work?

Timetables

When can I work?
Do I need a regular 'nine to five' timetable or can I work unsociable hours?
Can I be flexible, working as and when required?
Do I need to keep weekends and holiday periods free?

---

continued

Do I need a job that will fit around school hours or other responsibilities as a carer?

Students and colleagues

With which age group do I want to work?
Do I want to change sector?
Do I want to work with groups or individuals?
Do I want to teach adults or work with colleagues in an advisory or support capacity?
Would I prefer to work alone?

Stress and responsibility

What elements of my current job do I find stressful and would prefer to avoid in a new role?
What elements of my current job do I find enjoyable? Are there any jobs that would offer me similar experiences?
Am I wanting to decrease my levels of responsibility when I change roles?
Am I wanting to decrease my levels of stress when I change roles?
Am I happy to take on more responsibility?

Location

Do I want to remain working in a school or college?
Would I enjoy visiting lots of different schools or colleges?
Would I like the opportunity to work in locations other than educational institutions?
Am I happy to work nationally and stay away from home when necessary – on a regular basis or just occasionally?
Would I prefer to be based in a single workplace or am I happy to visit a variety of different workplaces?

Becoming self-employed

Depending on the career path you choose to take, you may find yourself joining the ranks of the self-employed. This can be a very different experience from working as an employee. As a self-employed worker, you will need to develop a completely different mindset and take total responsibility for all aspects of your working life – from administration and paperwork to time management, marketing yourself and negotiating contracts.

Administration, paperwork and other practicalities

When our case study, Karen (see Table 3), switched from being an employee to working for herself, she was amazed at how much she had to take on board. From invoicing clients to filling in her own self-assessment tax forms and organising stationery, running a business added a whole new dimension to her working life. We asked her what practical advice she would give to anyone thinking of following in her footsteps.

Get information: when I started, I knew absolutely nothing about running a business or becoming self-employed. Someone recommended Business Link (www.businesslink.gov.uk) and I had a session with one of their advisers. I was a bit anxious as I wasn't very knowledgeable about the field of business, but they immediately put me at my ease. They went through the basics and flagged up some issues that I would never have thought of – such as checking with my mortgage lender about working from home. They also recommended that I take one of their many courses, and I chose a start-up training course which covered issues such as planning, marketing, finance and accounting.

Another important source of information was the HM Revenue and Customs website and helplines (www.hmrc.gov.uk). Whenever I had to deal with official requirements such as tax and national insurance, I found it very reassuring to know that I could get information from 'the horse's mouth'.

Get professional indemnity and public liability insurance: if you are a freelance who works with a range of clients and/or visits different workplaces, it is essential to take out insurance. Professional indemnity insurance gives you cover if a claim is made against you for negligence, error or omission during the course of your work. Public liability insurance gives you cover in the event of any party suffering injury, disease or death as a result of your business activities. These insurances tend not to be cheap, but they are well worth budgeting for. You never know when something might happen, and it is one less thing to worry about if you know you are covered.

Find a good accountant: for me, getting an accountant was (and still is) an essential. I know it's another cost, but my accountant paid for herself within a year by ensuring that my self-assessment tax form was filled in correctly. She also identified outgoings that I could include as legitimate expenses – most of which I would never have thought of. Also, time is money! It would take me at least two days to get through what my accountant does for me. That's two days I can be out there earning, and as long as I am working at my usual rates, I can make enough to cover my accountant's fee. Even now, talking about 'my accountant' helps me to feel like a real businesswoman – and it's reassuring to have a trustworthy and knowledgeable professional on board, particularly when 'self-assessment' time is approaching.

Self-assessment tax forms: after years of having tax deducted at source (and trying not to think about what I was paying), filling in my own self-assessment form came as a bit of a shock. Mine is doubly complicated because I do lots of different jobs. I was glad to have my accountant around and very glad that I had kept meticulous records. My advice is to give yourself plenty of time and be organised. Mark the deadlines in your work diary and make sure you really do have all your records in order and to hand. If you end up passing the whole lot over to your accountant, do remember that it is still your responsibility to ensure that the form is accurate and sent in on time.

For more information on self assessment, visit www.hmrc.gov. uk/sa.

Paying National Insurance: National Insurance is something else I didn't have to think about as an employed teacher. National Insurance goes towards healthcare, benefits and pensions, and it is payable as a percentage of your earnings, above a certain threshold. There are four different classes of National Insurance contribution and the type you pay depends on whether you are employed or self-employed, how much you earn and whether or not you are an employer. I have to admit, I completely forgot about National Insurance for the first six months of my new working life! I suddenly realised I should be paying it and contacted HM Revenue and Customs in a panic. They were very helpful and supportive; they calculated what I owed in arrears and worked out what type of National Insurance I should be paying. They also offered me the option of setting up a monthly direct debit, a payment option I was very glad to take up!

For more information, visit www.hmrc.gov.uk/nic.

Budget for tax and National Insurance: putting aside money to pay your tax and National Insurance sounds obvious, but it's easy to end up being faced with large bills and insufficient funds to pay them. I make a point of saving as I go along and ensure that I have the bulk of the money put aside well before the deadline for payment. I am also very strict about not plundering my tax fund. I'm sure some people are able to keep on top of moving their finances around, but I need to keep things as straightforward as possible.

Keeping records: record keeping is a legal requirement, and filling in your self-assessment tax form depends on your records. From the moment I started working for myself, I kept everything. I probably go a bit over the top but I always feel it's better to be safe than sorry. The main items to keep are as follows:

- Receipts for any purchase linked to your working life: stationery, fuel, printer ink, business lunches . . .
- Records of bank statements and building society books (if you don't have a separate business account, you need to be able to demonstrate what is related to business and what is personal).
- Statements of interest earned from share dividends.
- Copies of invoices (see 'Getting payments', below).
- Electricity and gas bills for lighting and heating.
- Phone bills for both landline and mobile.

Different people have different ways of organising their records. My method has evolved through trial and error and I now have a simple sheet for each month with columns for income and expenditure [see Table 5]. I try to be strict about filling it in on a regular basis; it's amazing how quickly I lose track of what I did last week. Once the sheet is completed, I put it in a clear plastic pocket and then add that month's receipts, invoices and any other documentation such

Table 5 Karen Smith's expenses

Month: Feb-07

Income				Expenditure		
Date	Item	Amount		Date	Item	Amount
14.02.07	EXAMINATION FEE (INCLUDING MILEAGE)	£146		9.02.07	TRAIN FARE	£52.50
19.02.07	CONSULTANCY FEE	£300		6.02.07	UNDERGROUND FARE	£5.20
24.02.07	INSPECTION FEE	£800		6.02.07	POSTAGE	£5.20
				9.02.07	STATIONERY	£4.47
				14.02.07	FUEL	£10.08
				14.02.07	MEAL	£20.35
				19.02.07	ACCOMMODATION – B & B	£50
				21.02.07	FEES TO PROFESSIONAL BODY	£34
				22.02.07	FUEL	£25
				25.02.07	VIRUS SCAN FEE	£91.65
				25.02.07	PHOTOCOPIES	£1.20
				26.02.07	FUEL	£29
				26.02.07	COMPUTER CARTRIDGES	£14.97

as remittance advice slips. By the end of the year, I have twelve pockets (one for each month). It's a simple system but it works for me. The one downside is lack of space; if I have a busy month, the plastic pocket can get quite full!

The one set of paperwork I do keep separately is my gas, electricity and phone bills. When you are self-employed and work from home, it can be tricky to calculate what costs are generated by your working life and what counts as private usage. I now hand all the bills over to my accountant and she works out an appropriate percentage to be set against tax – yet another good reason for having an accountant.

Getting payments: after years of having a monthly salary paid directly into my account, chasing up payments was quite a departure for me. When I first started working for myself, I got behind with sending off invoices – which led to a few cash flow problems! Now I set aside one day a month for invoicing. In order to work out what I need to claim for that month, I go back through my diary and highlight the organisations I have worked for, along with the hours and the job; for example:

For invoices, I have a template on my computer which I fill in and either e-mail or print out and post, depending on what the company prefers (see Table 7). Some companies ask you to complete a claim form, and I always keep a photocopy to add to my files.

Once the cheques arrive, they have to be paid in, of course! I am strict about keeping my paying-in book counterfoils up to date and I also use internet banking so that I can get immediate access to my statements. When you have a diverse income like mine, it is particularly important to keep track of your account. I have a spreadsheet on the computer so that I can list all the invoices and claim forms I send out, and record when a payment arrives. It's surprisingly easy to lose track of a cheque, although life is getting easier on this front as more and more companies make payments via BACS (an electronic service that enables a company to transfer payments directly into your account, rather than having to send a cheque).

Storing your records: I was advised to hang on to my records for at least five years and also to keep a paper copy of anything that started out on paper, such as bank statements. Although I store all my invoices on the computer, I always keep a printout and I photocopy claim forms to add to my monthly records. Any significant e-mails get printed out and stored as paper copies. Even if you prefer to work

Table 6 Page from Karen Smith's diary

May 2006

8 Monday
a.m. – check NVQ assessment visits
1.30 to 3.30 Burton St John's School, student mentoring
late p.m. – write up note of visit for BSJ mentoring

9 Tuesday
Child protection course at Total Care Training: 10.00 to 4.30

10 Wednesday
9.30 – 3.30 Netherfield Training, NQT course
6.00 p.m – catch train to Wroxton

11 Thursday
1 day Wroxton High inspection (8.30 start)
6.15 p.m – train home

12 Friday
9.00 – 12.00 Kings School NQT assessment
2.00 Gym
4.30 hairdresser

13 Saturday
Meet Helen for lunch – 12.30 at The Bakehouse

14 Sunday
a.m. – catch up on additional note of visit for Fri / AST report
E-mail JS / TH / LM re conference

solely on your computer, I do think a printout acts as a useful safety net. It's also worth using software to make an automatic back-up copy for any computer files you create. If you lose vital records, it can cause a major headache when it comes to filling in your tax form.

Look into allowances and grants: it is well worth checking whether you are eligible for any support while you get yourself going. A change in your financial circumstances might affect your Child Tax

Table 7 Sample invoice

KAREN SMITH
14 WILLOW CLOSE
SHARPLEY
KENT
SH4 3ZQ

• •

INVOICE

To: Netherfield Training
Sharpley
Kent

Date: 31st October 2006

invoice number	date	task	fee
53	1st October and 3rd October 2006	*Assessment of 2 NVQ candidates (Gemma Jackson and Robert Timpson)	£200
		*Travel 20 miles @ 35p per mile	£7
		*Photocopying – 15 sheets @ 10p each	£1.50
	15th October 2006	*Child Protection Training – 1 day	£300
		*Travel – 45 miles @ 35p per mile	£15.75
		total	£524.25

Please make cheques payable to Ms K Smith

phone: 01333 777888
e-mail: ktraining@internet.com

Credit, and if you are on a low income you could be entitled to the Working Tax Credit. There may also be grants available for new businesses. When I started out, there was local help on offer for any business that could provide employment for up to six people and for small businesses with an environmental theme. As I didn't fall into either of these categories, I wasn't eligible for any support, but it's always worth checking. HM Revenue and Customs can give you information about tax credits, while Business Link will let you know what grants might be around.

Business stationery: I was advised to have my own headed paper, business cards and compliment slips. It does make you seem more professional, and I now regard it as part of my 'identity' as an educational consultant. It's worth spending a bit of time on colour and design and choosing something eye-catching and memorable. I would recommend contacting a local printer, who should be able to advise on design as well as produce your stationery for you.

Working from home: although I visit schools, colleges, training centres and companies in various capacities, I need to have a home-based office for preparation, paperwork and administration. This has turned out to be a little more complicated than I anticipated. Apart from keeping energy and phone bills for my accountant to offset against tax [see 'Keeping records', above], I also had to check insurance, mortgage and business rates. The advice I was given included the following:

- *Home contents insurance:* some insurance companies won't include work-related equipment in their house contents cover. Others have a limited threshold that you can quickly go over once you start totting up the value of items such as computers and furniture. Contact your insurer, and if you find that you are not adequately covered, consider asking an insurance broker to find you a policy designed specifically for home workers.
- *The mortgage:* rates for commercial loans are higher than those for domestic mortgages. If you are a sole trader using a home-based office, it is unlikely that your mortgage lender will charge you a higher rate. It is, however, a good idea to let them know that your usage is no longer solely domestic. If you rent your property, it's also advisable to inform your landlord.
- *Business rates:* if you use your home primarily to live in, you are unlikely to be charged business rates on top of your council tax.

However, as with your mortgage, it is worth checking where you stand on this one.

VAT registration: at last I have discovered why the petrol station keeps asking me if I want a VAT receipt! You have to become VAT registered once your 'taxable turnover' is more than a certain amount. At the time of writing, this was set at about £60,000 per annum, but you need to check with each budget, as the Chancellor changes the threshold from time to time. It is also possible to register even if you fall beneath the threshold, although registration does involve a lot of paperwork and you may need to set up new invoicing systems. As with anything 'official', seek expert advice as to what is required for your particular circumstances.

For more information, visit www.hmrc.co.uk .

Pensions: once you leave teaching, don't forget that you are no longer a part of the Teachers' Pension Scheme and that you will need to be making your own financial provision for retirement. See an independent financial adviser to explore your options. It is also worth discussing your pension with your accountant, as there may be tax benefits related to any pension payments you make.

Case study

From deputy head to . . . a portfolio career

'Working freelance', developing a 'portfolio career', becoming an 'education consultant' . . . these terms are regularly used for professionals whose jobs do not fit into a single, clear-cut category. But what do they mean? No two education consultants do the same job and no two portfolio careers have the same profile. When our case study, Karen, left her post as deputy head of a large comprehensive to move to a new area, she took the opportunity to change direction. We asked her to explain the motivation for her career shift and trace the development of what has become a wide-ranging and highly fulfilling working life.

continued

Q What do you say when people ask what you do?

A *It's always a difficult one. I usually call myself an 'Education Consultant and Trainer' (that is what I have printed on my business card). 'Education consultant' is rather a catch-all phrase, but it does cover the diversity of my working life. I think of myself as having a 'portfolio career' because my working week is filled with lots of distinct and separate roles. I could also be described as a freelance worker since my status is now fully self-employed, although I have been an employee for some of my roles in the past.*

Q So what made you decide to become an education consultant and develop a portfolio career?

A *It all began ten years ago when my husband and I moved areas, and I took a year out to organise our house move. Once the year was up, the prospect of going straight back into school didn't particularly appeal. I decided to look into other jobs, although I was always clear that I wanted to stay within the field of education. I was lucky in that my husband was able to support me financially for a short period while I explored my options, and I gradually came to realise that there were lots of jobs I could do. So – I didn't plan or set out to become an education consultant. It would be more accurate to describe my career as having 'gradually evolved' over the past decade – and this time next year, the profile of my working week could look quite different!*

Q How easy was it to get started and what particular jobs did you look out for?

A *My very first job was supply teaching. Although I wanted a change from the classroom, supply was a straightforward way of earning money and it also helped me to make a few contacts in an area that was new to me. I calculated the minimum number of days I had to do per month in order to manage financially. Once I was sure I could get enough work to cover the basics, it was then a case of going for anything that matched my skills and qualifications.*

Q How long did you work as a supply teacher?

A *In the end, only for one term, although I've always kept it in the back of my mind as a safety net (you never know when the work will dry up!) While working as a supply teacher, I spotted an advert for NVQ assessors in my local paper. At that point, there weren't a huge number of assessors around, and the company was offering to train successful candidates as part of the package. Free training seemed too good an opportunity to miss, and the chance to work with adults also appealed to me.*

Q Did it turn out to be all you'd hoped for?

A *It certainly did! In fact, it turned out to be my first experience of one thing leading to another – something that has happened throughout my career. No sooner had I got the job than I was invited to take on the role of operations manager for the whole company. My employer could see from my CV that I had management experience, and her permanent operations manager had just taken maternity leave. I was lucky enough to be in the right place at the right time.*

Q Was the NVQ assessor's training put on hold, then?

A *No, the operations management job was largely administrative; it didn't require me to have any educational skills or experience, and I was able to do my NVQ training at the same time. When the maternity cover came to an end, I carried on with the company as a freelance assessor. The management job was interesting and good experience, but it underlined my conviction that I wanted to remain within the field of education. Of course, when the contract ended, it meant the end of my salary. As I couldn't manage on assessing work alone, I had to look elsewhere to supplement my income.*

Q So what was your next move?

A *I signed up with a tutoring agency and quickly got enough work to fill my income gap. I mostly taught GCSE and A level. I also registered with the local authority home tuition service and worked with sick and excluded children and school refusers.*

continued

That was fascinating! Apart from having to teach the entire curriculum, I also had to draw on all my pastoral skills and experience. Although the tutoring provided a useful income strand, the biggest plus was the opportunity to keep up to date with my teaching skills and subject knowledge.

Q How did these different jobs fit together?

A *This was the point at which I really had to start organising myself and keeping a tight diary [for more on time management, see page 231]. All of a sudden I had to fit my NVQ assessing around my tutoring, and vice versa – not to mention the examining work that I had kept on from my teaching days. That gave me a very welcome income boost for the summer term, but I do remember having to plan my marking deadlines and examiners' meetings with great care and not book tuition or assessing sessions for crucial days. It was my first experience of combining jobs with set deadlines (the examining) and jobs where I could organise my own timetable (the tutoring and assessing).*

Q It must have been very different from school-based teaching. How well did you manage your working timetable?

A *After years of operating within the structured environment of a school, my 'piecemeal' working week took some getting used to! I do, however, think I am quite adept at time management, and my experience as a teacher certainly helped me to develop my organisational skills. I remember taking great pride in discovering little time- and money-saving tricks, such as spotting that a tutee and NVQ candidate were living or working in similar locations so that I could cut down on travelling. Now I love the flexibility of my working life and would find it quite difficult to go back to a set timetable within the one setting.*

Q It sounds as though you had quite a bit of travelling – and how did you cope with two such different jobs?

A *Yes, there was a lot of travelling – and if anything I do even more now! Fortunately, I like driving, but if you are not willing* to travel, you limit yourself as to the jobs you can take on. With regard to wearing several professional hats – again, I liked the variety of working with an adult NVQ candidate in an estate agency one minute and a 12-year-old at home with a broken leg the next. I did wonder how easy it would be to switch from one role to another, sometimes within the space of an hour or so. In practice, however, you just get stuck in with whoever you are teaching and, as always, respond to their particular needs – not really very different from the diversity of my role as a deputy head.

Q So how long did you do the NVQ assessing and tutoring?

A For three years; and very happy I was, too – but things move on. My husband came home with a leaflet advertising educational courses and conferences. As the company had a local base, he suggested I contact them to offer my services as a trainer. I did so, and they ended up offering me a job as a 'training director', designing, planning and marketing courses and conferences within the secondary sector.

Q Another example of applying for one job and being offered another?

A Yes! My motto is 'be open to anything as you never know where it will lead . . .' I did have to do a bit of negotiation as they wanted me to work full time and I didn't want to give up my other roles. Anyway, they agreed to a part-time permanent contract of two and a half days a week.

Q Why not just do the conference work full time?

A I did consider it, but I wanted to stay in touch with young people and learning. Organising conferences and courses, albeit for teachers, really does take you one step further away from the chalkface. I was also wary about putting all my eggs in one basket. Teachers get used to a high degree of job security, but once you start working freelance and taking on short-term contracts, you constantly have to keep an eye on your income and whether you are earning enough to get by. The more

continued

income strands you can gather, the more financial security you will have.

Q So what happened in the end with the tutoring and assessing?

A *I no longer seek tutoring, but I do take on pupils if I am asked. Nowadays, it's usually the children of friends, acquaintances, and contacts made through my other jobs. For example, I have just finished giving my god-daughter some extra help with her GCSEs. I gave up the NVQ assessing when I decided to train as an additional inspector for Ofsted.*

Q Why couldn't you keep both going? Was there a clash of interests?

A *No, not at all; it was simply a question of time and having to decide which direction to follow. I sometimes had to take days off from my work with the training company to carry out NVQ assessments and I didn't feel I could also ask for time off to do inspections.*

Q Was the company generally supportive about giving you time off?

A *Yes, they were. They recognised that employing personnel with a range of current skills and experience was advantageous for an education company.*

Q So your new working life involved working as a conference organiser, working as an inspector, doing some private tuition and examining work . . .?

A *Yes – and that remained my career profile for a couple of years until I spotted an advert for a temporary part-time teaching job. Although I carried on teaching as a tutor, the one thing I really missed was the 'performance' element of working with a whole class. I thought I would give it a go and see if I really did want to return to the classroom. I also thought it would be useful to refresh my teaching skills.*

Q Did you have to give up everything else in order to teach?

A No, and I probably wouldn't have taken the job if I couldn't have maintained my links with Ofsted and the training company. Having come this far, I didn't want to lose the option of slipping back into my non-teaching working life. Once again, the training company were very good and agreed to cut my hours quite considerably so that I could keep a foot in their door. The school was also very good in accepting that I might need time off for inspections. It helped that they needed me to teach a shortage subject and were desperate. As an ex-deputy head, I had total sympathy for their predicament and agreed that, wherever possible, I would only take on inspections booked for the days when I wasn't teaching. In the end, I taught for two terms and only had to take one day off. Negotiation has always been an essential part of organising and managing my career. I have generally found that people are willing to do whatever they can to facilitate the other aspects of my working life – as long as they know that I am equally willing to co-operate and give 100 per cent commitment when I am working for them.

Q So what happened with the teaching job?

A I loved it! But in the end I missed the freedom and flexibility of my portfolio career. When the contract finished after two terms, I decided to increase my hours with the training company once again, rather than look for another teaching job. It was at this point that the opportunities really started to flood in. A different branch of the training company was organising a mentoring scheme and I was invited to work as a mentor with underachieving pupils. As with inspections, this involved going into schools as and when required. Six months later, the training company underwent a shift of direction and it suited both of us to cut my hours as a conference organiser so that I could take on more mentoring and inspection work. It was at this point that I started working for them on a freelance basis and decided to become fully self-employed [for more on self-employment, see pages 207–15).

continued

Q Did becoming self-employed change your attitude to your work?

A *In practice, it doesn't make that much difference to my day-to-day working week, apart from having to keep on top of the business side of things. Becoming self-employed did, however, spur me on to seek more contracts. Ever mindful that opportunities can melt away as quickly as they appear, I decided to approach my local authority and offer my services as an education consultant. It was sheer good luck that they happened to need advisory support in my particular subject, and I was contracted to work for twenty-five days a year.*

Q What does that involve?

A *I do whatever is required. The work includes tasks such as assessing NQTs in schools across the county, providing departmental support and contributing to local authority conferences and meetings. Apart from providing me with work, the local authority contract has been hugely useful as a means of networking. I am now often asked to work on a private basis and I'm gradually building up a consultancy portfolio, providing services such as self-evaluation guidance and curriculum analysis.*

Q It sounds as though you have a dizzying amount of work to get through!

A *It's great! I do feel a sense of pride at having built up this career. I use my teaching and management experience daily, I work hard at being reliable and effective, maintaining my circle of links and contacts, and following up all possible leads. While it has been hard work, I do believe that this kind of career is open to any competent, committed and experienced teacher, if they want to follow a similar path.*

Q So what would be your advice for anyone who wants to follow suit?

A *I know it's a cliché, but I would simply say, 'go for it!' Work out the basic income you need to survive [see page 194], find* *something that will keep you going financially while you get yourself established and then follow up every possible lead. Don't be too downhearted by the setbacks (I've only described my successes in this interview – I've had my disappointments too!). Never forget that one small role can lead to . . . who knows what fabulous opportunities? Good luck to anyone who decides to give it a try!*

For more advice from Karen on developing a portfolio career, choosing to go freelance and becoming self-employed, see pages 207–15.

A different mindset

A school or college is a highly structured environment. Although teachers constantly have to respond to the unexpected, their overall working timetable follows a similar pattern from one week to the next, and much of their working day is mapped out for them. If you choose to leave teaching and become self-employed, all this will change. You will be solely responsible for managing your time; you will have to organise your own office equipment and workspace; you will have to seek out and maintain a wide range of work-based contacts . . . Working as a freelance or developing a portfolio career demands a different mindset from that of the teacher or manager, and brings with it a number of new tasks and responsibilities:

Getting work

Once you cease to be an employee, you will have to be proactive in finding work. If the prospect of seeking contracts is a little daunting, remember that you have marketed yourself to your pupils every single day. In other words, you have had more than enough practice at presenting yourself as a competent, trustworthy professional who deserves to be in employment.

Having taken the decision to embark on a portfolio career, try to follow up every existing lead and distribute your details as widely as possible. Sometimes work can come from the most unexpected places, and the more people who know about you, the more likely you are to be offered contracts (see 'Networking', below). One thing can also lead to another in the most unexpected ways. When education consultant Karen approached a school with her CV, the deputy head picked up on her experience of assessing business administration NVQs and offered to pass on her details to another school. As a result, she was asked to chair a panel of teachers discussing the development of GCSE business studies, a role that led on to an extensive contract supporting the management of vocational projects in schools and colleges. As she says, this was a perfect example of the network working in her favour.

When you first start out, it is also worth taking on any job, however minor. Karen's fee for chairing the business studies panel was modest, but it was a job well worth accepting because it led on to better-paid work. As your career progresses, you may reach a point where you can set a limit – no job under a certain fee, for example. At the same time, you never know when work might be a bit thin on the ground and you'll be glad that you kept even the smallest of avenues open. In the end, this is a decision that only you can make.

Although you will have to approach people and sell yourself, be sensitive to the reaction you are getting. Cold calling irritates many people, particularly when they are hard-pressed. Karen always approaches new contacts with a letter and CV, following up with a telephone call two or three weeks later. You can also use e-mail, but it is much harder to make an e-mail stand out from the crowd, and some professionals still do not take e-mails as seriously as the carefully written letter on good-quality headed paper. One curriculum leader told us that he only checks his computer inbox every two to three weeks, taking the view that people can write or ring if it's important. He also points out that he will file away a letter for future reference, but rarely gets around to storing or printing out and filing an e-mail.

Sending a flyer is another way of getting your details out and into the market. As with a letter, it needs to be well designed and eye-catching if it is to stand out from the crowd. It is also worth spending some time making sure that your flyer is appropriately pitched for your target market. Karen decided to approach schools in the independent sector and discovered that she needed to address her literature to the 'headmaster' or 'headmistress', not the 'headteacher'. She also discovered the importance of personalising her mail. Even though it takes a little time, she always tries to identify the person she wants to approach and addresses letters and envelopes with their name and title.

Once you have reached the stage of making telephone contact, Karen recommends liaising with a PA wherever possible. It is their job to receive and pass on information to their employer, and she usually finds them efficient, helpful and, perhaps most importantly, available. When you do get through to the person you are targeting, try to pick up on the signals they send out. If their response is clearly negative, it is a waste of your precious time to keep on trying – although it's always worth doing some *ad hoc* market research by asking why they are not interested in what you have to offer. If, however, they sound positive, don't give up. It took education journalist Helena two years to get work from one of the biggest magazines in her field. The editorial board kept expressing an interest and saying they would get back to her. When they didn't, she got back to them and the cycle would begin again. In the end, she (politely but firmly) asked if she was wasting her time and theirs, which spurred them into commissioning some book reviews. As with Karen's chairing of the GCSE business studies committee, the pay was not good, but she regarded it as an investment for the future, made sure she did a good job and now contributes regularly to the magazine.

Networking

Making and maintaining contacts within the field of education is one of the single most important ways of getting work. It is also a very useful means of keeping up to date with what is going on at the chalk-face. If you are operating in the area where you taught, you should already have a network of local contacts to draw upon. Make efforts to keep in touch with ex-colleagues and find out about their network of friends, colleagues and contacts. Do, however, be careful not to use colleagues simply as a source of information. Concentrate on maintaining friendships beyond the world of work, be appreciative of their support and treat them to coffee or dinner when picking their brains (a legitimate business expense!). Look out also for ways of offering a token of appreciation. Karen makes sure she organises a consultancy fee or free place for contacts who contribute to planning one of her training events, whereas Helena gives away copies of her review books as a 'thank-you' for any help she receives with an article.

Local authority and awarding body personnel can be another useful source of contacts. If you built up a good relationship with your local authority subject adviser or external moderator during your time as a teacher, get in touch with them, explain your new status and make sure they have your details on file. As part of their job involves the organisation of training and/or support, you could be a useful resource for them to draw upon in the future.

If you want to maximise work opportunities, you may have to try networking beyond your immediate area. As a starting point, scan the adverts in the education press, make a list of the companies that use education consultants and trainers, and try to get your details on their database. Attend as many education shows and conferences as possible and chat to other delegates and the personnel on the relevant stands. Always have your business cards, flyers and any other relevant literature ready to hand out to potential future employers. Just one word of warning: you do have to decide whether a particular conference or show offers enough networking and information-gathering opportunities to make it worth your while financially. As an employed teacher, such events are part of your working week and you will still receive the day's pay at the end of the month. As a self-employed freelance worker, you cannot be earning at the same time as attending an event. Always remember to factor in the loss of a day's earnings as well as the cost of the conference or show.

Initiating contacts is just the beginning. Even the most competent freelance worker can quickly drop off the radar if they do not maintain their profile with prospective employers. Find different ways to remind people of your existence and try to build up a friendly relationship with people who give you regular work. Helena mostly communicates with her editors and publishers through e-mail, but is aware of how impersonal the electronic communication can be. Once she has properly established contact, she gradually includes a few snippets of personal information (comments about the weather, references to her children or holiday plans). She quickly discovers who wants to focus purely on business and who is happy to develop a friendlier relationship – and regards it as no coincidence that she gets the most work from those with whom she shares a quick 'e-chat'! Sending Christmas cards is another straightforward and relatively cheap way of maintaining positive professional contact and/or showing appreciation for the work you have been given throughout the previous year. Karen also recommends checking the DCSF and QCA websites (www.dcsf.gov.uk and www.qca.org.uk) for new initiatives that link with what you have to offer. You can then get in touch with any relevant contacts to remind them that you have the necessary expertise to help them meet the demands of the new initiative.

Negotiating contracts and fees

Written contracts in the 'outside world' can be quite different from the standard teaching contract, and they also vary considerably from organisation to organisation. When you are first starting out, it's tempting to ask no questions and simply sign on the dotted line. Helena's contract for her first book stated that she had to give the publisher first refusal on any future books – something she regretted signing when she discovered that other publishers paid a much higher royalty percentage! Always read the contract carefully; it can also be worth asking a partner or friend to check through, as they may pick up on something you have missed. Watch out for any restrictive clauses, such as a time delay between leaving a company and working for a similar organisation, and make sure you think through all the implications. When Karen agreed to work part time for a training company, she was offered a contract that would have prevented her from doing training or advisory work with any other company. As this would have left her unable to earn a living wage, she decided to try negotiation before turning down the job. When she explained her circumstances to her potential employers, they accepted her point of view and agreed to remove the clause. Many companies have standard contracts but it is always worth negotiating, as they may be willing to fine-tune the details. It is also worth checking copies of annual contracts to see what changes a company might be making from one year to the next. If you are in any doubt whatsoever about a contract, seek professional advice – although you do need to set a solicitor's or accountant's fee against the overall monetary value of the work.

Of course, negotiation, keeping to a contract and being considerate is a two-way process. Once you start working for a number of different organisations, you have to be careful not to tread on people's toes. Karen had carried out some advisory work in an independent school via one of the training companies with which she had a substantial contract. When the school approached her directly the following year, she contacted the training company to ask if they were happy for her to accept the work on an independent basis. The contract was too small to make it worth their while and they were willing for her to go ahead. Although it ended well for her, it would have been worth losing the contract with the school to maintain a good relationship with the training company – and she ended up earning Brownie points for being honest and professional. She also points out the importance of confidentiality. A portfolio career will give you access to people in a number of different institutions and businesses, many of whom will know each other, and it is essential to be careful about the information to which you are privy.

Fees go hand in hand with contracts. Most teachers work in an environment where there is little room for negotiation over pay; salaries are standardised, and the monetary value of each responsibility point is generally public knowledge. As a consequence, the process of charging fees is unfamiliar to most teachers, and it can be difficult to know how much to ask once you decide to go freelance. If your fee is too high, you may not be offered further contracts; if it is too low, you may not be taken seriously. It can also be highly frustrating when a company responds to your estimate with surprised enthusiasm and you realise you could have asked for more! Many teachers also under-value their worth in monetary terms (just compare the cost of private tuition against a number of other professional and skilled services . . .). The starting point is to investigate the market. Find out what fees other people are asking for similar services and try to establish what schools, colleges and training organisations are willing to pay – always bearing in mind that this will vary, depending on the size of the establishment, the location, the sector and any extra money available for new initiatives.

When discussing work with a school or company, always have a rough idea of your daily or half-daily or hourly rate; you may be asked for an estimate of your fee, and if you are caught 'on the hop', you can end up making an inappropriate snap decision or, worse still, come across as disorganised. Once you have given a rough estimate, you can then take your time in getting as much information about the job as you can: how many teachers or students you are working with, whether you are working for a half-day or full day, the level at which you are working (students, NQTs, senior management), how much preparation is needed, whether a report is required and what expenses you will incur. You can then inform the school or company that you will get back to them in a day or two with a bespoke package to suit their requirements. Don't forget to be thorough in totalling up expenses, or you could find yourself out of pocket. Calculate carefully the cost of fuel, car use, meals, accommodation and photocopying, and either charge for them separately or make sure that they are fully covered by your flat rate.

Non-teaching job applications

Many jobs will involve an application process. Applications can range from CVs and covering letters to filling in application and/or CV pro forma provided by the employer.

As a first step, make sure that your CV is up to date and relevant. There are various styles you can adopt; to a large extent, you need to choose an approach that suits you and the job for which you are applying. Any CV should list your background in chronological order, preferably starting with the most recent. Make sure you cover the following sections:

- **Education**: include qualifications (usually from A level onwards), names of institutions, dates, grades and any relevant modules or courses.
- **Work experience**: include special responsibilities, achievements and interests, and any voluntary jobs that are relevant to the post (for example, your voluntary role as a youth worker could be just as relevant as your teaching experience if you are applying for a mentoring job).
- **Membership of professional organisations.**
- **Interests and hobbies**: give a *brief* explanation of the skills and experience you have gained.
- **Referees**: for a non-teaching job, you do not have to rely on a headteacher's or principal's reference. Choose different referees for different positions; for example, if you are applying for examining work, ask your awarding body subject officer from any previous examining posts. Unlike in teaching jobs, references are often not taken up until after you have been appointed. This means that your current employer need not know that you have been looking elsewhere until you are actually offered a job.

This is the standard approach to writing a CV. Another option is to base your CV on a series of skills headings, enabling you to outline your relevant skills. It is, however, essential that your skills are backed up by evidence. A statement such as '*good at planning*' needs further explanation, such as '*I was asked to take on the planning of the school timetable, a role that I have carried out for the past three years*'. A skills-based CV enables you to analyse the requirements of your new employer and focus on the skills that you think they would find useful. For example, if you are applying for a job as a subject adviser, it would be useful to include the following skill analysis in your CV:

An effective communicator: ten years as the Key Stage 3 Numeracy Co-ordinator at St Walter's Middle School has given me extensive experience of communicating with adults in individual and group situations:

- I present initiatives regularly to groups of colleagues and report back from conferences and local authority meetings.
- I support colleagues' numeracy teaching on a one-to-one basis.
- I give termly talks and presentations to parents, receiving consistently good feedback from my audiences.
- I communicate with parents individually at parents' evenings and have been asked by the school's NQT co-ordinator to support newly qualified teachers with parent liaison.
- I was elected for a second term as teacher-governor, a role that includes representing colleagues on the governing body and discussing school management.

Although the skills you choose to highlight will vary depending on your strengths and the job for which you are applying, some typical skill areas might include planning, research and resource preparation; working within a team; written communication; mentoring and counselling; showing initiative and working independently; problem solving; ICT skills, and specific subject skills such as linguistic or numerical ability. You will also need to list your qualifications, employment history, interests and referees.

There are many companies that will write your CV for you. Although this will involve you in costs, it may be worth looking into if you find yourself continually falling at the first fence. Many of these companies are now web based. Try doing an internet search for 'CVs' or 'curriculum vitae' to find out what options are available.

Non-teaching job interviews

Anyone who has worked as a teacher will have successfully undergone at least one demanding interview. The selection process for teachers tends to follow a fairly set pattern: an interview with a panel consisting of the headteacher or principal, teaching staff, governors and, in some cases, older students; teaching an observed lesson; and, for management posts, making a presentation. Interviews for jobs outside teaching can vary enormously and they won't necessarily follow a pattern or be what they seem. Bear in mind that an invitation for 'an informal chat' can be an interview in disguise, as can a telephone conversation. Alternatively, you may be asked to participate in a much more formal seminar-style situation with set topics to discuss, a facilitator and an observer taking notes. Be prepared for anything, and always be aware that any contact with a potential employer could be contributing quite significantly towards the selection process.

Time management

Although teachers have to be skilled at time management, organising your working day as a freelance can present some quite different challenges. Schools have structured timetables, with one week very similar to the next in the sense of what you have to get done. This means that even the most disorganised person can build up a routine. Not so once you decide to develop a portfolio career! No two days will present you with same set of tasks; you may have both short-term and long-term contracts to juggle, you may need to be in completely different places at different times and you may also have to get used to working for stretches of time at home.

The first step is to be organised about dates and deadlines. As part of timetabling your visits to schools, colleges, training centres or business establishments, don't forget to include days for preparation, follow-up work and travel. For example, if you are leading an INSET day in a school at the other end of the country, you will need to set aside two or three days for preparation and travel. In other words, a one-day event can generate a working period of up to four days, and you need to make sure that any follow-up work for one job doesn't overlap with the preparation for another, particularly if you have a tight deadline to meet. Karen also recommends doing follow-up paperwork as quickly as possible. If, like her, you are undertaking several different roles, it can be surprisingly easy to mix them up. For example, she recently had to do some NQT assessments followed by a school inspection. She knew there was a risk of muddling up the information for the two jobs, and even though she had a couple of weeks before the NQT report deadline, she planned her timetable so that she could get the report written up and out of the way before starting the inspection. Some people find it easy to plan ahead in this way – and others don't. The golden rule is to be absolutely clear about what each job will involve, make sure you allow enough time for each job, keep your diary up to date and never organise anything without first checking your availability. Your reputation for being reliable and keeping to deadlines is every bit as important as your competence when it comes to getting more work!

Once you have sorted out your timetable and got to grips with meeting deadlines, how you then choose to organise your working day depends on what suits you. Helena knew that time management was not her strong point and she did some research into how to plan her work. Everything she read suggested that a set routine was the approach to take, and she tried her very best to start writing at 9.00 a.m. and finish at 3.00 p.m., with an hour off for lunch. On some days her timetable worked perfectly; on other days, she was constantly interrupted or found that she needed several breaks to refocus her thoughts. She now works to whatever timetable feels right for a particular day – and if that means writing at midnight, or writing in short twenty-minute bursts in between walking the dog and putting on the washing, she is happy as long as she meets her deadlines. She also discovered that she can write through the night if she absolutely has to, and will occasionally do so in order to meet a particularly pressing deadline. On the other hand, Karen knows that she cannot push herself beyond a certain point, and always plans a routine that gives her plenty of time to finish off important projects. One of the joys of self-employment is the freedom it gives you to adopt your own, personal working pattern.

Managing your time as a freelance also involves making decisions about when not to work. Self-employment enables you to take time off when you need to, and you can also choose to book holidays during off-peak periods. However, if you are working within the field of education, you may miss out on opportunities if you are away during term-time. Unlike the employed teacher, you will also not be paid during the school holidays. Decide whether you need to plan ahead for this through budgeting or boosting your summer income by teaching in a summer school (see page 35) or marking examination scripts (see page 76). You can also use the holiday periods to catch up on tasks such as administration, reading and research or planning new talks, courses and inset days.

Saying 'yes' or 'no'

In the early stages of your new working life, you probably do need to say 'yes' to just about anything – unless you genuinely don't have the experience to pull off a job. If your inclination is to turn down an offer of work, take a moment to think through where the 'no' is coming from. Perhaps you do have the skills and capabilities to speak at that conference, present that paper to your local heads' association or make a difference to that school in special measures. Perhaps all you need is a bit more courage . . .

At the same time, you need to be realistic about what you have to offer. Karen was recently asked to do some training with a group of FE tutors. Knowing that she could draw on her knowledge of generic teaching skills, she thought long and hard about accepting the work. However, in the end she turned it down, as she did not feel that she had enough experience of the FE sector. She advises thinking carefully about the difference between lack of confidence and lack of competence. There's nothing worse for your reputation and self-esteem than agreeing to do something and then making a bad job of it!

As you become more established and better able to choose the work you take on, it is also worth taking a few moments to think through what a job involves:

- Do you have the time to fit it in and follow it through properly?
- If you are only paid for contact time, to what extent do the preparation and paperwork eat into your hourly rate?
- Are you being offered plenty of other work, and so can afford to say no to a job you are not sure about?
- In spite of your resolution to stretch yourself, is this job going to cause you so many sleepless nights that it's not worth the stress?
- Is it one of those jobs that, while not particularly appealing, could lead to other, more interesting or better-paid work?

Over the years, Karen has developed a technique to buy herself thinking time. Unless she is immediately certain about a job, she makes a response such as: *'That sounds really interesting! Can I just check my diary and get back to you . . .'* She then focuses on the pros and cons of the job, makes a decision and contacts the person offering the work as quickly as possible. As she says, any job offer is a huge compliment, and even if she has to turn something down, she always tries to show genuine appreciation.

Clothes

Depending on how you chose to dress as a teacher, you may need to develop a new wardrobe to fit in with your new role. Although Karen always liked to look smart as a deputy head, she now dresses as a businesswoman, with an emphasis on suits and appropriate accessories. She regards herself as a consultant who is marketing herself as a competent professional, and she believes that a businesslike appearance helps her clients to have confidence in her. In contrast, education writer Helena works mostly from home, and her 'smart' wardrobe has dwindled to the point where she struggles to find anything to wear on the rare occasions when she does have to attend a business meeting. For her, this is one of the many advantages of her new working life. As a part of preparing for your new role, think about how you want to present yourself and the impression you wish to create, and start building up an appropriate wardrobe.

Self-motivation and working alone

For many people, having a large group of like-minded colleagues is one of the great advantages of teaching. Most staffrooms are friendly and supportive places, particularly for teachers working in more challenging areas. Whether you need to let off steam, bounce ideas off a fellow professional, seek support or advice, or simply share a Friday night drink, many teachers will find the social contact they need among their colleagues.

Once you decide to go freelance, you will lose the luxury of the staffroom with its ready-made social circle and the daily contact it affords. For some people, this is not a problem. Education journalist Helena rather enjoys her solitary working life, although she knows that her peaceful day will end at 4.00 p.m. when her family come home from school. She also values the opportunity to have complete control over her working day, with no distractions or interruptions.

There are, however, disadvantages. You need to put real effort into networking, and keeping up with ex-colleagues and other contacts. As an education consultant, trainer, inspector, conference speaker or writer, you need the oxygen of other people's ideas, experiences and perspectives on new initiatives. If you are by nature a sociable person who thrives on human contact, you also need to make sure that you don't become too isolated. The telephone can be a lifeline. Do, however, keep an eye on the phone bill and look into cost-effective packages if this becomes a problem. Karen cites another aspect of working alone that needs to be factored into your working day: unless you have jobs that include administrative support, you will have to do all your fetching and carrying for yourself. She now realises how much she relied on the school office to sort out and send her mail, and her curriculum assistant to type up letters, photocopy and carry out other time-consuming administrative tasks.

PA support services

There are a growing number of individuals and small companies offering 'remote' PA support services. If you find yourself overwhelmed by administration and paperwork, it may be worth getting help – particularly if it frees you up to take on more fee-earning contracts.

For Karen and Helena, the need to develop friendships beyond the workplace is a positive outcome of their new working lives. As school-based teachers they both relied to a great extent on their colleagues for a social life. Once they started working for themselves, they were forced to develop non-work-related friendships and make a point of arranging social engagements during their working week. As a result, they both feel that they have achieved a better work–life balance and developed a much wider and more diverse group of friends and contacts.

Chapter 6

Staying in teaching . . . managing your stress levels and work–life balance

Although this book sets out to offer some new and different possibilities for those who want to move beyond the classroom, there is another option: to stay where you are and address whatever might be causing your dissatisfaction. This chapter looks at:

- reasons for staying in teaching;
- techniques for managing your stress levels;
- improving your work–life balance.

Why stay?

If you are unsure about leaving teaching, try listing all the advantages of the job. A reminder of just how much teaching has to offer may be all you need to give yourself a renewed sense of purpose. Use the following list as a starting point. Ignore any of the points that fail to resonate with your particular experiences and add any of your own that come to mind:

- **Making a difference**: teachers make a huge and significant contribution to society. When we asked our 'complete career change' case studies to describe the disadvantages of their new jobs, many of them mentioned that they missed doing something that 'really mattered'.
- **A sense of satisfaction**: finally making a breakthrough with a child who has difficulties; getting to grips with a challenging class; having a group enraptured and 'eating out of your hand' . . . even if these moments are rare, there are few work experiences that can match the sense of satisfaction when everything in your classroom is going according to plan.

- **Creativity**: the sky's the limit when it comes to researching and trying out new ideas, preparing resources and putting up classroom displays. Although teachers often feel that they have never done enough, the flipside is the chance to be endlessly creative. When you try out a new idea and an enthusiastic voice pipes up, '*this is really good, Miss*', it is music to the ears!
- **Spending time with children**: at the risk of sounding like an advert for the teaching profession, children and teenagers really can be fun, fascinating, quirky, challenging and highly stimulating individuals with whom to spend your time. If you find 'human nature' endlessly fascinating, there are very few jobs where you come across so much of it within a single day.
- **Boredom thresholds**: although marking can be tedious and some teachers do eventually become jaded, the greater part of the average teacher's day is anything but boring. Every child is different, every class is different, every day is different. Most teachers simply don't have time to get bored. While the prospect of taking on mundane work may seem appealing at times, for some people a tedious job can be more stressful than a highly pressured, responsible job.
- **Structure**: although every day is different, teaching follows a structured timetable. For those who need it, teaching offers routine and the familiarity of going to the same workplace and working with the same individuals every day.
- **Colleague camaraderie**: staffroom camaraderie is another aspect of teaching that many of our case studies missed. The links that teachers form with their colleagues can be remarkably strong, particularly if they are working in a tough area and need to rely on each other for support. In small schools, the staffroom tends to be cohesive, whereas larger schools offer a wide social mix. Whatever the size of school, most teachers will find a group of colleagues with whom they can get along.
- **Autonomy and teamwork**: although many teachers feel that they have had their autonomy eroded over the past few years, you still have more individual control than is the case with a number of jobs. When you are in your classroom, you are in charge. At the same time, teaching involves enough teamwork to prevent you from feeling isolated. For many people, the balance is about right. You have the opportunity to work with colleagues, but not to the extent that you are constantly in each other's pockets.

- **School holidays**: there is no question that teachers need holidays to recuperate from the pressures of their working week and catch up on planning and preparation. If you are seriously considering a move to a different job, you may be happy to swap holidays for a more regulated and less intense job. However, it is worth thinking about how much the holidays mean to you; although they come at a high price for teachers, you may ultimately decide that the price is worth paying.
- **Career structure**: unlike many jobs, teaching has an established career structure. If you are ambitious, you can plan your move up the ladder with a relatively good idea of what each rung will involve and where you might end up. Teaching can also lead to a variety of different options, as we have demonstrated in Chapters 1–4. If you are in the early stages of your career, it may be worth staying in teaching for a bit longer so that you can develop your CV in preparation for a future job move.
- **Job security**: teaching is a relatively secure job. Unless you demonstrate a serious degree of incompetence or work in a school with falling rolls, you are unlikely to be made redundant. With such a large number of schools throughout the country, you will not have difficulty finding jobs to apply for if you need to move location, want a change or are looking for career development. You will also have less competition in certain geographical areas, and for some subjects. Even during times of job shortages, most teachers eventually find work.
- **Income**: it is a moot point as to whether teachers are paid fairly in comparison with other professions. However, teachers' salaries still compare well with national averages, and although you can earn more in other jobs, you may equally find yourself struggling to match your income as a teacher. This is certainly something to think about if you need to earn a reasonable living wage.
- **Income security**: when asked about the disadvantages of their new role, most of our self-employed case studies cited the loss of income security: '*Will there be enough money at the end of the month to cover the bills?*' is how one individual put it. As a teacher, you know what your pay cheque will be at the end of each month and you know approximately what you will be earning in five years' time, so you can plan ahead. If you need a mortgage or loan, you are generally regarded as a 'good bet' for these very reasons.
- **Teachers' pensions**: although a pension can seem of minor importance in the early years of your career, it is nevertheless a

factor to consider when deciding whether or not to stay in teaching. The Teachers' Pension Scheme, as it currently stands, offers better provision than many private pensions, including cover for your spouse in the event of your untimely demise. There are many retired teachers or teachers approaching retirement who are glad that they stuck with teaching for the pension alone!

- **Familiarity**: teaching is what you trained for. It is the career you chose to go into and a world whose language and culture you understand. Other career areas, such as business, have a different philosophy from teaching and can take some getting used to.

Think carefully about whether you truly want to give up teaching. If you have any doubts, read through the rest of this chapter and explore some of the 'coping' strategies before making a final decision.

Stress or pressure: where are you at?

If you are considering leaving teaching for any reason other than straightforward career development, it is possible that you are suffering from a degree of stress. Teaching is generally accepted as one of the most stressful jobs you can do, with work-based stress cited as the top reason for teachers seeking support. But what does stress actually entail, and how can we recognise the difference between 'pressure' and 'stress'?

A certain amount of pressure provides the necessary motivation to get up in the morning, get ourselves into the workplace and strive both to achieve and to improve on our performance. It is when pressure becomes excessive that it leads to stress. Stress is the negative reaction to too much pressure, and it can result in a wide range of physical, emotional and psychological symptoms. The point at which pressure tips into stress varies from one person to another. In a sense, it doesn't matter how much pressure other people can manage or whether you 'should' be coping with the demands of your job. If you are struggling with the symptoms of stress, it means that your circumstances are having an adverse effect on your health and well-being, and something needs to be done.

It is essential that you do not ignore stress symptoms until you have reached crisis point. It is equally essential to accept that stress is *not* a sign of weakness. People who finally admit to having difficulties are often surprised at how much support and understanding they receive from colleagues, friends and healthcare professionals. If the people who know you best are expressing their concerns about you, listen to what they have to say. Make yourself stop and think through how you really feel. What are your current attitudes to yourself . . . your work . . . your behaviour . . . your relationships . . . your leisure pursuits? Have you changed in recent times? Are you more irritable, more withdrawn, unusually fatigued, sleeping more badly than usual? Stress can manifest itself in many different ways, and each individual will react differently. If you are suffering from a number of the following symptoms, it is time to take action.

Physical symptoms

- Recurrent aches and pains; tight, tense muscles, particularly in the neck and shoulders.
- Lethargy and feelings of weakness and fatigue.
- Insomnia and disturbed sleep.
- Reduced immunity, leading to greater susceptibility to colds and other infections.
- An increase in headaches and migraine.
- Digestive disturbances, irritable bowel syndrome and diarrhoea.
- Increased difficulty in controlling long-term conditions such as eczema, asthma, diabetes and migraine.

Occasionally, the above symptoms can indicate a physical disease and should always be checked out by your GP.

Emotional and behavioural symptoms

- Difficulties with concentration and increased levels of forgetfulness, loss of reliability, problems with timekeeping, proneness to accidents.
- Erratic eating habits.
- Over-reliance on stimulants such as nicotine, alcohol and caffeine; use of recreational drugs and addictions such as gambling to blot out feelings of anxiety.
- Difficulties with personal relationships, increased irritability, excessive and unprovoked outbursts of anger.
- Depression: lack of enthusiasm for activities that previously gave pleasure; lethargy and fatigue; feelings of hopelessness; greater difficulty waking up and getting out of bed than normal; increased difficulty with ordinary, everyday tasks such as organising the weekly shop.

- Anxiety: inability to relax; racing thoughts; worrying about imaginary disasters; panic attacks, including increased heartbeat and hyperventilating.

Any symptoms of depression should not be left for longer than two weeks before seeing a doctor.

Strategies: what can you do?

If your stress levels have reached crisis point, you need to get support from your employer and medical help as a matter of some urgency. It is, however, far better to take action before you reach this stage. As a starting point, make a list of what you find difficult about your job. Perhaps you are exhausted by an excessive workload; perhaps you feel frustrated about the unreasonable demands placed on you by senior management; perhaps your confidence and self-esteem have been battered by constantly having to deal with challenging children. In each case, a different set of strategies is required and you will need to tackle the cause of the problem, explore how you handle it in a practical sense and think through your attitude to your work. For example, if you are struggling with your workload, you can take practical steps to address the situation by offloading non-essential tasks and improving your time-management skills; you can change your mindset and learn how to adjust your expectations of yourself in relation to your work; and you can increase your energy and fitness levels through relaxation, exercise and improving your diet and sleep patterns. Alternatively, feeling 'stale' may be more of a problem than an excessive workload. In this instance, you need to find ways of breathing new life into your teaching. Try out some fresh ideas in the classroom; get involved in a project such as a drama production or organising a charity theme day; start an MEd or look into the possibilities of teaching a different subject. In the end, each individual needs to create a bespoke package of strategies to match their personality, their way of working and the particular difficulties they are experiencing.

The following list of strategies has been compiled from tips, advice and suggestions given to us by practising colleagues. Some of the ideas will be new to you, some you may already have tried and some will act as a reminder of what you know you should be doing if you are to regain control of your job. Check through the list and try any of the ideas that you think might work for you:

Managing your workload

- Make a list to establish the core elements of your job. What is essential and what is the icing on the cake? Pick one or two minor tasks and put them to one side. After a week or so, assess whether you are doing a less competent job as a result. If the answer is 'no', these tasks are clearly not worth your time and effort, and you should at least consider the possibility of ditching them.

- Always remember that you are the only one who knows the full extent of the work you do. If you feel that your workload is excessive, log everything so that you have a comprehensive record of your tasks and responsibilities. Starting on a Monday, compile a record for each day, listing every activity and how long it took. By the end of Friday, you can add up your workload for the week and how many hours you actually worked. Apart from providing evidence, a written record will help you to identify whether you truly have an unreasonable amount of work or whether you could lessen the problem by using your time more efficiently.

- Have you become bogged down with extra-curricular responsibilities? Helping to run the PTA or taking girls' rugby twice a week after school are laudable activities, but they are not essential if your health and well-being are at stake. Don't feel guilty about dropping whatever you can. If you find it hard to give up extra-curricular activities, perhaps it is time to consider why you need to overburden yourself in this way.

- Consider whether you can afford to go part time. If you love your job but feel stressed and overburdened, part-time hours will free you up to stay on top of the work. Just one word of warning: don't fall into the trap of cramming a full-time job into part-time hours, or end up being overloaded with extras because you are the one with the 'spare' time!

- Consider whether you want or need to climb the career ladder. Although the current culture of career development within education is a positive thing for those who want to progress, it is not appropriate for everyone. If you suspect that a promotion would shift you too far beyond your comfort zone, don't be afraid to stick with your current position and simply focus on performing to the best of your ability.

- Consider whether you still need to hold a position of responsibility. If you are in the later stages of your career and not planning to progress any further up the ladder, is the extra money worth the additional pressure? Many teachers downsize in the latter years of their working life and end their careers focusing on what they most enjoy: classroom teaching. Just one word of warning: check how a reduction in income will affect your pension before making a final decision.

- If possible, get to school early. Peter, a head of maths, is always in his office by 7.00 a.m. He is at his best in the mornings, and an early start enables him to take time out to relax at the end of the school day. Ample pre-school preparation time also means that you are not rushed for briefing meetings or registration. If you have your own children to sort out in the morning, look into making use of a breakfast club or employing extra help with childcare.

- Could you be making more constructive use of free periods, PPA and non-contact time? It is frighteningly easy to let an hour slip away without achieving very much – and that means you have to spend the evening or weekend catching up on what could have been done in school. Try making a list of tasks and allotting yourself a set amount of time for each task. Keep an eye on the clock as you work; it really does help you to operate more efficiently if you are constantly aware of how time is passing.

- Give priority to keeping your classroom, office and stock cupboard tidy and well organised. If your pupils know where in the classroom to find resources and can follow your established routines independently, it makes your life much easier. Similarly, if you can always lay your hands on the equipment you need, it will cut down on your preparation time and help you to avoid a last-minute panic.

- Aim to mark work as quickly as possible. Regardless of subject or age group, marking is much easier if the task is still fresh in your own mind. Year 3 teacher Carole always marks her pupils' maths books as soon as they go off for lunch. If she ever has to leave the marking until later, it hangs over her, takes twice as long and she struggles to remember who was having difficulties and whose work needs special attention. Not only does efficient marking make her life easier, but it also enables her to do a better job – and that helps to keep her stress levels in check!

- Work out a marking regimen that suits you. If you mark a set of work once a week, it may take an hour. If you mark a double set of work once a fortnight, it may only take you an hour and half, with an overall saving of thirty minutes over the two-week period. However, having to plough through two weeks' work can seem much more of a burden than weekly marking sessions. Decide which approach works better for you and plan a weekly timetable for your marking. Although your timetable will need to be flexible, if you can stick to it as closely as possible it will help you to feel in control of your work

- Wherever possible, get pupils to mark two-thirds of their work in class and take in the books to check the remaining third. This approach has the threefold advantage of cutting down on marking, giving pupils responsibility for assessment and enabling you to get a regular overview of their books. It works best for subjects such as maths, language vocabulary tests, single-answer and multiple-choice questions, and spelling tests.

- Be pragmatic about taking the occasional short cut. As an example, science teacher Matthew describes his rationale behind presenting a paragraph of factual information to a class of GCSE students:

    Dictation is the quickest and easiest approach, but not always ideal for pupils with literacy difficulties. Presenting the information in a dynamic form via the interactive whiteboard may be more motivational for the pupils, but it takes a lot of preparation. For me, the choice is simple. If I'm overburdened with work, I use dictation and accept that the best educational approach sometimes has to be sacrificed in order to keep my head above water.

- Whenever you are planning and preparing resources, give some thought to the future. Prepare resources that can be kept and reused. Make sure you file copies of handouts, notes and activity sheets so that they can be duplicated in subsequent years. Although you should continually develop and update your teaching materials and aids, you can save yourself a lot of work and effort by building up a reusable collection of resources.

Colleague relationships

- However much pressure you are under, set aside time during morning and lunch breaks to sit down and relax with your colleagues. Many studies have shown that good work-based relationships help to protect against stress.

- Share problems, experiences and funny anecdotes. Letting off steam with trusted colleagues is an important safety valve in a highly pressured job such as teaching. Do, however, be wary about becoming overly involved with other people's personal disputes. If you choose to confide in a colleague, be sure that your revelations will remain confidential. If you are a senior manager, you have to be particularly careful about choosing your confidant(e)s.

- Be honest with colleagues and admit your mistakes. If you are an NQT or inexperienced teacher, it is much easier for a mentor to help you if you are open to advice. If you are in a leadership position, colleagues are more likely to respect you if you admit that you got something wrong rather than trying to engage in a frantic cover-up operation. If you feel you are making too many mistakes, take a look at your stress levels. An increase in forgetfulness and uncharacteristic incompetence are common signs of stress, and may be an indication that you should be seeking help and support.

- Try collaborative planning. If a number of staff are all teaching Year 8 maths, or you and a colleague have parallel Year 4 classes, collaborative planning has the potential to halve your workload. Working with others can also be a lot more enjoyable than working on your own, and the cross-fertilisation of ideas and resources can only enhance your teaching.

- Learn to say 'no'. At the same time, think carefully about each individual request. In the long run, it may be not a good idea to say no to someone who gives you a lot of support. Some tasks are also an inherent part of your job. If you find yourself unable to manage tasks that you really should be undertaking, arrange a meeting with your line manager to discuss your job description and workload.

- Treat ancillary staff (lab technicians, classroom assistants, secretaries, caretakers, cleaners) with respect. All teachers rely on their support and assistance, and it will make a significant difference to the smooth running of your day if you can establish a good working relationship.

- Make appropriate use of the support provided by curriculum assistants. As part of your planning, identify tasks that you can delegate, for example photocopying, typing, directed resource preparation, collating data and preparing displays. If you don't have a curriculum assistant, lobby your senior management team to provide practical support for your subject. Do, however, spare a thought for the curriculum assistant's workload. Teachers tend to operate individually and are not always aware that, collectively, they are making unreasonable demands.

Health, fitness and lifestyle

- Drink water throughout the day. If you suffer from fatigue and/or headaches, you may be able to solve the problem simply by rehydrating yourself.

- Eat regularly and choose foods that give you long-lasting energy: lean protein, wholegrains, nuts and seeds. Avoid snacking on sweet foods, as they will give you a quick sugar hit followed by an energy slump.

- Watch your tea and coffee intake. Although several black coffees throughout the day may give you a temporary boost of energy, too much caffeine is bad for your long-term health and leads to fatigue.

- Get fresh air and sunlight, particularly in the winter months. Primary school teacher Helen noticed that she felt livelier and more energetic on the days when she did playground duty. She now tries to get outside for a few minutes during every break-time. If you are prone to seasonal affective disorder (SAD), look into positioning your office or classroom desk so that you are facing a window.

- If you have a stressful lesson or a difficult encounter with a colleague, try deep breathing. Inhale through the nose, exhale through the mouth and breathe right down to the diaphragm. Intersperse several slow, deep breaths with normal breathing while you are in the tense situation. As you become more practised, you will start to feel the tension melt away with each breath. Deep breathing can also be used to help you manage the after-effects of a difficult event.

- Some people are invigorated by social events; others need privacy and their own space in order to recharge their batteries. Find a way of relaxing that suits you. Take up yoga, learn to meditate, have aromatherapy massages, make time to meet a friend for coffee at the weekend, go shopping, kick everyone out of the house on Sunday morning and enjoy being by yourself. Once you have discovered what works for you, make relaxation time an absolute priority. Always remember – relaxation is not a treat, but an essential part of a healthy and balanced lifestyle!

- Take up exercise. We all know it is good for us and will ultimately lead to greater energy levels and a more cheerful disposition. This is fine if you love your weekend rugby or pounding round the gym, but more of a problem if you struggle to find anything you enjoy. If you are not a natural exerciser, explore ways of building it painlessly into your life. Park the car in the space furthest away from the supermarket entrance; take the stairs rather than the lift; put your back into housework; accept with good grace being the one to walk the dog, and make it a 'power walk' rather than an amble. Even marching on the spot and swinging your arms for ten-minute bursts while watching the television is better than nothing.

- Insufficient sleep will eventually grind down even the toughest of individuals. If you are having difficulty sleeping, do your very best to find a solution. See your doctor to discuss the problem; avoid tea, coffee and alcohol at night; avoid eating too late or doing vigorous exercise within two or three hours of going to bed; check that the temperature in your bedroom is neither too hot nor too cold and make the room as dark as possible. Alternative and complementary therapies also work for some people. Learn a relaxation technique and try camomile tea or a warm bath with a few drops of lavender essential oil before bed.

- Get help in the home. You may already have a cleaner, but how about employing a gardener or someone to do the painting and decorating? Make a rule: if tasks such as ironing or walking the dog are therapeutic and enhance your life, do them yourself; if they are a burden, pay someone else to do them for you. Your work as a teacher is stressful and demanding, and you need to protect your relaxation and leisure time.

- Make your working environment as beautiful as possible. Although this is not always easy in the average school, pictures, cushions, mobiles, plants and flowers are quick and straight-forward ways of brightening up an office or work area.

Changing attitudes and building self-esteem

- Teaching is a never-ending job. Whenever you are assessing your preparation for any task, ask yourself, '*Have I done all that I can in the time available?*' If the answer is '*yes*', put the task to one side and move on to something else. One early years practitioner remembers a 4-year-old in her class holding up his picture and announcing, '*This is not my best painting, but it's the best I can do today.*' There are many adults who could do with taking a similar attitude to their work.

- Once you have established what you find stressful, accept that you may not be able to change certain aspects of your job. For example, there is not much you can do about attending after school meetings, having to mark homework or teach a challenging class last thing on a Friday afternoon. Focus on finding practical solutions to those problems that can be addressed and ignore the rest. You may find that fine-tuning the areas you *can* change will lift just enough pressure to make everything else seem more manageable.

- Don't assume that you can solve every problem. Although teachers often feel that they should be able to handle anything, in practice some pupils' difficulties lie beyond the scope of the school. This does not mean that you should stop trying, or cease to make proper use of all the available support systems. It is, however, important not to let your self-esteem become adversely affected by those pupils you are unable to help.

- Focus on your successes. Although you should always analyse and address those aspects that haven't gone to plan, don't let a bad event colour the whole day. If you have had a difficult time with one pupil, remember the other twenty-nine for whom you are doing a good job!

- Do you have letters from grateful parents? Secondary school teacher Diana recently received a letter from an ex-pupil who had suffered from anorexia. Now grown up and healthy, the pupil wanted to let Diana know that she wouldn't have been where she is today without her support. Diana makes a point of reading this and other letters of appreciation whenever she feels disillusioned or overburdened.

- As long as your workload is not too much of a problem, getting involved with extra-curricular activities can help to lift your relationship with your pupils to a new level. Going on school trips, organising a theme day or starting an after-school club can also give you a new lease of life if you are feeling a bit jaded.

- Seek professional help and support from others. Talk to your line manager, mentor or union rep, or contact the Teacher Support Network (www.teachersupport.info). For some people, a good counsellor can literally be a life-saver. For others, simply having the chance to unburden themselves to a trained listener is all that is required to get them back on track. Cognitive behavioural therapy is another alternative. It places less emphasis on exploring the source of your problems and more on finding new and better ways of managing stressful situations. See your doctor to discuss possible strategies and try to get recommendations for therapists from friends and acquaintances. If one therapist doesn't work for you, don't be afraid to stop seeing them and try someone else.

- Watch out for self-destructive tendencies. Be honest with yourself: do you find it difficult to give things up? Do you deliberately overload yourself? Some people do not feel they are doing a 'proper job' unless they are constantly on the go. If you think you fit into this pattern of behaviour, make serious efforts to prune your workload (see 'Managing your workload', page 242). If you have difficulty cutting down, seek help from a trusted work-based mentor or counsellor.

- Teaching is a vocation. It is much more than simply a means of earning money, and in order to survive, you need to take satisfaction from the fact that you are 'making a difference'. Keep reminding yourself that you are enhancing the lives of your pupils and that your input is essential to their future health, wealth and happiness.

- Go on a stress management course. Work-based stress is increasingly being recognised as a serious problem, and there are plenty of excellent courses to choose from.

NQTs and inexperienced teachers

- Become a magpie. Keep an eye out for those teachers who seem to cope well with the situations you find difficult, for example staying on top of marking, using ICT in the classroom or managing challenging pupils. Chat to them in the staffroom and make a note of their tips and advice. They may also be willing (and flattered!) for you to observe them teaching a lesson.

- Write things down. When you have a session with your mentor or someone comes up with a useful suggestion, make a note of their advice. You also need to check your notes regularly. With so much to think about, it is surprisingly easy to forget even the best ideas.

- Whenever you get the chance, spend time with other NQTs. If most of your colleagues are experienced, you can end up feeling demoralised by what you perceive as your lack of skills. Sharing your experiences with people in similar circumstances will help you to keep things in perspective. If you are a secondary school teacher, your local authority should also be able to put you in touch with NQTs teaching the same subject in other local schools.

- Don't be afraid to make judicious use of established disciplinary networks. For example, if your school has a 'time out' system, find out how and why it operates and use it to help you manage challenging pupils. Never feel that seeking support is a sign of weakness. Even the most experienced and effective teachers regard whole-school disciplinary support systems as integral to their success in the classroom.

- At the same time, take care not to become too dependent on external support. Work at developing your own disciplinary techniques, as well as using whole-school systems. Discuss this issue with your mentor to check that you are getting the balance right.

- Find out in advance who to contact for support if you are struggling with curriculum and planning, experiencing difficulties with discipline or having personal problems. Don't let problems pile up. Teachers are, on the whole, a kindly bunch of people who will be happy to give personal support if you ask for it. Remember – every teacher was once an NQT!

- Plan as thoroughly and as comprehensively as possible. Although many teachers fly by the seat of their pants from time to time, in the early stages of your career you need to have everything at your fingertips. Disciplinary problems often occur when pupils are unoccupied, either because there is a breakdown in your planning or because you haven't provided follow-up tasks for the quick workers and/or high attainers.

- Always remember that you are in a position of authority over your pupils, even if you are fresh out of college and teaching a Year 13 class. Although developing a friendly relationship with your pupils is important, you should not attempt to be their 'friend'. The most effective teachers prioritise doing a competent and professional job above being popular with their pupils.

- Smile and look cheerful. If your pupils perceive you as happy to be in the classroom, it helps them to feel positive towards you.

- Some teachers can be very territorial about the staffroom and lay claim to 'their' chair or 'their' cup. Even if you find it irritating, accept that you are the newcomer and try not to tread on any toes. The support of your colleagues is essential in teaching, particularly in the early years of your career. Do whatever it takes to build up sound relationships in the staffroom.

Dealing with inspections

- Once you know that an inspection is imminent, make last-minute checks to ensure that you are well organised. Always have inspections in the back of your mind whenever you are sorting out your records, planning and other paperwork. In the lead-up to an inspection, you can then keep on reminding yourself that you are as well prepared as it is possible to be.
- Don't ever feel that you 'should' be taking things in your stride. Accept that everyone finds inspections stressful, and be kind to yourself by organising as much practical support as possible, both before and during the inspection. For example, if you have young children, draft in a supportive friend or relative to help out, and ask your partner to take responsibility for evening meals.
- If you are concerned about a particular aspect of your teaching, such as behaviour management or special needs provision, don't be afraid to seek help and guidance well in advance of any inspection. If you are a curriculum leader and you are worried about your department as a whole, request a departmental review from your senior leadership team, a local authority advisory team or an education consultant with appropriate expertise and experience.
- Don't plan to do anything out of the ordinary just to 'impress the inspector'. Stick with your tried-and-tested teaching methods and what you know you can do well. If the inspection does flag up that you need to introduce a wider range of approaches, try to take it as a positive opportunity to improve your teaching.
- Have lesson plans ready. They may seem a bit of a chore, but they will help you to keep on top of things while you are being watched. They also give you a good opportunity to highlight all the positive aspects of your lesson, for example how you are extending the gifted and talented, supporting special needs and differentiating during the lesson; what opportunities you are providing for assessment; the details of your objectives; and how you are pacing your lesson.
- In each lesson, have a chair ready for the inspector along with a copy of your lesson plan. Apart from making the inspector feel welcome, it is far less disruptive if he or she can slip into the room, sit down straight away and look over your lesson plan without having to interrupt you.
- It is particularly important that you follow a good health and fitness routine during an inspection (see 'Health, fitness and

lifestyle' on page 246 for some suggestions). If you know that you find it difficult to eat when you are anxious, prepare small snacks to keep your blood sugar levels up, and make sure you maintain your water intake. If you have the opposite problem and overeat when anxious, try to avoid sugary snacks. It is also a good idea to watch your caffeine intake. Too much coffee, tea, chocolate or cola can make you even more jittery than you already are.

- Be prepared for a debriefing with the inspector and try to avoid taking a defensive stance in the face of any negative comments. Be open to suggestions; many inspectors have a wealth of experience and may be able to give you some very positive and useful advice. Bear in mind also that this is a professional dialogue. Try not to take any criticism personally, and remember that there is no such thing as the perfect lesson.
- Don't be unnerved if an inspector leaves part-way through a lesson. In many cases, the inspector will be visiting at least two different classes within one period and his or her sudden disappearance is no reflection on you or your teaching.
- If an inspector doesn't give feedback because they leave in the middle of the lesson, make sure you find them later. If you haven't been told where in the school the inspectors are based, find out from your curriculum leader or senior leadership team. If you cannot find them, leave a message asking to speak to them before they leave the school. You have a right to feedback, and there is nothing worse than worrying about their assessment of your lesson when a quick dialogue would probably set your mind at rest.
- If you feel that an inspector has behaved unfairly or unreasonably, talk to your head of department, line manager or senior leadership team. At the very least, this will help you to 'get things off your chest', and further action may be required. Inspectors also need feedback on their performance!

Coping with school trips

- A trip is perhaps the one school-based event where it is worth giving in to your neurotic tendencies. Imagine the worst and then prepare for it! If you know that you have covered all eventualities, you will find it much easier to relax and take everything in your stride on the day.
- Make sure you are following all local authority and school procedures for trips so that you are covered should the worst

happen and something goes wrong. It is also essential to check for any change in policy or regulations before you start the planning process.

- Plan the practicalities down to the last detail. Have spares of anything essential, such as packed lunches, water, clipboards, stationery, and even clothes if your children are young. Make a list of equipment such as the mobile phone, the first aid box and the register, and remember to check your list before you set off.

- Ensure that children have their inhalers and any other essential medication they might need. If medication has to be administered by a staff member, check that you have written parental permission and that the medication is in its original container along with the prescriber's instructions. For the most recent guidance on administering medicine, double-check your school and local authority policy. Regardless of the age group, prepare for the possibility of a child succumbing to travel sickness.

- Your adult: child ratio is important, both from a safety point of view and to ensure that the children receive sufficient adult input to make the trip a success. Ask a couple of people to stand by in case a colleague is sick and can't join you.

- For local trips, make every effort to visit beforehand so that you know where you're going and can work out the practicalities. For example, if the route from the coach park to the attraction involves a busy road, do you have enough staff to supervise children on a potentially hazardous walk? Although you must not take fewer than the statutory number of adults, you can always take more.

- Work out a timetable and stick to it as closely as possible. Always make sure you have enough time for each stage of the trip; there is nothing more stressful or likely to lead to problems than having to rush sixty youngsters!

- If you are not very confident about supervising pupils beyond the school premises, make sure you take along someone who is. The presence of a colleague with good discipline and lots of experience of school trips will help you to feel calm and in control of things.

- Make sure you communicate effectively with parents about the trip. For overnight or residential trips, consider holding a parents' meeting. Give them plenty of time to complete permission forms, and check that all forms have been returned in good time. Be clear about timings and take along parents' contact details so that you can get in touch if there are any delays.

- Never assume that all parents will read letters. Nursery school owner Sarah recommends giving parents the same piece of information in as many different ways as possible. For a forthcoming trip, she sends home a letter, puts up a notice and aims to tell each parent individually as they come to collect their child.

- Let colleagues know well in advance that you are planning a trip and that certain pupils will be missing lessons. Try to be considerate about when you plan your trip. Many of your colleagues won't particularly appreciate your whisking their GSCE class out of school when they are under pressure to finish the syllabus before revision leave.

- Think through the dates for an evening trip if you have to book something several months in advance. A post-Christmas theatre outing can seem a very good idea in September, but come January when the weather is awful, it may not be such an appealing prospect.

Parents' evenings and meetings

- If you find parents' evenings a source of anxiety, keep reminding yourself that many parents will be feeling just as nervous as you, particularly if they have negative memories of their own school days. Do everything you can to present a relaxed front. Smiling, making immediate eye contact and shaking hands will help to get things off to a positive start.

- As with any potentially nerve-racking situation, plan and prepare well in advance. Notes, records, mark books and reports are important evidence of the comments you wish to make, so double-check that you have everything to hand. If you have some difficult messages to deliver, think through the wording you intend to use. Always try to offer a positive along with the negative (there is no child who does not have at least one redeeming feature!) and accompany any negative messages with practical strategies.

- Teachers often have to deal with anxious parents, and it can be emotionally draining when parents find it hard to let go of their anxiety. In the long run, a sympathetic approach is usually the least stressful for both you and the parent. Always take their concerns seriously, even if you privately think that they are being over-anxious. Although some parents may have good reason to feel concerned, as a detached professional you can help them to keep things in perspective and cope with whatever is causing their anxiety.

- Having to deal with angry parents is a major source of stress for those in the teaching profession. In many cases, parents' anger arises from the belief that they are not being taken seriously. Try to give parents the opportunity to let off steam; often this is all that is needed to diffuse their anger so that you can then go on to discuss the problem more calmly. As with anxious parents, focus on practical strategies and working in partnership with the parents. Reassure them that you and the school will keep them informed of how the strategies are working, and prioritise keeping your promise.

- If you feel that parental anger is getting out of hand during any parents' meeting, don't struggle on alone. Contact your curriculum leader or a member of your senior management team and ask for support. If prior to a meeting you anticipate that your personal safety might be at risk, always make sure that you have another staff member with you. A witness to the meeting can also be useful for taking notes, particularly if there is likely to be any dispute over what was said.

- If you are new to teaching, remember that parents' evenings will get easier with experience. One primary NQT had a difficult parent to deal with during her first parents' evening. After the meeting was over, she discussed the exchange with her headteacher, who pointed out that when she had conducted as many parents' evenings as he had, the occasional (and inevitable) negative parent would no longer worry her! Slowly but surely, she discovered that he was right. She also discovered that some parents have a tendency to be suspicious of a new and inexperienced teacher, and as she became more established at the school, the parents became less challenging.

Index